The Changing Face
of Christianity

The Changing Face of Christianity

Africa, the West, and the World

EDITED BY
LAMIN SANNEH AND
JOEL A. CARPENTER

OXFORD
UNIVERSITY PRESS

2005

OXFORD
UNIVERSITY PRESS

Oxford University Press, Inc., publishes works that further
Oxford University's objective of excellence
in research, scholarship, and education.

Oxford   New York
Auckland   Cape Town   Dar es Salaam   Hong Kong   Karachi
Kuala Lumpur   Madrid   Melbourne   Mexico City   Nairobi
New Delhi   Shanghai   Taipei   Toronto

With offices in
Argentina   Austria   Brazil   Chile   Czech Republic   France   Greece
Guatemala   Hungary   Italy   Japan   Poland   Portugal   Singapore
South Korea   Switzerland   Thailand   Turkey   Ukraine   Vietnam

Copyright © 2005 by Oxford University Press, Inc.

Published by Oxford University Press, Inc.
198 Madison Avenue, New York, New York 10016

www.oup.com

Oxford is a registered trademark of Oxford University Press

Library of Congress Cataloging-in-Publication Data
The changing face of Christianity : Africa, the West, and the world / edited by Lamin Sanneh
and Joel A. Carpenter.
p.   cm.
Includes bibliographical references and index.
ISBN-13 978-0-19-517727-5; 978-0-19-517728-2 (pbk.)
ISBN 0-19-517727-4; 0-19-517728-2 (pbk.)
1. Church history—Twentieth Century.   2. Church history—Twenty-First Century.
I. Sanneh, Lamin O.   II. Carpenter, Joel A.
BR481.C47 2005
270.8'3—dc22   2004008859

9 8 7 6 5 4

Printed in the United States of America
on acid-free paper

To Andrew Walls
In esteem and gratitude

Preface

Joel A. Carpenter

One of the most important but least examined changes in the world over the past century has been the rapid rise of Christianity in non-Western societies and cultures. In 1900, 80 percent of the world's professing Christians were European or North American. Today, 60 percent of professing Christians live in the global South and East. Christian thought and expression are being framed within these regions' cultures; they are by no means merely exported from the North Atlantic region. Christian people and institutions in places such as Brazil, the Philippines, and Nigeria are engaging the personal, social, and political dimensions of life and seeking to redirect them in light of the Christian gospel. Today, Christianity is a global faith, but one that is more vigorous and vibrant in the global South than among the world's richer and more powerful regions. It presents a remarkable case of "globalization from below" rather than an imposition from the world's great powers.

Christianity in Africa has become a salient part of this story because it poses perhaps the most dramatic case of rapid growth, local variation, and culture-transforming influence. In 1900, there were only about 9 million Christians in all of Africa. By 1945, however, this number had more than tripled to 30 million. By 1970, this number had more than tripled again to more than 115 million. Today, there are an estimated 380 million Christians in Africa.[1] African influence on the world Christian scene is growing, and it is becoming much more common to see Africans leading Christian agencies and shaping Christian thought. The newly elected executive of the World Council of Churches is Samuel Kobia, a Kenyan. The chief

officer for the World Alliance of Reformed Churches is Setri Nyomi, a Ghanaian. The presenter of the prestigious Stone Lectures at Princeton Theological
Seminary in 2003 was Kwame Bediako, also a Ghanaian. Africa is fast becoming a heartland for world Christianity, and anyone who would understand the
dawning of this new dispensation in world religious history would do well to
study its African dimensions.

African Christianity, like Africa itself, is a huge generalization. Although
this book must work with some sense of what African Christianity might mean,
it is not our intention to offer either a definitive or a comprehensive account.
Rather, we have chosen some cases that are more illustrative and suggestive
of the themes and realities that must factor into any larger accounting. Among
the themes we find are belief in an active and densely populated spirit world,
a faith that delivers the faithful from the fear and power of the spirit world as
well as from poverty and despair, and a faith that sustains hope for peace and
solidarity in a strife-ridden continent. Our intent is to foster interest and debate
on the nature of Christianity in its African and other manifestations rather
than to attempt any grand synthesis. Indeed, some of our authors disagree
with each other, most notably the two who focus on Ghana.

We also believe that the best way to understand Christian manifestations
in Africa is to put them into a global and historical context. Thus we offer an
essay on the rise of new Christian cultural forms in the Caribbean amid the
African diaspora there. We also present three essays on enduring issues in the
modern history of Christian expansion. Each of these chapters addresses a
theme in Westerners' encounters with Asians and vice versa. In the conclusion,
we argue that the interaction between the Christianities of the West and the
rest of the world will be tense and sometimes explosive. At present, it seems
difficult for Western observers to find even categories in which to place the
Christianity of their African counterparts. As much as we appreciate some early
attempts to do this, we are convinced that labels such as "conservative" or
"fundamentalist" or "medieval" distort the African Christian reality and probably reveal more about the post-Enlightenment eyes of the beholders. Uniquely
African types and categories are now emerging, and they deserve their own
places on the conceptual maps or, more likely, their own maps.

Just as the charts of Western modernity are inadequate for exploring African Christianity, so are the modern divisions in scholarship. This book offers
a thoroughly interdisciplinary approach. It assembles the work of scholars from
a variety of disciplines, notably anthropology, history, literary and popular culture, philosophy, religious studies, and theology. More important, it refuses to
partition off the questions and insights of Christian theology from these other
fields of knowledge. In this way, the contributors not only try to understand
the outlook of African Christianity but also try to acknowledge its influence.

We must acknowledge some other things as we go to press. First, this
project began as a research seminar on world Christianity that was conducted

at Calvin College during the summer of 2000. Half of the chapters in this book began as papers delivered at a followup conference at Calvin in April 2001. These essays were sharpened by the constructive critical reading of the other participants, notably Katherine Brueck, Paul Hiebert, Robert Mc-Cuttcheon, Vincent McNally, Kim Paffenroth, Brendan Pelphrey, Charles Taber, Christian Van Gorder, and Andrew Walls.

The generous support of the Pew Charitable Trusts underwrote this project, which was conducted through the Calvin College Seminars in Christian Scholarship. We cannot offer enough praise for the former director of the seminars, Dr. Susan Felch, and her capable staff, who have underwritten and undergirded us with their warm hospitality and expert management. We are particularly grateful for the help of seminar staff members past and present: Krista Betts Van Dyk, A. B. Chadderdon, Anna Mae Bush, and Kerry Schutt Nason, who assisted with the project's coordination. Heidi Rienstra and Amy De Vries, also at Calvin, lent their expertise to the preparation of the manuscript. Finally, we must thank Thomas Byker, Bradley Schrotenboer, Leigh Tickner, Julie Vander Zwaag, and Teresa Woolworth, the Calvin students who prepared the maps, and Johnathan Bascom, their professor, who organized the effort.

The dedication page acknowledges the enormous debt we owe to Andrew Walls, who has encouraged and inspired us to see the great movements of Christian history.

—Grand Rapids, Michigan
February 2004

NOTE

1. David B. Barrett and Todd M. Johnson, "Annual Statistical Table on Global Mission: 2004," *International Bulletin of Missionary Research* 28 (January 2004): 25.

Contents

Contributors, xiii

Introduction: The Changing Face of Christianity:
The Cultural Impetus of a World Religion, 3
Lamin Sanneh

PART I. Christianity as a Non-Western Religion: Studies from
Africa and the African Diaspora

1. Religion Bridge: Translating Secular into Sacred Music:
   A Study of World Christianity Focusing on the U.S.
   Virgin Islands, 21
   Patricia Harkins-Pierre

2. Culture, Christianity, and Witchcraft in a West African
   Context, 45
   Todd M. Vanden Berg

3. Shall They Till with Their Own Hoes? Baptists in
   Zimbabwe and New Patterns of Interdependence,
   1950–2000, 63
   Isaac M. T. Mwase

4. A View of Ghana's New Christianity, 81
   Paul Gifford

5. The Role of Churches in the Peace Process in Africa:
   The Case of Mozambique Compared, 97
   G. Jan van Butselaar

6. Christian Witness in the Public Sphere: Some Lessons and Residual Challenges from the Recent Political History of Ghana, 117
Kwame Bediako

PART II.   Reflex Impact: World Christianity and the West since 1850

7. Interpreting Karen Christianity: The American Baptist Reaction to Asian Christianity in the Nineteenth Century, 135
Jay Riley Case

8. Missionary Thinking about Religious Plurality at Tambaram 1938: Hendrik Kraemer and His Critics, 159
Richard J. Plantinga

9. Contextual Theology: The Last Frontier, 191
Wilbert R. Shenk

Conclusion: The Current Transformation of Christianity, 213
Lamin Sanneh

Index, 225

Contributors

Kwame Bediako is the director of the Akrofi Christaller Memorial Centre for Mission Research and Applied Theology in Akropong, Ghana. He is also professor and director of the program in African Christian Theology for the University of Natal at Pietermaritzburg, South Africa. Best known among his theological works is *Christianity in Africa: The Renewal of a Non-Western Religion* (1995).

Joel A. Carpenter is the provost and a professor of history at Calvin College. His research field is American religious history, with special expertise in the study of evangelical Christianity. He is the author of *Revive Us Again: The Reawakening of American Fundamentalism* (Oxford University Press, 1997).

Jay Riley Case teaches history at Malone College, Canton, Ohio. He works in the field of American religious history and the history of foreign missions. He recently published "From the Native Ministry to the Talented Tenth: The Foreign Missionary Origins of White Support for Black Colleges," in *The Foreign Missionary Enterprise at Home*, edited by Daniel H. Bays and Grant Wacker (2003).

Paul Gifford is professor in the Department for the Study of Religions at the School of Oriental and African Studies (SOAS) of the University of London. His research area is contemporary African Christianity. He is the author of *African Christianity: Its Public Role* (1998).

Patricia Harkins-Pierre is associate professor of English in the Humanities Division at the University of the Virgin Islands in St. Thomas, U.S. Virgin Islands. One of her areas of research is the development of Christianity as a world religion in the Caribbean.

Isaac M. T. Mwase is a faculty member of the Tuskegee University National Center for Bioethics Research and Health Care. Although trained as a philosopher of religion, and an ethicist, he pursues many scholarly interests, including contemporary African Christianity.

Richard J. Plantinga is professor of religion at Calvin College in Grand Rapids, Michigan. His research area is Christian responses to religious plurality. His major publication in this field is *Christianity and Plurality: Classic and Contemporary Readings* (1999).

Lamin Sanneh is professor of history and D. Willis James Professor of World Christianity at Yale University. His most recent book is *Whose Religion Is Christianity? The Gospel beyond the West* (2003).

Wilbert R. Shenk is the Paul E. Pierson Professor of Mission History and Contemporary Culture at Fuller Theological Seminary. He researches and writes in both of these fields. His most recent work is *Enlarging the Story: Perspectives on Writing World Christian History* (2002).

G. Jan van Butselaar has been teaching at the theological colleges in Butare, Rwanda, and Rikatla, Mozambique, and was general secretary of the Netherlands Missionary Council. Today, he is concentrating on the study of African church history and on the state of religious freedom in the world. He is the author of *Church and Peace in Africa: The Role of the Churches in the Peace Process* (2001).

Todd M. Vanden Berg is associate professor of anthropology at Calvin College. His special interests include intercultural communication and the interaction of traditional religious systems with modernity. His field research has been in northeastern Nigeria, focusing on the Longuda people. He is the author of "'We Are Not Compensating Rocks': Resettlement and Traditional Religious Systems," *World Development* 27 (February 1999): 271–283.

The Changing Face
of Christianity

Introduction

The Changing Face of Christianity: The Cultural Impetus of a World Religion

Lamin Sanneh

Few developments in our day have been more striking and less anticipated than the emergence of Christianity as a world religion. Why does this fact appear so dramatic? First, the colonial empires that were Christianity's accompanying frame were waning when the religion commenced its surprising forward thrust. New faith communities came into being without a colonial order there to maintain them. Instead of Christianity fading away along with the empire, it unexpectedly grew and spread. Second, the denominational pattern of missions has made it well nigh impossible to conceive of Christianity surging and prospering outside denominational structures. The relatively recent nature of worldwide Christian growth also has given us not much time to take stock or to overcome the ingrained Euro-American analytical habits. The rising prominence of Christianity has failed to make an impression on our conventional frames of mind, and furthermore, against the culture wars now raging in our midst, news of Christianity's expansion abroad gets drowned out.

In the wake of the worldwide Christian resurgence, societies and cultures on every continent and in most countries continue to be attracted to the church. Preindustrial primal societies in the Southern Hemisphere that once stood outside the main orbit of the religion have become major Christian centers. They are inducing cultural movements and realignments that only now are coming into their own, especially those in the new urban centers of the global South and East. The resurgence is not simply a matter of new names being added to the rolls, but of the accumulating pressure to accommodate new ways of life and thinking that are creating massive cultural shifts. By contrast, Europe and, to some extent, North America, once considered Christian strongholds, are in marked recession or retreat. The communities of the North Atlantic are fast becoming the church's arid land or at least its shrinking base; meanwhile, the societies of the Southern Hemisphere are emerging as new Christian strongholds. In the case of North America, only new religious immigrant groups have varied the pattern of decline and retreat by masking the extensive structural reverses that the culture wars have inflicted on organized religion.

The New Landscape

A few keen observers in the past century hinted at the coming new reality. Aware that Europe's energies were at the time absorbed in war, Archbishop William Temple nevertheless observed in 1944 that the global feature of Christianity was "the new fact of our time," a prescient observation. An impressive picture now meets our eyes: the exploding numbers, the scope of the phenomenon, the cross-cultural patterns of encounter, the variety and diversity of cultures affected, the structural and antistructural nature of the changes involved, the shifting *couleur locale* that manifests itself in unorthodox variations on the canon, the wide spectrum of theological views and ecclesiastical traditions represented, the ideas of authority and styles of leadership that have been developed, the process of acute indigenization that fosters liturgical renewal, the duplication of forms in a rapidly changing world of experimentation and adaptation, and the production of new religious art, music, hymns, songs, and prayers. All of these are featured on Christianity's breathtakingly diverse face today.

These unprecedented developments demand that we reexamine the serial nature of Christian origins and expansion—here today, there tomorrow—and account for the cycles of retreat and advance, of attrition and expansion, of decline and awakening, and of a pull here and a push there that have blazed the religion's trail from its origin. In earlier eras, the many faces of Christianity were carryovers of family traits, with new denominations perpetuating old quarrels; today, the faces are fresh.[1]

The pattern of contrasting development and forward momentum is occurring simultaneously in various societies on a world scale, with Christianity in its twilight Western phase contrasting strikingly with its formative non-Western impact. Christianity has not ceased to be a Western religion, but its future as a world religion is now being decided and shaped by the hands and in the minds of its non-Western adherents, who share little of the West's cultural assumptions. It is no longer fanciful today to speak of the possibility of, say, an African pope, with all that that means for the cultural repositioning of the church. Yet barely a generation ago, such a prospect was unimaginable, so astonishing has been the distance we have traveled from the position of the West as the impregnable citadel of Christianity, in fact, as its intellectual cradle. The church militant was the West triumphant. Hilaire Belloc, for example, thought he was expressing a mere truism without need of elaboration when he declared, "Europe is the faith," meaning that Christianity, race, and territorial Europe were identical. Europe's civilizing mandate was Christianity's mission, too, and vice versa. As Benito Mussolini put it, it was the Italian cultural genius that salvaged Christianity, "a wretched little oriental sect" in an undistinguished corner of the world, and raised it above the flood mark. It is another truism needing much elaboration to state that today that is no longer the case, with challenging intercultural implications.

The pattern of the current worldwide accelerated Christian expansion and acculturation has not been that of the faithful replication of a model whose original exists in Europe and which can be transplanted elsewhere without alteration. The variety of forms and styles, the complex linguistic idioms and aesthetic traditions, and the differences in music and worship patterns show world Christianity to be hostage to no one cultural expression and restricted to no one geographical center. More languages and idioms are used in reading the Christian scriptures and in Christian liturgy, devotion, worship, and prayer than in any other religion. The unity of Christianity, however defined, has not been at the expense of the diversity and variety of cultural idioms and of models of faith and practice in use at any one time and in any one church tradition. Christianity today is not just a changing face; its leaders and personalities are changing.

On its own terms, what is happening in the story of Christianity is nothing short of a fundamental historical shift in the character and fortunes of the religion and of the social modes appropriate to it. It is the contemporary replay of themes and issues familiar to us under the rubric of Christian origins in the Mediterranean world and beyond, but without the corresponding Roman and Hellenic compass to guide our thinking and give us the symmetry of reason and revelation. Great social instability is threatened from the meeting of such diametrically opposed cultural systems.

Diverse Tracks and a Moving Center

The essays gathered in this volume offer evidence of that cultural gap but also offer samples of the stunning variety of the story of Christianity with regard to its polycentric roots and its world scale. Without trying to be comprehensive or representative, the chapters suggest different methodological strategies for exploring and interpreting the data. They pay attention to forces on the ground and in the air and to rhythms and continuities in multiple settings. Patricia Harkins-Pierre describes the world of Caribbean culture and its vibrant fusion of literary and musical styles into a contemporary pulsating anthem of testimony, praise, and prayer. She describes the new eclecticism of combining secular and religious themes to produce new strains of music, drama, and poetry. The Caribbean's position between North America and South America and between Africa and Europe makes it a fulcrum of historical confrontation, as well as a unique crossroad in the transmission and mediation of culture. As a diaspora community of peoples, ideas, and influences, the Caribbean has engaged issues of global resonance. In the words of a Caribbean song, "Though we function differently, / We got one identity, / Because as children of God we're / Re-building identity."

Appropriately, Christianity fits, and is perceived to fit, into that Creolized world of new and changing identities and of "imagined" island communities summoned for battle with the hosts contending for their allegiance. The Caribbean's history of colonization, slavery, migration, dependence, and freedom represents a confluence of cultures kept alive by a vigorous process of blending, assimilation, and interaction. Grassroots churches have sprung up and, with local leadership, have varied the patterns of worship and prayer by adopting improvised participant styles to expand set forms of the prescribed liturgy.

Taking the path of conciliation and responding with a strategy of if you can't beat them, join them, Catholic churches have turned to African charismatic missionaries as leaders of worship, and they have incorporated revival-style hymns, songs, and music in worship. By thus enlarging its liturgical boundaries, the Catholic Church could avert the culture clash otherwise threatened by the global Christian resurgence. At any rate, in the new religious movements, vernacular Creole and standard English are juxtaposed in preaching, testimony, and storytelling. Jesus is depicted as a person of color, and the ideal Christian disciple is described as a radical soldier, suitably fitted out with rhythm guitar, bass guitar, harmonica, keyboard, drums, and the other accoutrements of the itinerant vocation and poised to join the Knight Errant into the fray. The emphasis is on the people's idiom: simple, direct, minimalist lyrics that stand above the swirling sound and vibrating music of the instruments. It is art from below in the service of truth from above: humble work here directed to a high purpose there. Harkins-Pierre weaves all these themes into the many voices united in one message.

In his chapter on witchcraft in Africa, Todd Vanden Berg, an anthropologist, beats a different drum when he describes the war being waged on local Christian grounds against powers unseen and its displacement of the main mental furniture of Western Christianity. Vanden Berg brings the theology of religions, contextual theology, and philosophical generalization to bear on the perennial controversy concerning witchcraft. It is a taboo subject in mission-related churches, he observes, because missionaries took a top-down view of indigenizing the church in Africa, in contrast to the grassroots approach of the Africans themselves. Vanden Berg questions the value of a top-down view of contextualization for long-term effectiveness, as he also questions the value of having theologians and other Western theorists jump-start the process.

The popular roots of indigenous renewal movements in Christianity defy the clinical categories of philosophical generalization and their elitist view of the church. At the level of the people's lives, evil and the spirit hosts are daily realities encountered in the course of normal living. Abstract religious thought, however, avoids any mention of these realities and so postpones confronting the corresponding issues of intercultural encounter.

It turns out, says Vanden Berg, that churches are major venues for the process of adaptation and synthesis that is going on among local Christians; and therefore, these churches offer an excellent place for studying issues of social change and culture clash. Social scientists and especially anthropologists, according to Vanden Berg, would have to overcome their presuppositions about so-called primitive cultures as an organic unity to take seriously the positive effects of an external influence like Christianity, particularly because the absence of a uniform response to Christianity among local populations shows that there is no hegemonic power at work. The problem, he notes, is that anthropological presuppositions about primitive societies have assumed the posture of a nonnegotiable dogma, much like the hegemonic, top-down claims they ascribe to Christian missions. He senses the potential culture clash in this area and calls for self-criticism to advance genuine understanding and engagement with the local manifestations of an alternative Christianity.

Vanden Berg shows the reality of witchcraft beliefs among the people he studied in Nigeria. The reality of the world of witches is connected to belief in spirits and, it turns out, to confidence in the power of Christianity to protect people from harm and to intercede on behalf of the afflicted and those at risk. In population centers where the original people are mixed and intermingled with numerous groups of outsiders, there are likely to be many and persistent occasions of social tension, personal strife, and suspicion and recrimination. That was the case, Vanden Berg found, in one Nigerian village where Longuda people were host to some ten different exogenous ethnic groups. Such tensions broke out into witchcraft accusations in the face of personal tragedy, sudden or severe reversal of fortune, and other bad occurrences. Witchcraft beliefs remain pervasive and persistent, and no amount of denial can shift that reality, at least in Christian Africa.[2]

According to Africans, whether Christian or not, we are not alone in the universe, which is inhabited by the devil and by a host of spirit forces that are ever attentive to us. We should also be ever attentive to them if we are sensible. The stripped-down universe of a post-Enlightenment Christianity is a small fit for this larger world that Africans live in. That small, disinfected universe of the West is fine for the conventional rhythms of the regular day, but not when the legion of ancestors, the spirits, and the living dead come calling. Accordingly, witchcraft beliefs function like an explanatory model for why bad or evil things happen, a worldview that also tells people what they can do for remedy and safeguard. It is not a fatalistic worldview; instead, people are surrounded by an active, dangerous spirit world that requires constant and vigilant intervention to be safe and whole. Nothing, observes Vanden Berg, is a product of random chance, and so any prevarication or compromise might put a person at risk by suggesting a pact with the devil.

Vanden Berg's account of witchcraft belief contradicts the claim by scholars since the 1930s that magic or, in our case, witchcraft is merely "mysticism in the fetters of fixed idea." It also weakens the claim of evolutionary theory that "polytheist" beliefs normally dissolve in the stages immediately preceding accession to monotheist faith. As Sir James Frazer put it, religion is the despair of magic and merely succeeds it in time. The actual situation on the ground, however, appears a lot more complex than that clinical view would suggest. The new Christianity has not evaded the issues of a crowded, dynamic universe of persons, souls, spirits, and evil. On the contrary, it has embraced that world without reservation and thereby defined a significant front line in the culture clash with the West.[3]

The financially precarious position of the small community of Baptists in Zimbabwe, founded by American Southern Baptists in 1950, offers a study in contrast. Isaac Mwase calls for continued American support of the work in the face of the precipitate withdrawal of American missionary personnel after independence in 1980. Local Baptists were saddled with maintaining a costly infrastructure of missionary hardware, and, in spite of repeated requests for help, their American founders more or less abandoned them. At one time, the Americans maintained 80 missionaries in Zimbabwe, a Baptist publishing house, a seminary, a hospital, a media center, bookstores, a primary school, and a secondary school. Mwase argues that local Baptists had a right to expect continuation of this work, with financial support from the United States maintained at equivalent levels. But that has not happened, and he feels that the Americans' cessation of investments in ministry represents an impoverished understanding of Baptist solidarity and a failure of partnership.

Mwase suggests several reasons for the breakdown in relations. Zimbabwe as Southern Rhodesia was fraught with the politics of race, and the white supremicist regime in 1965 under Ian Smith worsened an already bad situation. When the Southern Baptists' mission board decided to introduce a plan of subsidy reduction until a fully self-supporting local church could be phased in over a 10-year period, the postcolonial context framed the mood of Zimbabwe's Baptist leaders. For them, the language of self-support smacked of abandonment. Support for the seminary was scaled back so drastically as to call its viability into question. The resourceful principal of the seminary, Henry Mugabe, found some alternative funding sources in America, but they are no match for the prior levels of support. Mwase's case study reveals a facet of mission history that differs strikingly from the standard image. In the case of the Baptist mission in Zimbabwe, it was not paternalism and domination that were at issue, but the local demand for missionary investment that was unjustifiably ignored. Yet Mwase affirms that Baptist work continued to prosper, with "a church that is alive with excitement and growth." That has not, however, assuaged feelings between Zimbabwean Baptists and their Southern Baptist coreligionists. At the minimum, the story suggests that excitement and growth are due to factors other than missionary finance and oversight, which, according to a standard definition, are what *extraversion* is about. It also indicates an estrangement in Baptist polity that can only widen with the culture gap.

In the midst of dire challenge and danger, the churches of Africa have not relinquished control of their affairs into the hands of the churches in the West. Drawing on educated leadership in the congregations and on the Christian contribution to democratization, the churches feel entitled to play a public role in state and society. With the dreams of independence turning sour and their societies plunged into war and persistent instability, many church leaders are addressing urgent issues of peace, reconciliation, and justice, as Jan van Butselaar describes for Mozambique in his chapter.

As a Portuguese colony with a strong Roman Catholic influence, Mozambique developed the habits and complexes typical of the church-state affinity that underpinned its history. In the ensuing turmoil of an armed nationalist uprising that marked the painful decolonization process, however, the church was squeezed between a desperate, brutal colonial suppression and a violent liberation campaign. Samora Machel, the triumphant Marxist leader of the anticolonial struggle, denounced the Catholic Church as a colonial, antirevolutionary tool on the occasion of the country's independence in 1975. The church beat a long overdue retreat, unable to deny its role as an ally of Portuguese rule and at the same time unable to offer a credible alternative to the ideology of Marxist repression. It paid the price of compromise with the colonial state.

The state of limbo into which the churches were driven was lifted only when Frelimo, the governing party, began to overheat from the excesses of revolutionary vengeance. A fractured and disaffected civil society combined with a profoundly disenchanted rural population to strip the government of any popular support. With apartheid South Africa hovering in the shadows and ready to pounce on the government for giving support to Nelson Mandela's outlawed African National Congress, some of whose fighters were based in Mozambique, Frelimo was constrained to climb down from its lofty perch and adjust its revolutionary posture by giving the churches some slack.

The Catholic Church's well-known connections with Renamo, Frelimo's ideological bête noire, became an asset in the negotiations to end the civil war. After the death of Machel in an airplane crash in 1987, the momentum of peace and reconciliation picked up. At its seventh General Assembly meeting in Addis Ababa in October 1997, the All Africa Conference of Churches called

for a peaceful settlement of the war, to little avail, Butselaar notes. The intervention of the Catholic Church the following year brought old faces onto the
new stage, and that moved the peace process forward significantly. The Catholic
Church was able to mobilize the considerable resources it commanded and
draw on its dominant influence in the country to help broker a peace deal.
Butselaar describes how two churchmen, a Catholic and a Protestant, were
honored for their work toward peace and reconciliation.

One of the chapters about Ghana is by Kwame Bediako, a Ghanaian theologian and head of the Akrofi-Christaller Memorial Centre in Ghana, a theological research and education institute. Advancing from premises of his own,
Bediako shows the need to reconnect the new Christianity in Africa to the
preceding cultural heritage, with its accommodating, pluralist ethos. The
changing face of Christianity reflects patterns of renewal grounded in local
priorities rather than in the superpower center of gravity of American dominance. Contemporary analyses have, nevertheless, continued to use a geopolitical and Enlightenment rationality to explain Third World Christianity.

The influence of the Enlightenment and the social sciences has made it
difficult to adjust intellectually and take the full measure of Christianity in its
African setting, Bediako argues; we do not see in Christian religious thought
and practice the seeds of a theological rationale for a revitalized civil society
and responsible state power. The notional bridge that may exist between a post-
Christian West and a post-Western Christianity is strained further by the reas-
sertion in Ghana of Christian public values that the West has long abandoned.
Ghana's religious pluralism, Bediako insists, has reinvigorated the democra-
tizing impulse. The newly elected Catholic president of the country stood
alongside his Muslim vice president as a lay Methodist chief justice administered the oath of office, first on the Bible and then on the Qur'an. It is precisely
as a predominantly Christian society that Ghana has been hospitable to religious tolerance, with a multiplicity of associations and expressions flourishing
there. The churches have continued to offer a religious critique of power rather
than, as a prickly West fears, grasping for power to use against dissenters.

In another chapter on Ghana, Paul Gifford sets forth a challenging inter-
pretive view of Ghana's new Christianity by reviewing new forms of religious
life that depart radically from the style of the old-line churches. Here the emphasis is instrumental, with the scene dominated by faith-healing groups, prosperity churches and assemblies, and charismatic and Pentecostal groups. A
running theme in these new religious groups is success and doing well materially, with heavy reliance on Old Testament scripture. The rule of interpretation is narrative: the words of scripture addressed to individuals here and
now, with the idea of miracles happening now to fulfill their wishes.

At least in their popular organized forms, there is little sense in these
groups of the afterlife and judgment, only of winning in this life, as the Winners' Chapel, founded in Lagos, Nigeria, in 1983, teaches.[4] With 400 branches

in Nigeria and in 38 other African countries, the Winners' Chapel owns the Faith Tabernacle in Lagos, which seats more than 50,000 every Sunday, making it one of the biggest congregations in the world. Ministry in this context means removing the blockage and impediments preventing full realization of earthly blessings. Many of these groups are prominent in the media. They own TV and FM radio stations. One group, that of Mensa Otabil, established the first private university in the country, where he inculcates his message of hard work, planning, vision, and social reform. His emphasis reveals the modern outlook of these new groups and sets them at odds both with the mainline churches that eschew Pentecostal and charismatic claims and with nativistic groups that stress the importance of traditional therapeutics. But controversy does not constrain these groups.

A comparison with Muslim Africa should shed light on the wider use of religion for worldly ends. The Mouride Brotherhood, a Senegalese Sufi order founded in the early 1900s, has spawned an active network of groups and cells in West Africa and beyond, cells that are remarkable for their solidarity and work ethic. (The word *mouride* is Arabic for "disciple, novice.") The order, with Touba in Senegal as its founding center, has branches in several U.S. cities. On the occasion of the visit to the United States of Shaykh Mourtada Mbaké, an 83-year-old surviving son of the founder, Amadou Bamba (d. 1927), disciples and supplicants flocked to see him at his private quarters to seek blessings for success and to bring gifts. The blessings sought took many forms: Arabic prayer phrases delivered into cupped hands and sprinkled over the face to assure worldly advancement, measured quantities of holy water for the owner to douse on the premises of her restaurant to attract business, and the personal saintly aura of the shaykh believed to be imbued with potency to preserve. "Others, asking for a blessing, said they had in mind its powers to bring prosperity, health, maybe a green card that would allow them to settle legally in the United States."[5]

Even the Mouride work ethic is used to measure success in an ungrudging, precise way. A devotee testified that a small increment in effort at work, say, from 75 percent to 80 percent, being the result of the shaykh's blessing, might be the 5 percent margin a person needs to move up a rung on the ladder of health and prosperity. The shaykh's blessing provides a narrative of power and self-improvement; it is charisma in the service of a worldly ethic. That is why, the devotee pleads, one should never begrudge a blessing. The collections taken for the shaykh, as the earnings of a life of dogged persistence pounding the New York City sidewalks peddling wares, are acts of *do ut des,* an investment of the type "I give to him so that he may give in return," a calculated exercise in self-interest.

New York's City Hall might not care to associate with those for whom the City of God is no less tangible than Times Square and the Brooklyn Bridge, but in accord with political self-interest, it has declared an Amadou Bamba

Day in Harlem, complete with mayoral blessing and a street parade.[6] Mouride religion that combined so successfully with African ideas and practices now finds in its American transplanting a new opportunity for reinvigoration. New York City has become New Touba in the New World. The Mourides have mobilized to make maximum use of the occasion to promote their shaykh and their brotherhood. News of that is spread through the brotherhood's network to galvanize communities of devotees spread in numerous countries, including Italy, France, Germany, the Netherlands, and Britain.

It is a prominent article of Mouride teaching that religion bridges the distance between eternal reward and worldly blessing, between the Muslim *barakah* and the Wolof *bayré*.[7] Work and obedience to the shaykh in this life have become valued emblems of faith and devotion to God in the life hereafter. A prayer to capture that mood might end with "as on earth here, so let it be in paradise there." The worldly and the religious are equally realities for the Mouride,[8] as they are for many other Muslims. Accordingly, in adopting the language of the prosperity gospel, the anointed leaders of the new Christianity may be drawing on a venerable vein that occurs also in Africa's encounter with another ancient world religion.

Part II of this book turns from contemporary Africa to the history of Christianity in modern Asia. It highlights the emergence of some themes that have come to full flower in present-day world Christianity. The focus of Jay Case's chapter is on the implications of the nineteenth-century work of American Baptists among the Burmese Karen tribe for developments and tensions in mission and in religious thought among U.S. Baptists. Case commences his story of American Baptist missionary work among the Karen people with the significant point that the initiative to introduce Christianity among the people was their own and that it was they who pressed the Americans to enter the culture and promote the interest in Christianity that they had shown. With challenging implications, Christianity had preceded civilization among the Karen people, upsetting the sequence that most people had come to expect. Equally tellingly, the evangelical impulse had stirred among the people long before American evangelicals had given it any thought. The export variety of American religious activism had been preceded by strains of the phenomenon on the ground, to the discomfiture of planners and strategists in the United States.

Karen Christians mobilized behind the oral tradition to field the new religion among their people. They employed old myths and narratives to anticipate the coming of missionaries and thereby promoted Karen culture as the frame for receiving and transmitting Christianity. It was a pointed demonstration of the indigenous discovery of Christianity rather than the Christian discovery of the indigenous culture. When, accordingly, the New Testament appeared in translation in 1853, there was a stampede for it. The Karen initiative was rewarded with its own scripture, and so the path for expansion could be resumed with renewed energy and confidence. The Karen evangelists had in the Bible a primer for spreading the religion and naturalizing it among their own people. They had a warrant, too, for their struggle of cultural identity.

American Baptists scrambled to make sense of such news from afar, unable as yet to grasp the cultural implications of Christianity buoyant beyond the West. Apart from ad hoc rules for missionaries' field practice, anthropological science was scarcely conceived at the time, and little else existed by way of intellectual resources to explain the spectacle of a resurgent Christianity outside the frame of civilization as the West understood it. The insights of the social Darwinism of a later age would have yielded conclusions no more enlightening and no less disconcerting. Hierarchical notions of society were deeply ingrained in the West, and so the possibility of unsupervised faith among so-called primitives in acephalous cultures was discounted a priori. The undeniable evidence of a vigorous Karen Christianity therefore threatened a major disruption of accepted ideas about staged development and missionary oversight.

It fell to Francis Wayland, a moral philosopher, an ordained Baptist minister, and a president of Brown University in Rhode Island, to explain how reports of Karen Christianity as a lay, grassroots, popular movement might be reconciled with American Baptist ideas of lay participation and a democratized culture. Beyond that, Karen Christianity demonstrated the success of Christianity in a non-Western frame and proved that Western culture was not a prerequisite for Christian conversion—such were the early precursors of what we know today as the challenge of multiculturalism. The Karen people did not have to become like Americans to be Christian, Wayland insisted. Rather, the Karen people must be encouraged to cherish their own language, for that was the channel God chose for conveying truth and affirming the people. As such, God had preceded the missionaries into the field, an accurate religious insight that nevertheless was too radical for the proponents of civilizing mission to accept. But that did not stop it from being true, especially for the relevant local populations.

The balance of opinion among contemporary Baptists, however, was on the side of those who supported mission by conventional routes and rules: schools, books, schoolteachers, and the funds necessary for their success. These could do for the natives what vernacular languages alone could never do. Wayland, accordingly, became less representative of the broad band of missionary thinking. An educated elite, sufficiently Christianized, it was accepted, would carry forward the work of Western civilization more effectively than anything else of local vintage. With that went the view that missionary oversight was required to guard the store and keep up the momentum. Arguments for superior missionary oversight coincided with the era of Jim Crow legislation in the American South and white supremacist ideas in America to sharpen the color-coded, paternalist impulses of mission.

Forces on the mission field, driven by local agency, continued to generate dissenting views. The proven capacity of indigenous ministry, said one experienced missionary, showed we could dispense with smothering the gospel in the swaddling bands of Western civilization. To be viable or credible abroad, Christianity did not have to depend on the sending boards. In fact, observed a missionary critic acidly, civilization and Christianity might not be a winning combination abroad after all. Although it would take another hundred years or so for the results to show fully, the pattern and its implications were evident to keen observers like Francis Wayland.

Richard Plantinga picks up the theme of the theology of religions and expounds it in relation to the ideas of Hendrik Kraemer, the Dutch scholar who lived and worked in Indonesia in the 1920s and '30s. Kraemer's influential book, *The Christian Message in a Non-Christian World*, written in 1937 and published the following year, propounded a theory of mission that took critical account of other religions—in particular, Islam—in relation to Christianity. The book stirred a vigorous intellectual debate worldwide and became a defining moment of the ecumenical movement. Kraemer's South Asian missionary experience allowed him to bring Third World ferment into the otherwise tranquil deliberations of his Western colleagues, who responded by accusing him of religious colonialism. Yet the clarity and force of Kraemer's statements have continued to earn him the attention of the ecumenical world. As late as 1988, Kraemer's ideas still stirred debate and defined positions on the place of other religions within Christianity's own broad economy.

Plantinga refers to Lesslie Newbigin's defense of Kraemer as a Christian advocate in the presence of other religions, an issue that has remained prominent as Third World immigration swells the ranks of non-Christian religions in the West. All of that makes Kraemer's work of continuing pertinence, however controversial his ideas were. Even his critics have conceded that Kraemer had in general laid down the essential elements of the alternatives of any theory of religions vis-à-vis the challenge of interreligious encounter.

There has been no generally accepted view of the rationale of religious pluralism. Kraemer's exclusivist position that Christ alone is the true way to God, for example, sets off alarm bells among liberals without resolving the paradox of universal truth claims expressed as particular, specific religions, each valid in its own eyes. In that sense, the universal and the particular do merge quite naturally, for instance, as Buddhism, as Hinduism, as Islam, as Judaism, or as Christianity, rather than as an indistinct, amorphous synthesis. What such religions have in common is that they make universal truth claims, for otherwise they would lose title to their particular name and to their reason for being. Even in the mundane world, memory and recognition are impossible without a name to summon. That was the conclusion of a famous clinical research project carried out by a leading African psychiatrist. Religion is no different.

Kraemer dramatized that paradox for Christianity, but the same could be said of the other religions, too. We are familiar with the paradox today as the tension between diversity and difference, with *diversity* understood as tolerance of all religions and cultures and *difference* as exclusion and, thus, as intolerance. But that polarity creates a morale-sapping cultural muddle by requiring all religions and cultures to submit to diversity as the final truth, and by requiring that they also abandon all claim to those of their teachings that deviate from the creed of diversity. Diversity thus behaves like a truth claim by proscribing difference. Difference, for instance, that will not yield to a prescriptive synthesis—whether such difference is of race, tribe, gender, language, nationality, neighborhood, education, lifestyle, taste, or creed—is ipso facto condemned as intolerance. Yet it is hard to defy difference and uniqueness without risk to diversity itself, and it is hard to embrace diversity without a truth claim. Achieving diversity as a desired good seems to sacrifice difference as a necessary good. The culture wars of the West are fueled by that smoldering contradiction, which may help explain the continuing preoccupation with the issues Kraemer raised so sharply. The very worthy goals of mutual tolerance in one human family, which for the time being is necessarily spread among diverse religious truth claims, still await an acceptable, viable vehicle to advance mutual trust.

In his chapter on the theological response to Christianity in the non-Western world, Wilbert Shenk turns to a different challenge, centered on intellectual developments in the post-1945 world. The setback for missions in China following the Communist revolution led to their withdrawal and also to a searching inquiry into the reputation of Christianity as a Western religion that is considered foreign and unwelcome everywhere else.

Because carrying the Christian name became a burden, especially in China, Christian Asians drew upon the idea of "contextual theology" to make the case for a naturalized Christianity in Asian culture. The first phase of their task was to strip Christianity of its Western accoutrements and its reputation of cultural betrayal before moving to the second phase of their task, which was the constructive one of rehabilitating the gospel in the idiom and priorities of indigenous societies. Only local leaders and theologians could legitimately or effectively undertake such a two-prong task, and only in that way could an authentic Christianity emerge, Shenk argues. Yet, as Vanden Berg shows, theologians are loath to engage with the local if doing so means taking local ideas of evil and spirit power such as witchcraft into account.

In any case, the challenges of contextual theology are not just matters of internal acceptance and local legitimacy but of Western control as well. The West is disinclined to take seriously ideas and methodologies that are not its own, and overcoming that resistance is a formidable obstacle in the way of freeing local theological potential. Those local theologians who might pioneer contextual theology, for example, find themselves drawn to the West to advance their careers because of lack of opportunities at home. With their departure, the initiative they should seize is conceded to the West. Third World Christianity continues, for that reason, to be enmeshed in the ramifications of Western economic and intellectual power, supporting the view of Christianity abroad as an extension of Western dominance.

That symbolizes the irony of Roland Allen, an English missionary Shenk mentions, who became an intellectual proponent of making Christianity truly indigenous. Allen hoped that indigenization would enable Chinese and other Third World Christians to assume responsibility for missions without the stigma of foreign conspiracy. Yet, Allen's was a top-down view of rendering Christian mission authentic. Because of its roots in Western sensitivities, the cause of legitimate indigenization, accordingly, remained vulnerable to charges of not being authentic enough. Local advocates embraced the radical nationalist project to insulate themselves against such a charge, a position that still failed to solve the problem of Christianity seeking to hide its foreign nature under a Chinese costume. In his concluding theological reflections, Shenk argues that contextual theology, where it has been successful, led to effective mission and to a revitalized church, something that should have a salutary effect on the West, too, he contends.

Rules of Scholarship and Obligations of Experience

The chapters of this book are the results of the fruit of new research and fresh critical thought on the fast-developing story of Christianity beyond the immediate shores of Europe and North America and of the impending culture clash with a post-Christian West. They examine the religion in its familiar Western mode and pursue variations on the theme in new settings and cultural transpositions. The studies pause here and there to recall familiar themes and directions in Western Christianity and to reveal new facets from Christianity's encounter with indigenous idioms and other religions.

The authors have not tied themselves to the futile search for the Holy Grail of one comprehensive explanatory theory, one all-encompassing answer for the riddle of one universe of facts. Nor have they flinched from offering, where that is warranted, a reasoned hypothesis for the nature of the culture gap that trails the global Christian resurgence. They have confronted the evidence critically but sympathetically and then ventured theoretical generalizations stringently but responsively. They offer no shibboleths and preclude no outcome that is consistent with a reasonable account of the evidence.

The multidisciplinary team of scholars assembled here is intended to demonstrate that we need not only new tools and methods to expound the story of world Christianity but also new combinations of skills and expertise if our work is to rise to its greatest potential. In all of this, we have sought not to lose sight of the subject of our study and not to become lost in the arcane maze of scholarly discourse. Talking to one another as experts should be enhanced by all of us remaining engaged with those whose lives, work, and stories captured our interest in the first place. We owe an undeniable obligation to rules of intellectual scrutiny no less than to the veracity of experience, because something of our own meaning and value is invested in the tools and ideas we bring to our subjects. Accordingly, the channels we fashion with our particular disciplinary tools should serve to convey the subject matter of what we encounter and, in so doing, make the means serve the end.

NOTES

1. Andrew Walls writes with respect to Africa, "For African Christianity is undoubtedly African religion, as developed by Africans and shaped by the concerns and agendas of Africa; it is no pale copy of an institution existing somewhere else. . . . African Christianity must be seen as a major component of contemporary representative Christianity, the standard Christianity of the present age, a demonstration model of its character. That is, we may need to look at Africa today in order to understand Christianity itself. . . . Africa may be the theatre in which some of the determinative new directions in Christian thought and activity are being taken." Walls, *The Cross-Cultural Process in Christian History* (Maryknoll, NY: Orbis Books, 2002), 119.

2. In a contrasting case, under the Kano State and Zamfara State penal codes in Nigeria, Shariʿah Islamic sanctions apply to anyone found guilty of witchcraft, including possession of what is described as juju and related charms and amulets. But witchcraft accusations carry a legal peril, for falsely making them renders one liable to penalties for *qadhf* under Sharīʿah. Still, providing criminal sanctions proves the reality of witchcraft practice, as it also proves that hard cases make bad law.

3. Andrew Walls points out that medical missions made their earliest and strongest impact in those societies, as in the West, where healing and religion could be mentally separated with ease and that, conversely, such missions were less prominent in premodern cultures, where healing and religion were most intimately connected. It shows that medical missions were part of an Enlightenment system of rationality and progress and to that extent had limited scope in traditional societies. Walls, *The Missionary Movement in Christian History: Studies in the Transmission of Faith* (Maryknoll, NY: Orbis Books, 1996), chap. 16, 219.

4. It is pertinent to the issue to recall the major theological statement on faith and suffering by the Sudanese scholar Isaiah Majok Dau in his book *Suffering and God: A Theological Reflection on the War in Sudan* (Nairobi: Paulines Publications of Africa, 2002). Dau is senior pastor of the Sudan Pentecostal Churches and principal of a Pentecostal Bible school in Kenya. He said he first learned to read and write at age 17 before going on to earn a doctorate in theology, surmounting great obstacles in the process. His book is arguably the first substantial theological study by a Sudanese on the war and the suffering it has engendered. His work shows how his African experience has reshaped the triumphalist note normally associated with Pentecostalism.

5. The *New York Times* front page report, "In Harlem's Fabric, Bright Threads of Senegal," July 28, 2003.

6. The Smithsonian Institution has issued a music CD called *Badenya: Manden*

Jaliya in New York City (Smithsonian Folkways Recordings, SFW #40494, 2002), devoted to West African immigrants in the city.

7. Camilla Gibb describes the role of saints in social life. Her study is based on East Africa. "Baraka without Borders: Integrating Communities in the City of Saints," *Journal of Religion in Africa*, 29: 1, (1999):88–108.

8. See Ed van Hoven, "The Nation Turbaned? The Construction of Nationalist Muslim Identities in Senegal," *Journal of Religion in Africa*, 30: 2 (2000): 225–48; and also Beth Anne Buggenhagen, "The Prophets and Profits: Gendered and Generational Visions of Wealth and Value in Senegalese Murid Households," *Journal of Religion in Africa*, 31: 4 (2001):373–401.

PART I

Christianity as a Non-Western Religion

Studies from Africa and the African Diaspora

I

Religion Bridge: Translating Secular into Sacred Music: A Study of World Christianity Focusing on the U.S. Virgin Islands

Patricia Harkins-Pierre

Make a joyful noise unto God, all ye lands.

—Psalm 66:1

Sing praises to the Lord . . . proclaim among the
nations/ what He has done.

—Psalm 9: 11

In the last decades of the second millennium, modern culture, particularly in the West, has been highly secularized and often unsparingly critical of religion. Looking into the near future, novelist Salman Rushdie spoke for many public intellectuals when he proclaimed, "The third millennium must be the age in which we finally grow out of our need for religion."[1] Elsewhere in the world, however, religious faith—and Christianity in particular—is vibrant and growing. At the turn of the new millennium, this disparity of religious interest and commitment was dramatic indeed. Andrew Walls, the eminent historian of African Christianity, observed that

> already more than half the world's Christians live in Africa, Asia, Latin and Caribbean America, and the Pacific. If present trends continue, at some point in the twenty-first century, the figure could be two-thirds. It seems that the repre-

sentative Christianity of the twenty-first century will be that of Africa, Asia, Latin and Caribbean America, and the Pacific. . . . The events that, for its weal or for its woe, will shape the Christianity of the early centuries of the third millennium are those already taking place. . . . If we are to know the whole story, we must explore a Christianity formulated by a whole series of cultures with histories of their own.[2]

Within the wide-flung geographical and cultural region of the Caribbean, a dynamic concept of world Christianity is revitalizing the twenty-first-century church. This reality is becoming increasingly evident in one Caribbean community—the U.S. Virgin Islands—where Christianity in its Western colonial form has been rejected by much of the population. To study the phenomenon, I first explore the history of Christianity in the Virgin Islands within the wider context of its historic and contemporary expansion. Next I focus on how a recent musical titled *Jankombum*, by Caribbean playwright Eddie Donoghue, reflects the root causes of the crisis Christianity is now experiencing in the U.S. Virgin Islands. Finally, I focus on the work of Caribbean gospel artists in the Virgin Islands whose "confident adoption of vernacular speech as consecrated vessel," to borrow an apt phrase from Lamin Sanneh, has placed them "squarely at the heart of religious change."[3]

Christianity and Conquest in the Caribbean

The U.S. Virgin Islands comprise one group of the many Caribbean islands that in several ways find themselves caught in the middle. Geographically, they are caught between North America and South America. Culturally, they are caught between Africa and Europe, a fact extensively referred to in Caribbean music and literature. Religiously, they chart a course between rejection and renewal of Christianity. To understand the present dynamic within the U.S. Virgin Islands community, we must keep in mind that in the Caribbean, the record of Christianity's foundation and expansion is set within a history of conquest, slavery, ongoing oppression, ambivalence about religion, cultural ambiguities, and in-betweenness. It is a complex history, the story of a deeply troubled place rich in drama and tragedy.

Christianity was introduced to the Caribbean at the very beginning of its contact with Europeans, when Christopher Columbus explored this part of the world for Spain. On his second voyage to the so-called New World in 1493, Columbus encountered what we know now as the U.S. and British Virgin Islands (see figure 1.1). He was so struck by their beauty that he named the region for St. Ursula and the radiant virgins who, according to legend, were martyred with her. Even today, these islands have a reputation of being a paradise because of their lovely beaches and the clear, fertile seas in which they

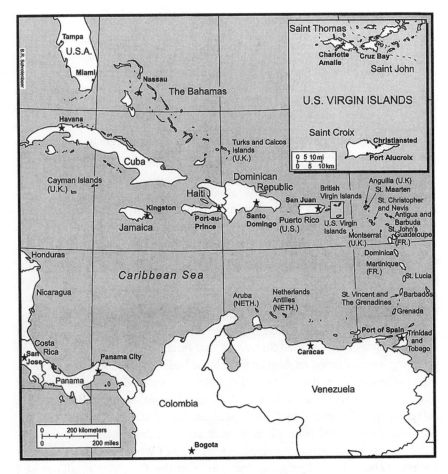

FIGURE I.I. U.S. Virgin Islands

are set like four green jewels. Columbus soon encountered people from the same Taino culture group he had earlier described to his sponsors on his first voyage of discovery in search for a new trade route to India:

> They should be good and intelligent servants; for I see that they say very quickly everything that is said to them; and I believe that they will become Christian very easily, for it seems to me that they have no religion. Our Lord pleasing at the time of my departure I will take six of them to your Highnesses in order that they may learn to speak [a "civilized" European language].[4]

Within 50 years from the November day when Columbus sailed up Salt River in St. Croix, nearly all the island tribespeople in the region we now call the West Indies had been enslaved and then exterminated by disease and ill treatment, but not before most of them had been converted to Christianity by Catholic missionaries. At the beginning of the twenty-first century, the language of the Tainos, Arawaks, and Carobs who first settled the Virgin Islands survives only in some place names. The traces of their tribal nature worship are preserved in just a few stone zemis (tiny, intricate statues of their gods) and rock carvings, such as those found on the island of St. John.[5] But the artifacts and legends of their once vital, widespread culture are honored and studied today by U.S. Virgin Islanders.

After Columbus's initial landfall, Spanish, Dutch, French, and English privateers and pioneers fought more than 200 years for ownership of St. Croix, St. Thomas, St. John, Water Island, and their neighbors. But it was the Danes who finally gained control of the "four sisters" by 1734. The pattern of exploitation, slavery, and conversion of non-Europeans begun by the earliest European explorers and settlers in many ways foreshadowed the fate of the Africans the later colonists brought to the Caribbean as forced labor for their lucrative cotton, sugar, rum, indigo, and spice plantations. However, unlike the indigenous peoples whom the Europeans destroyed, the African population that displaced them as slaves managed to survive in spite of terrible suffering and even managed to preserve many traces of their various tribal cultures.

During World War I, the Danish government sold this beautiful cluster of tropical islands to the United States.[6] By that time, the rich colonial plantation economy initially based on African slave labor had collapsed, because of changing markets and a series of natural disasters. In spite of these setbacks, the islands seemed an ideal location for U.S. naval bases, strategically located to safeguard the Panama Canal. As is still the case today, the majority of the population descended from Black African slaves, although much of the economic and political power remained in the hands of White people of European ancestry. The politics, literature, and music of the U.S. Virgin Islands still reflect the long, often bitter, sometimes violent strife between these two groups.[7]

Only because of an amazing will to live, and ability to adapt, did any slaves transported from Africa to the Virgin Islands as plantation workers during the eighteenth and nineteenth centuries survive the harsh treatment they received.[8] Eventually, like the Amerindian slaves before them, most of the African slave population converted to Christianity because of the efforts of both Catholic and, increasingly, Protestant European missionaries.[9] Gradually, the descendents of the original African slaves forgot nearly all the words their ancestors had brought to the Caribbean from the Mandinga, Kalabari, Amina, Kongo, Akanda, Popo, Nupe, Kawaku, Loango, Sokaot, Amina, Mokko, Ibo, Bambara, and Ashanti languages.[10] "Gaan . . . Gaan . . . Gaan," African captives aboard a slave ship aimed for St. Croix lament in the opening scene of Caribbean playwright Eddie Donoghue's recent musical, Jankombum.[11] Over the years, the slaves, their children, and their grandchildren learned to speak—and sing— in the European languages imposed on them by their oppressors. But the grammar and syntax they used among themselves retained marked character-istics of their African heritage, evolving into Danish Creole, still occasionally heard in the U.S. Virgin Islands until the late twentieth century,[12] and English Creole, with its distinctive Cruzan, St. Thomian, and St. Johnian dialects.[13] These dialects together make up the "nation language" currently spoken by many Virgin Islanders.[14]

Christianity, Slavery, and Resistance

Today Christianity is at a crisis point in the U.S. Virgin Islands. Black Carib-bean playwright Eddie Donoghue, born on the island of Montserrat but now living and working in the U.S. Virgin Islands, reflects on the root causes of this crisis in *Jankombum*, a well-researched historical drama written on St. Thomas and first performed there in March 2000. In an article featured in a local paper, the *Independent*, Donoghue said the musical was written "to cele-brate the end of the millennium while paying tribute to the traditional lives of African slaves in the Caribbean." Although the title has been translated into English as *Jim Crow*, the playwright has stated that the word *Jankombum* is the proper name for the hero of his musical, whose character is based on "the mythical son of the African god Borriborri," the creator god of the Amina nation. [15] The unpublished play is set in 1741, although the playwright's stage directions acknowledge, "We have taken license to embody a number of his-torical events from a [slightly] later period [in the same century]."[16]

The Danish planters rule St. Croix, St. Thomas, St. John, and Water Island. Conditions are not easy for either the planters or their slaves. Dengue fever, malaria, smallpox, and other diseases debilitate both the oppressed and their oppressors. The European settlers so far from their own homelands find the sometimes scorching heat and the yearly threat of hurricanes and earthquakes almost unbearable at times (as the historical documents show), but they are determined to succeed in their quest for economic gain.[17]

In the opening act of *Jankombum*, Mrs. Carstens, a rich planter's wife (based on a historic character) is having a conversation with another character adapted from history, Paul Erdman Isert.[18] This German surgeon has just dis-embarked from the slave ship *Christenborg*. During their encounter, the play-wright establishes the two central themes that resonate throughout the story of Christianity in the U.S. Virgin Islands: (1) the forced Diaspora of Africans, leading to their subsequent struggles to reestablish cultural identity and func-tional communities of hope, and (2) the ambivalent relationship of European mission–founded Christianity to Afro-Caribbeans.

Carstens tells Isert, "All of our slaves are Christian. I must credit Brethren Martin and the other Moravian missionaries for bringing Christianity and civ-ilization to the heathens."[19] Later in the same scene, the surgeon reflects that the slaves on St. Thomas are "captives in a strange land. The pawns of religion." Isert is immediately berated by Carstens, her husband, and their friends for his subversive speech. Martin, one of the Moravian missionaries who founded the Church of the Brethren in the Danish West Indies, self-righteously retorts, "As witnesses of Christ we are charged . . . to go throughout the world and instruct all nations."[20] The clergyman advises the doctor to devote himself to saving bodies and "allow me to minister to the souls of heathens." The minister goes on to describe "the ideal bondsman," who remains faithful to his master, suffering yet serving willingly. He tells Isert, "They are not fruits that grow of themselves. They are nurtured by the missionary. They are the result of divine grace."[21] This missionary represents the same viewpoint as the colonial administrator in Nigeria that historian Lamin Sanneh described, who "said that Christianity was giving Africans the wrong ideas of equality and justice."[22]

How the White slave owners and their missionary allies in the musical respond to even the mildest criticism of their lifestyle in the Danish West Indies is summed up by one sanctimonious line they sing together in a chorus: "We civilize, Christianize, we baptize." They decline to admit any guilt or remorse about the practice of slavery. Isert's response is emphatic: "I feel sick! I am sick!" He confesses to the unsympathetic planters and clergy how bitterly he regrets having paid for passage to the Danish West Indies by serving as surgeon aboard a slave ship, where he daily witnessed the "tormented minds" and physical abuse suffered by the African captives. "The evil we perpetrate exceeds the limits of humanity," he moans. Before he leaves the room, Isert sings, "Spare us O Lord from error and misunderstanding / From hypocrisy and fanaticism / From pride and vanity / From unbounded ambition."[23] He becomes an abolitionist, much to the disgust of the Carstens and their missionary allies, who fear a slave rebellion in an area where the Black bondsmen far outnumber the free Blacks and Whites. They believe that any such revolt would be sparked by the same "religious idea" that, as Sanneh has noted, "gave Africans the political notion that they were equals of Europeans."[24] Indeed, during the eighteenth and nineteenth centuries, slave revolts were not uncommon throughout the Caribbean, and the Virgin Islands were no exception. Donoghue has stated in an interview that his play is "a composite picture based on the story of David, a slave who participated in the aborted 1759 revolt on St. Croix."[25] For our purpose of understanding the crisis that Christianity is facing in the U.S. Virgin Islands at the beginning of the twenty-first century, it is imperative to realize that the Black population within this society has a well-established history of fighting against bondage and racism that has helped many of them retain a strong sense of self-respect in the face of many challenges.

As Eddie Donoghue's play progresses, we learn that the slaves themselves often quarrel over the role of missionaries and Western Christianity in their lives. Some of the slaves, especially those who listen to the Lutheran missionaries, genuinely believe in the salvation of Jesus Christ and have faith that a glorious future in heaven awaits them. That hope—that eager expectation of good—is based on the same two premises that Lamin Sanneh pointed out in discussing the history of slavery in Africa during a *Christianity Today* interview: "African captives" (like Caribbean slaves) had hope on earth because evangelical missionaries taught them, first, that "we are each made in the image of God" and, second, that "the stigma" of slavery "is dissolved in the blood of Jesus."[26] Other slaves, including the protagonist, Jankombum, "know there is such a thing as a spiritual life" but totally reject all missionaries, especially the Brethren, whom they believe are controlled by the planters.[27] They resent having to communicate in the language of their oppressors and refuse to praise Christ in any language, especially any African language, unlike the Christian slaves who, at one point in the play, break out into spontaneous songs praising and worshiping Jesus Christ in their native African tongues of Mokko, Ibo, and Karabari. Today, Jankombum and his cohorts would accuse the Christian converts of being merely hypocritical syncretists, rather than being transformed through their faith in Christ.[28]

The conflicting attitudes toward Christianity in the Black community of Donoghue's musical are still very evident in U.S. Virgin Islands society today, a point to keep in mind as we move from the colonial to the so-called postcolonial era. The polarization these attitudes can lead to is personified most fully in Donoghue's drama by a comely house slave named Rebecca and her suitor, the rebellious Jankombum. Rebecca teaches the slave children about the baby Jesus, "how he was born in a manger . . . how the wise men visited the stable," and then leads them in her favorite Christian European hymns with lines such as "Assist and teach me how to pray, / Incline my nature to obey" or "Comfort every sufferer / Watching late in pain; / Those who plan some evil/ From their sin restrain."[29] But when she tries to convert Jankombum to the gospel of forgiveness and reconciliation in which she finds spiritual strength and freedom, he resists. "Why don't you ask God to forgive you for all them lies you fool the children with?"[30] He taunts the woman he finds so alluring and yet so exasperating, deliberately using English Creole rather than the Standard English Rebecca favors. In response, she reads to him from Isaiah 1:18: "Come now, and let us reason together, saith the Lord; though your sins be as scarlet, they shall be as white as snow." Deliberately misinterpreting the meaning of this scripture, he declares he does not want to be made "white as snow" because he is proud to be Black and of African descent. When she talks to him about the joys of heaven Christians look forward to and their fear of going to hell unless they are redeemed, he renounces any belief in such a place as heaven and scornfully declares hell must be "the same as down here where all you Christians rape, steal, kill, fornicate."[31] Jankombum and Rebecca powerfully embody the problematic to which our study of the U.S. Virgin Islands responds: Is the mission-founded Christianity of Afro-Caribbean culture a source of liberation or a prop for the status quo? Is this faith a deceptive panacea that

in reality fails to resolve such persistent, deeply rooted problems as racial prej-
udice?

Jankombum not only expresses his rebellious spirit through his choice of
dialect but also through a type of musical expression, African drumming and
dance, that Rebecca spurns, just as he spurns the European Christian hymns
the missionaries have taught her. Donoghue scripts African-derived drumming
and its compelling rhythms only for Jankombum and the other radically rebellious slave characters who are planning a revolt against their European masters and the Christian missionaries.[32] As Jankombum flirts with Rebecca,
tempting her to at least abandon her Europeanized code of decorum if not her
Christian faith, he reveals that he is planning a slave revolt.[33] Rebecca is aghast,
terrified for her mistress, Mrs. Carstens, who has been kind to her. Justifying
his hatred of White European planters and those merchants, soldiers, and
missionaries who choose to be their allies, Jankombum points to his mutilated
leg. Although she is sad about the crippling punishment he received for running away from his master, Rebecca leaves, refusing to listen further to what
she calls "diatribe" that "borders on blasphemy!"[34]

Postcolonial Christianity

Jankombum is a fictional work set in the eighteenth century. However, the
opinions and concerns the playwright expressed are historically accurate. Moreover, they even now continue to affect people living in the U.S. Virgin Islands—
the territory promoted as "America's Paradise"—as well as people living elsewhere in the Caribbean. Even though the slaves in the Danish West Indies
demanded and received their freedom in 1848, Western Christianity, with its
bittersweet relationship to European and then U.S. missions, has been constantly under attack, particularly during the last 30 years. This is true in spite
of the fact that the majority of Virgin Islands residents, especially among the
African-Caribbean community, continue to identify themselves as Christian,
as census figures clearly show.[35] This ambivalence is complicated by the current
political status of the U.S. Virgin Islands, which, unlike some of its Caribbean
neighbors, has still not gained political independence. The four sister islands
together form a territory of the United States, with the same status as Guam
in the Pacific. According to the United Nations, the U.S. Virgin Islands remains
a colony in a supposedly postcolonial world. Although the citizens of the territory are also citizens of the United States and have their own locally elected
governor and legislature, they are not allowed to vote in national elections. This
kind of inequality sometimes causes bitter resentment, especially because the
tourist economy of the territory, so dependent on the continuing goodwill and
wealth of mainland U.S. citizens, is fraught with environmental and social
problems.

Many of the Christian congregations in the Virgin Islands are still closely affiliated with the historic mainline churches mentioned in *Jankombum*: Dutch Reformed, Moravian, Lutheran, Anglican, and Roman Catholic. Christian missionaries and evangelists, usually from the United States, have continued their work in the U.S. Virgin Islands up to the present day. Baptist and Methodist mission teams, for example, are common there. Baptists have established not only a highly respected primary school but also the Blue Water Bible College and Institute, which attracts students from across the Caribbean for training in Christian ministry. Since the 1960s, as in sub-Saharan Africa, the mainline Protestant missionaries have been superseded by conservative evangelical and Pentecostal missionaries. The financial and moral support from mission teams coming from the U.S. mainland during times of economic and social crisis, such as those immediately following hurricanes Hugo in 1989 and Marilyn in 1995, have been much appreciated by most U.S. Virgin Islands residents. Nevertheless, given the history of the territory, it is no wonder that today Christianity is often viewed by Black Virgin Islander "resistance" leaders, such as writer Mario Moorehead and politician Adelbert Bryan, as "the propaganda tool of White colonizers from Europe and the United States, intended to keep the Black populace in mental bondage."[36] The catchphrase *cultural imperialism* is commonly used by the local media and intelligentsia to highlight the pervasive and, in their view, usually pernicious influence of the United States on every aspect of contemporary life in the U.S. Virgin Islands. Proliferating violence is blamed on the influence of the powerfully subversive gangster rap from the U.S. mainland secular music industry, for example, and the constant tensions between the Black and White segments of the local population are blamed on the racist attitudes with which the White-dominated media bombards television, movie, and Internet consumers. The establishment of the Independent Citizens Movement Party signals a small but significant grassroots initiative for political freedom. Despite of the constant criticism, the truth is that most people in this community are proud of the territory's regional reputation for relative prosperity and the economic and educational opportunities that come from its close ties with the United States.

Even so, growing numbers of so-called grassroots churches have responded to the accusations of cultural imperialism by breaking away from denominational control in favor of local leadership and power.[37] This response is reminiscent of the African Independent Churches movement during the twentieth century in sub-Saharan Africa as a sign of spiritual independence from outside dominance.[38] Another response has been the increasing number of Virgin Islanders who have turned to Rastafarianism, originally from Jamaica, with its own Creolized language system and its African-based rituals, including chanting and drumming, such as that portrayed in *Jankombum*. Islam and Hinduism have also established a strong presence in the Virgin Islands; so have Santeria, the worship of the Yoruba god Ogun in the form of St. John;

Vodun, or "voodoo," a hybrid of Catholic and African religious practices orig-inating from Haiti; and Shango, a form of obeah or fetish worship imported from Trinidad.[39]

Since the beginning of the twentieth century, emigrants to the U.S. Virgin Islands have included a large number of Spanish speakers from Puerto Rico and, for the last 10 years, from Santo Domingo. "Native" Virgin Islanders (those who were born here and whose parents and grandparents were also born in these islands) complain that French Creole speakers from Dominica, St. Lucia, St. Martin, and Haiti also seem to outnumber them, "taking over" their jobs and their churches.[40] During the past 20 years, emigrants from India and the Middle East have become increasingly common, often owning small but lucrative businesses, a fact that the native Virgin Islanders often resent. Unlike most of the other emigrants, they do not consider themselves Christians but rather Hindus or Muslims.[41] The Moravian church is still influential in the community, however, and the Moravian missionaries are still given credit for being the first group to promote literacy among the Black inhabitants.[42]

In fact, the Virgin Islands today seem to have a Christian church on nearly every street corner, a fact often alluded to in conversation and in the local media.[43] However, many of the congregations are aging, and they often com-plain of not attracting enough new, young members to revitalize them. One reason for this is the frequently lamented "brain drain" that a native Virgin Islander, businessman Lawrence Baschulte, refers to in his July 2002 guest editorial for the territory's best-selling newspaper, the *Daily News*: "For as long as I can remember we have been selling the Virgin Islands to tourists as Amer-ica's paradise; and I agree for one or two short weeks, to an outsider, the Virgin Islands can be paradise. But for those of us who live on the islands, life here is not easy task."[44] For hundreds of years, dengue fever, earthquakes, and hur-ricanes have threatened those who lived here. Add to these the modern chal-lenges of frequent power outages, unemployment, and the exorbitant cost of living, and many parents feel driven "to send our children away for a higher education and not expect or encourage them to come back to the Virgin Islands to improve our paradise." Baschulte warns, "Without our young people to shape our future, we will have no future."[45] To make matters worse, pastors, such as Leayle M. Benjamin, who shepherds Covenant Christian Center com-plain that frequently those in the community who "profess Christianity with their mouths are backsliders in fact," while others are "Christmas-and-Easter Christians or enter our churches for weddings and funerals only."[46]

So what are Christians doing about these problems? The Catholic churches in the U.S. Virgin Islands today are meeting the challenges posed by "indif-ference, disenchantment and hypocrisy" head-on.[47] They have done so by turn-ing to charismatic African missionaries, for instance, and radical young priests from Dominica who use French Creole and lively music in their services to attract new converts and foster a spirit of revival. The twenty-third annual Dominica National Independence Celebration, held on Sunday, November 11, 2001, at the Holy Family Parish Church on St. Thomas, is a perfect example of these initiatives at work. The celebration is organized by a committee of laypeople drawn from the large percentage of Dominican immigrants and descendants of Dominican immigrants in the congregation. Each year they bring a priest from Dominica to celebrate Mass at the event. This year the visiting celebrant was Monseigneur William John-Lewis. He was assisted by the pastor, Simon Peter Opira, a missionary originally from Nigeria, and John K. Mark, a young, newly ordained priest born and raised on St. Croix, now the parochial vicar of Holy Family Parish on St. Thomas.[48] The church literally overflowed with enthusiastic worshipers of all ages, social classes, and ethnic backgrounds as the service progressed.

Music was an integral part of the celebration. The large choir wore colorful costumes reminiscent of those commonly worn in Dominica a hundred years ago. The congregation joined them in the songs that complemented the Mass. Choir and congregation were accompanied by a small group of skilled musicians, playing an electronic keyboard and electric lead, rhythm, and bass guitars. The lyrics of all but 3 of the 24 songs included in the program were in French Creole with a Caribbean beat, starting with the entrance hymn, "Minon Mi Nou Dominchen" ["Look, We Are Dominicans"], and concluding with the recessional hymn, "Merci Bondie" ["Thanks to God"].[49] "Together We Are Christ's Body," one of the few songs with English lyrics, was printed and sung in English Creole rather than in Standard English. Excerpts indicate its message:

> Together we are Christ's body, no
> Longer slaves but free. . . .
> (1) We cannot do nothing if Christ
> Ain't inside o' we,
> We can' be His body if we ain'
> Loving as He. . . .
> (2) If our actions too selfish we gonna
> Be in a mess,
> We ain't to compare who is better
> Or who is best. . . .
> (3) Though we function differently,
> We got one identity,
> Because as children of God we're
> Re-building identity.[50]

The simple words of this song bear witness to the same healing Gospel message preached so eloquently in John-Lewis's sermon (which he delivered almost simultaneously in both French Creole and Standard English):

Today we celebrate independence, but friends, there is no freedom except in Jesus Christ! Liberation from the powers of darkness—allowing nothing to be a stranglehold about our necks, keeping us from seeing the beauty of Christ in those around us. . . . Sin is true slavery; in Jesus Christ is true independence and liberty to love Him with our whole heart and to love our neighbors as ourselves. Until we hear and act on this our true freedom is far from us.

The monseigneur's sermon contained traditional Bible references, and its theme was based directly on scripture. But his delivery took him out of the pulpit, striding up and down the aisles, cordless microphone in hand; he was equally at ease in two languages, telling jokes, inserting personal anecdotes, even singing from and promoting his album of hymns displayed on a table outside the main entrance to the church. "As you can, see music is a big part of my ministry," he said at one point. The crowd applauded, laughed, and sang along with him—and after the service rushed to get a tape or CD of his *The Journey of the Soul*, which though on sale was given freely to those who said they could not afford to buy it. When they play the album, his audience may at first be surprised to discover that it consists wholly of old English or American standards such as "Amazing Grace" and "I Surrender All," though "Amazing Grace" does open with the thrumming of what the artist hopes "sounds like African drums." At the feast after Mass, John-Lewis told Caribbean gospel artist Glenworth Pierre and his wife that his activities as a recording artist only enhance his vocation as a Catholic priest "in this technologically sophisticated age we live in." He added, "In my next CD I will put French patois and an island beat. I must."[51] This gospel artist's comments acknowledge the importance of using regional dialects and rhythms as means of bridging the gap between secular Caribbean culture and the modern church in order to attract— and keep—the interest of Caribbean people.

Other denominations in the Virgin Islands today are also reaching out to people in many ways, including the music in their services, programs, and concerts. At St. Thomas Assembly of God, for instance, Pastor George E. Phillips has not only an organ in his church but also a full set of drums, electric guitars, and a state-of-the-art keyboard. These instruments have become basic equipment for many Christian musicians in the Caribbean, as in the United States, over the past few decades. But Phillips also allows the youth ministry to praise the Lord through rap music and contemporary Caribbean music, especially in their evangelistic concerts, "so long as the lyrics have a clear Christian message" and the performers "dress appropriately, not immodestly."[52] In this time when so many young people struggle with identity issues and how to survive in an often hostile world, Christian churches in the U.S. Virgin Islands want to help local youth realize that the best way to resolve their struggle about being Caribbean or American is to decide "I am Christian. I am first and foremost a citizen of God the Father's kingdom, adopted into his family through Jesus Christ, whose ambassador I am to his honor and glory, in the power of the Holy Spirit."[53] They know the importance of music to most of the young people they want to help, and they realize the power of music when it is used to praise and worship God.

The music ministers and pastors understand the need all people have for both individuality—uniqueness—and yet community. That is precisely why even usually conservative U.S. Virgin Islands congregations, such as Pastor Amaran Williams's Seventh Day Adventist Philadelphia Church, are changing their tune—at least to a certain degree. Prominent long-time member Professor Violeta Donovan explained in an interview: "We do recognize music to be a very important part of our worship service and have always had several choirs, and some wonderful soloists, as well as congregational singing." On reflection, she added:

> We believe that Christian music is not necessarily Christian, how-
> ever, simply because of lyrics; in our church we try to make sure the
> rhythms and melodies are appropriate. It isn't always easy to do.
> Our eleven o'clock main service is more conventional. We use mu-
> sic most of us would agree to. But when the youth group sings, they
> often choose pieces that many of us may not recognize as being as
> Christian as we would like. Sometimes only a few words are re-
> peated loudly over and over, or the instruments may be so loud they
> drown out the words completely. Sometimes the words of the songs
> don't even seem scriptural or even necessarily Christian. It is a diffi-
> cult situation.[54]

As a dedicated Christian and mother of two teenagers herself, Donovan's concern about some of the music young people in her congregation choose for praise and worship reflects the conservative theological position many members of her denomination share. She does not want to alienate the youth group singers, but she believes they should choose only music that is fitting and proper for the church setting she shares with them. She knows that the youth group is following the musical fashion of their time and generation, but she agrees with John Calvin's remarks in the preface of his 1545 Psalter: "Care must always be taken that . . . there be a great difference between music which one makes to entertain men at table and in their houses, and the Psalms which are sung in the Church in the presence of God and his angels."[55] She desires order and harmony in church music to reflect her concept of Christian values, whereas the young people might protest that they are responding in faith through their music to a time of chaos and rapid, constant change. Perhaps both the younger and older members of this U.S. Virgin Islands church family would benefit from the following insight into similar conflicts within the Body of Christ occurring all over the world today:

Further, if it is indeed true that deep in human beings is a desire for fittingness between their deepest convictions and their art, then one can predict that the zealous young musician . . . who steps into a congregation determined to reform its musical taste is probably doomed to fail. If he is politically adroit and has powerful people supporting him, the music itself may change; but unless the religious self-understanding of the people is also reformed, their taste will alter less rapidly than their resentments build up.[56]

Caribbean Gospel

Some of the other Christian churches on the two larger islands in the territory—St. Thomas and St. Croix—have been open to a more radical spirit of change, reflected in their choice to abandon denominationalism and evolve into independent units. Like the Catholic pastors Opira and Phillips, the pastors of these churches also frequently feature Jesus as a man of color in their sermons, their Bible studies, and the bright artwork that adorn the walls of their church buildings.[57] The Danish planters of the eighteenth century would have been outraged, and their slaves amazed, at this radical shift in values and biblical interpretation. What would they say if they could see these congregations openly celebrating the African ancestry that most of their members share by dressing in clothes reflecting their heritage? Covenant Christian Center, New Visions Ministries, V.I. Christian Ministries, and Kingdom Life Christian Center are prominent examples of independent churches in the U.S. Virgin Islands that celebrate Christianity in this way. During their services, congregations, choirs, and soloists may sing a variety of songs, everything from standard hymns such as the nineteenth-century classic "Blessed Assurance" by Fanny Crosby of the United States, to any number of contemporary praise and worship songs by U.S. artists on the Integrity recording label. But more and more often, they also sing Caribbean gospel songs by Virgin Islands Christian songwriters: "Perfect Love," from Glenworth Pierre's 2001 album, *Anointed Worship*, or "Going God's Way," from Bernard Smith's 2001 album of the same title.[58]

Such works are part of a new flowering of sacred music in the Caribbean. It poses some challenges to other styles and offers instead a new Christian aesthetic. Yale University philosopher Nicholas Wolterstorff writes about such processes in Christian communities. Aesthetics, he insists, including musical expression, need to be biblically grounded. Songwriting should be sensitive to the beauty and inspiration of diverse styles without losing its responsibility to "be of benefit to us . . . giving us delight and building the community."[59] Wolterstorff explains the potentially provocative role of creative Christian artists in this way:

If the community of artists is truly to make a contribution to human welfare, however, they cannot each take a poll of what certain people say they like in art and then deliberately shape their work so as to satisfy them. Some, at least, must be an advance guard striking off in new directions, trusting that if they find something new in which they themselves take aesthetic delight, others among their fellows will find this delight as well—but never really knowing, taking the risk. . . . If human fulfillment is to be served and shalom [the peace of God] established, artists cannot all be obedient followers and timid calculators. Explorers are needed too.[60]

As the editors of *Voice Print: An Anthology of Oral and Related Poetry from the Caribbean* comment, Caribbean music today, whether secular or sacred, "has become the container of a wealth of alternative rhythms" to the older "standard" hymn and ballad rhythms with strict "iambic tetrametric quatrain shapes" imported from Europe and the United States.[61] A University of the Virgin Islands student, Viola Clarke, further identified the purpose behind the music of the "radical new" Caribbean artists. She wrote: "It gets the attention of people who are not really interested in Jesus Christ, and provides Christians with an opportunity to witness."[62] This Afro-Caribbean gospel music movement is gaining popularity and wide acceptance throughout the Caribbean—and beyond.

The music's main themes, revealed through the lyrics, convey the character of the new cultural identity and the communal ethos that is being forged in the new independent and Catholic charismatic churches. Harriet Mason, probably St. Thomas's best known Christian character actor and comedian, is the wife of the dynamic Caribbean evangelist Stan Mason. Two years ago, she discussed the state of Christianity today in the Caribbean and the role of music in revival and evangelism on her weekly radio show *Lighten Up*. She began by asking her audience to call in with their responses to the question, "What is Gospel music anyway?" She followed the ensuing conversations with her own definition: Gospel music "is people of God singing for the Lord. It's designed to set you free. Every kind of beat, from every place in the world. African—we have it; reggae (my favorite, I'll be honest); jazz—and every contemporary beat today from rap to hip-hop. The intention of the heart and the testimony of the mouth make up gospel music. . . . We can all keep our culture without losing our souls." Then she asked her featured guest, Caribbean songwriter and music minister Glenworth Pierre, to address the concerns of "those sincere Christians in the Caribbean who wonder if contemporary popular Caribbean beats and rhythms can really be used in the service of the Gospel today." He answered:

Not everything called gospel music *is* gospel music. The music in itself is neither good or bad. The Bible tells us it's always the intentions of our hearts and how our words match up with the living

Word of God that counts. If the words don't line up that way, I'm sorry; it's never gospel music, no matter what beat you've used. That song some of us sing, "I'm going up the rough side of the mountain," is not gospel no matter what old religious spirit tells us it is. What makes gospel music unique is the anointing. It cannot be music filled with doubt or unbelief. It cannot be lacking joy and full of complaint instead. Paul and Silas didn't sing about how rough life is; they sang with joy and faith and the angel of the Lord set them free.

Harriet Mason responded to his commentary, "Glen is known to be radical, folks. . . . And I have to agree with what he's saying."[63]

It is no longer uncommon for gifted musicians who live and work in the U.S. Virgin Islands to minister not only in Standard English but also in their own English dialect or in French Creole. Their decision to do so is the direct result of what Virgin Islands scholars George F. Tyson and Arnold R. Highfield describe as "the long, syncretic process of creolization, whereby Africans were eventually transformed into West Indians."[64] An array of "nontraditional" Christian Caribbean music ministries, which translate secular contemporary music styles into sacred music, have affected the U.S. Virgin Islands during the past 10 years. Among them are Joseph Niles from Barbados; from Jamaica, the Grace Thrillers and gospel artists Lester Lewis and his wife, "Singing Rose"; King Short Shirt of Antigua; Harella Goodwin from St. Croix; solo artists Glenworth Pierre and Bernard Smith, originally from Dominica; a trio from the Bahamas, System 3; the Turnbull sisters, particularly Judy Turnbull, from Grenada; and Kingdom Crew and Naomi Toussant, from St. Thomas. Like the European White missionaries who first came to the Caribbean hundreds of years ago, these Caribbean-born Black Christian songwriter-musicians have not only heard Christ's command to spread the Gospel but also have acted on it. Christianity, "the fruit of the Western missionary movement," has been transformed by contemporary Caribbean artists into the promoter and preserver of Caribbean people's cultures and languages.

A perfect example of this "radical" evangelism by contemporary Caribbean gospel artists occurred in April 2001. The calypso legend, King Obstinate, performed in concert at one of St. Thomas's largest churches, Church of God of Prophecy, with Bernard Smith as his opening act. The success of this concert had to do with many factors, but paramount among them was the timing. April is carnival month in St. Thomas, a time of extended revelry and often debauchery that includes weeks of celebrations featuring alcohol, local food, beauty and talent shows, and music competitions. The carnival festivities culminate in two days of elaborate parades. Before he had a stroke and decided to "get right with God his healer,"[65] King Obstinate was famous for the many calypso contests he won throughout the Caribbean. He still draws enthusiastic fans who would never otherwise attend a gospel concert, especially one held in a church. Calypsos grew out of the rich oral tradition of the Caribbean, which the editors of *Voice Print* identify as "a heritage of song, speech and performance visible" in a wide variety of "folk forms."[66] They are often associated with Trinidad's long and well-publicized carnival history, but St. Croix ("Cruzan") scholar Gilbert Sprauve noted that in the Virgin Islands as well "Carnival beckons today's singing troubadours—the calypsonians—from near and far in the region to compete in Calypso tents." Calypso, he states, is "only sung in Creole . . . in a cycle of perennial festivities. . . . Carnival can be seen as the foremost manifestation of Culture in the Virgin Islands and elsewhere in the region."[67] Calypsos became popular as satires on Caribbean society, songs of "celebration, praise, censure, erotic desire, ridicule."[68] In the hands of King Obstinate today, the classic calypso beat, reinforced by steel pans, drums, and brass, is set to lyrics with a Christian message. His focus now is on evangelizing audience members who are not Christian and sparking revival among his Christian listeners.

Lester Lewis and Singing Rose of Jamaica have been pioneers in the field by integrating several popular types of contemporary Caribbean music, especially reggae, with what they believe is "the good, the very good news of salvation through 'The Winner Man,' Jesus Christ."[69] Reggae began in Jamaica during the 1950s and early 1960s, evolving out of ska and rock steady, what West Indian poet and historian Kamau Brathwaite called "the native sound at the yardway of the cultural revolution that would eventually lead to . . . reggae."[70] Since Bob Marley's explosion on the international music scene more than 30 years ago, reggae has been considered the "roots" music of the Caribbean. According to cultural scholars, including the editors of *Voice Print*, reggae grows "directly out of the speech and music rhythms of Rastafari."[71] "The very nature of reggae, heavy bass-line and space between voice and 'riddim' with horns or synthesizer muted in the middle range, generally means that one can hear every word of the performance. Sound is stripped down to the skeleton of riddim, with the superimposition of the flesh of voice in performance."[72] Lester Lewis and Singing Rose have used the worldwide popularity of reggae as a vehicle to successfully carry their gospel message to nearly every continent. And even as their own music ministry grows, they continue to mentor others whose goals are similar. They have actively encouraged the young artists in the Bahamian trio System 3, for example, to master new styles, including dance hall, the most recent variant of reggae, in order to reach other young people throughout the Caribbean. In a song titled "Even Da Go" (1990), System 3 "translate" the words of the New Testament Great Commission into language framed by a beat their audience will listen to and understand.

Among the many Caribbean gospel songwriters striving to develop international audiences, few have managed to dedicate their talents to full-time ministry in a time and place that are often hostile to such a lifestyle. Most of these Christian artists, whether amateur (part-time) or professional (full-time), are multigifted, not only composing lyrics and melodies but also singing, playing, and performing their original music "to the glory of God and to reach a hurting world with His love."[73] Two of the best known and respected Afro-Caribbean professional gospel artists in the Virgin Islands, Glenworth Pierre and Bernard Smith, both originally from Dominica, now live in the territory as naturalized U.S. citizens. The vision and ministry of Glenworth Pierre is a blend of familiar and unique elements. In his written testimony, he reports: "I've been singing ever since I was a little child. From the day the Lord saved me He gave me a new song and from that day I have been singing the Gospel."[74] The title of one of his most recent releases, for example, *Anointed Worship* (2001), reflects the artist's belief in "the vital importance of the Holy Spirit's inspiration."[75]

Like his friend and mentor Lester Lewis of Jamaica, Glenworth Pierre was not a Christian as a young man. He was born on the island of Dominica and brought up in a Catholic family, but in the book he is presently writing, *Man's Reject Is God's Best*, Pierre relates some painful facts from childhood and adolescence. He is one of more than 50 "outside" (illegitimate) children fathered by a Dominican cricket player. When he was five years old, his mother left for the United States, where she married and started a new family. He never saw her again. "I'm a living witness and example of being a reject," the psalmist writes in his spiritual autobiography, "But I grew up to be a very blessed young man."[76] When he left home at the age of 17 for the island of St. Martin, where he was to live for 17 years, however, he was not searching for God. In spite of hard-won success as a guitarist and soloist there, by early 1985, because of a gambling addiction, Pierre did not have "even a cent to my name. . . . My back was against the wall."[77] Alone in a rented room one Sunday night in February, he experienced a dramatic conversion after he suddenly felt an overwhelming desire to read the entire Book of Psalms. He burned the manuscripts of all the songs he had written before he became a "born-again believer." He began to attend a Pentecostal church, and he no longer smoked marijuana, drank, or gambled. He stopped defining himself as an angry, oppressed young Caribbean Black man "living in darkness and longing for the light," and began seeing himself as "a new creation living in the light, letting that light shine through me, attracting others to Jesus Christ and freedom from self, sin and death."[78]

In 1998, Pierre produced his first album, *Radical Soldier*. To date he has released ten tapes, six CDs, and one music video. He has become an ordained minister of music who describes his ministry in this way: "I am a psalmist. My styles include reggae, soca, calypso, cadence—a big featured variety. I also write, and arrange all my songs. I play rhythm guitar, bass guitar, harmonica, keyboards [and drums]."[79] He creates some of his lyrics in standard English, but most of them are in Dominican English dialect or Dominican French Creole (which he still calls patois). In 1999, he opened a recording studio on St. Thomas, Lifeline International Music Ministry, as part of the evangelistic work he now shares with his wife. Pierre has appeared in concert throughout the Caribbean, sometimes as the featured artist and sometimes performing with other notable Caribbean gospel songwriters and singers, including Mary Powell of St. Kitts, Jerry Lloyd of Dominica, and Piper Laundry of St. Martin. "Give your heart to Jesus," he pleads with his listeners whenever he is in concert; "I pray that [my] songs will be a great blessing to everyone who hears them."[80]

The Internet and jet travel, two of the chief instruments of globalization, have propelled these Caribbean Christian songwriters and recording artists out to distant regions. A decade ago, Pierre foresaw that "Caribbean Gospel Music is going to make a crossover into the United States of America. . . . I see the way the people in America are responding to my ministry. . . . I see a bright future for Caribbean Gospel Music."[81] In a 1994 interview, he added, "The time is right for international growth in ministry. When I was in England, people were listening to Caribbean music everywhere."[82] Lester Lewis and Singing Rose would agree that their friend is a good prophet. Three years ago, for example, "Winner Man," a song they wrote for one of their albums, became a hit all over the Christian world when international gospel star Ron Connoly sang it on one of his releases. Today many of the tapes, CDs, and videos Caribbean songwriters and gospel singers produce are available throughout the United States and England and in countries on every continent as well. One innovative secular St. Thomas radio station has recently begun promoting Caribbean gospel music on its Web site.[83]

Glenworth Pierre's life story and music ministry are essentially similar to that of many other contemporary Afro-Caribbean male gospel artists, full of pathos, drama, pain, defeat—and redemption through sudden conversion to Christianity. His quest as a messenger of hope, not only to the island community where he lives but also to "a dying world"[84] far beyond its boundaries, is like that of fellow professional gospel songwriters and singers Lester Lewis of Jamaica, Piper Laundry of St. Martin, and Bernard Smith. Each of these men have emerged from "the darkness of despair and poverty into the light of Jesus Christ" and have since then dedicated their lives to his service, reaching out to all other "lost and hurting people of this generation."[85] No wonder they resist the label of "local" artists. Their dynamic ministries are reminiscent of an observation Lamin Sanneh has made:

> The most important thing we need today is moral character and leadership. . . . You find such people not among the privileged but among what you might call the flotsam and jetsam of society. These are people who have been to the depths of human experience and have come to their faith in Christ in a way that places them at the very center of God's moral redemption of the world.[86]

Their work provides a "Religion Bridge"[87] between Christian believers and nonbelievers throughout the Caribbean and beyond. Moreover, their ministries provide an important bridge that Western born and educated Christians may choose to cross in a quest to understand Christianity as a world religion. They are a powerful instance of what Sanneh terms "the vernacularization of the Gospel in the idioms of the folk, the people of the world."[88]

NOTES

1. Salman Rushdie, "Rethinking the War on American Culture," *New York Times*, 3 May 1999, A–21.

2. Andrew F. Walls, "Eusebius Tries Again: Reconceiving the Study of Christian History," *International Bulletin of Missionary Research* 24 (July 2000): 105–6.

3. Lamin Sanneh, *Translating the Message: The Missionary Impact on Culture* (Maryknoll, N.Y.: Orbis Books, 1989), inside front cover.

4. *Diario* of Christopher Columbus, quoted by Barbara Helfgott Hyett, *The Double Reckoning of Christopher Columbus: 3 August–12 October 1492: Poems* (Urbana: University of Illinois Press, 1992), 98.

5. Michael Paiewonsky's beautifully illustrated *Conquest of Eden 1493–1515: Other Voyages of Columbus, Guadeloupe, Puerto Rico, Hispaniola, Virgin Islands* (Rome: MAPes MONDe, Editore, 1990) shows a photograph (139) from the Royal Danish Library in Copenhagen of the Reefbay petroglyphs of St. John; the carved rock and its reflection in the water form an Arawak god.

6. The United States first flexed its muscle as a world imperial power in the Caribbean. After its victory in the Spanish-American War the United States gained control of the island of Puerto Rico. It also occupied Cuba (1895–1902 and 1906–1909). Then it seized power in Haiti (1915–1934) and the Dominican Republic (1916–1924). The United States purchased what would become the U.S. Virgin Islands from Denmark in 1917 to establish a naval base. For provocative glimpses of the European colonial and American imperial legacies through the eyes of contemporary Caribbean critics, read Derek Walcott's essay "The Muse of History" in a collection titled *Is Massa Day Dead?* (New York: Doubleday/Anchor, 1974), as well as his Nobel Lecture, *The Antilles: Fragments of Epic Memory* (New York: Farrar, Straus, Giroux, 1992). See also *The Colonial Legacy in Caribbean Literature*, edited by Amon Saba Saakana (Trenton, N.J.: Africa World Press, 1987).

7. The often-troubled relationship between the United States and the Caribbean has been exhaustively discussed by Caribbean writers. See Selwyn Cudjoe's seminal study, *Resistance and Caribbean Literature* (Athens: Ohio University Press, 1980); Governor Charles Turnbull's paper "Progress Towards Decolonization in the United States Virgin Islands, 1917–1992" (fourth meeting of the Latin American Social Science Council, U.V.I., June 1992); and perhaps the liveliest and most in-depth scholarly work on this issue in popular culture, Carolyn Cooper's *Noises in the Blood: Orality, Gender and the 'Vulgar' Body of Jamaican Popular Culture* (London: Macmillan Caribbean, 1993).

8. One of the most useful and accessible sources of information concerning the harsh conditions most slaves suffered in the Virgin Islands is *The Kamina Folk: Slavery and Slave Life in the Danish West Indies*, edited by George F. Tyson and Arnold R. Highfield (St. Thomas, V.I.: V.I. Humanities Council, 1994). Some of the most pow-

erful fictional accounts of slavery in the English speaking Caribbean are *Psyche* (London: Macmillan Caribbean, 1956/1980) and *The White Witch of Rosehall* (London: Macmillan, Caribbean, 1958/1982) by Jamaican writer Herbert deLisser, and *I, Tituba* (New York: Ballantine, 1992) by Maryse Conde, set on the island of Barbados.

9. Dale Bisnauth's *History of Religions in the Caribbean* (Kingston, Jamaica: Kingston Publishers, 1989) is a well-researched, concise study of how various religions, including Christianity, arrived and developed in the Caribbean. Other helpful studies include Armando Lampe, ed., *Christianity in the Caribbean: Essays on Church History* (Kingston, Jamaica: University of the West Indies, 2001) and Arnold R. Highfield and Vladmir Barac's translation of Moravian missionary C.G.A. Oldendorp's classic account of his sojourn to the Danish West Indies in 1767–1768, *History of the Evangelical Brethren on the Caribbean Islands of St. Thomas, St. Croix and St. John* (Ann Arbor, Mich.: Karoma, 1987).

10. Vincent O. Cooper, professor of English and linguistics at the University of the Virgin Islands, shared his perspectives on the pervasive, sometimes elusive influence of West African dialects on the history and culture of the Virgin Islands. See his chapter, "St. Kitts: The Launching Pad for Leeward Islands Creoles" published in *St. Kitts and the Atlantic Creoles: The Text of Samuel Augustus Matthews in Perspective*, edited by Philip Baker and Adrienne Bruyn (London: University of Westminster Press, 1998–99). On the development of Caribbean English, see Kamau Brathwaite's groundbreaking study, *History of the Voice: The Development of Nation Language in Anglophone Caribbean Poetry* (London: New Beacon, 1984), and another excellent source, Peter A. Roberts's *West Indians and Their Language* (Cambridge: Cambridge University Press, 1988).

11. This unpublished play has been performed only once to date, in March 2000 at the Reichhold Center for the Arts, St. Thomas.

12. Dr. Gilbert Sprauve, noted Crucian-born scholar of Caribbean culture and modern languages at the University of the Virgin Islands, brought the last known speaker of Danish Creole in the Virgin Islands as his guest to a Humanities Division senior seminar during spring semester 1990. The elderly lady could be prevailed upon by her daughter to speak only a few words of Danish Creole for the students and faculty (including myself) who were present. Since then, she has passed on.

13. Roberts, *West Indians and Their Language*, 13.

14. Brathwaite, *History of the Voice*, 13.

15. Eddie Donoghue interview, *Independent*, 24–25 October 1999.

16. Donoghue, *Jankombum*, ms., 1999.

17. Johan Lorentz Carstens, *A General Description of All the Danish, American or West Indian Islands* (St. Thomas, V.I.: V.I. Humanities Council, 1994); Caryl Phillips, *Cambridge* (London: PICADOR/Pan, 1992); and Pat Gill's novel *Buddhoe* (New York: Wentworth Press, 1976/1985) are fictional accounts of conditions and relationships on West Indian plantations. See also Neville Hall, *In the Danish West Indies: St. Thomas, St. John and St. Croix* (Kingston, Jamaica: University of the West Indies Press, n.d.), especially the chapter "Empire without Dominion: The Danish West Indies, 1671–1848."

18. See Isert's account, "Voyage to Guinea and the Caribbean," in *The Kamina Folk*, edited by Tyson and Highfield, 103–10.

19. *Jankombum*, Act 1, Scene 2.

20. Ibid.

21. Ibid.

22. Lamin Sanneh, interview, *Christianity Today*, 10 July 2000, 43.

23. *Jankombum*, Act 1, Scene 2.

24. Sanneh interview, 43.

25. Eddie Donoghue, *Independent* interview.

26. Sanneh, interview, 42.

27. *Jankombum*, Act 1, Scene 3.

28. But see Lamin Sanneh, *Translating the Message*, 36–48, a discussion of the role of syncretism in the first century of Christian history for an enlightening insight into how this term can be applied in a positive sense.

29. *Jankombum*, Act 1, Scene 3.

30. Ibid.

31. Ibid.

32. Altogether, there are 20 fully developed songs and many song fragments woven into this drama. Of these, 12 were specially composed by Donoghue. Donoghue, "Lyrics: First Line, Script Page, Type, Source," *Jankombum*.

33. The slave revolt on which this musical is based was a short-lived conspiracy that never came to fruition, but ended in imprisonment, torture and execution for the Black slave leaders implicated in the plot. Engelbret Hesselberg, "Account of the Negro Conspiracy on St. Croix, 1759," *Kamina Folk*, 53–60.

34. *Jankombum*, Act 1, Scene 3.

35. Frank Mills, "Immigration Patterns in the U.S.V.I.," U.V.I. Award for Excellence in Research Lecture, University of the Virgin Islands, spring term, 2000.

36. Gilbert Sprauve, untitled essay, University of the Virgin Islands, spring semester, 1993, p. 3.

37. Stewart Brown et al., eds., *Voice Print: An Anthology of Oral and Related Poetry from the Caribbean* (Kingston, Jamaica: Longman, 1989), "Introduction," 3.

38. Paul Gifford, *African Christianity: Its Public Role* (Bloomington: Indiana University Press, 1998), 324–25.

39. Dale Bisnouth, *History of Religions in the Caribbean* (Kingston, Jamaica: Kingston Publishers, 1989), chaps. 4, 6, and 7. I must acknowledge also Professor Gene Emmanuel, my colleague at the University of the Virgin Islands, for insights into the practice of Rastifarianism, Santeria, and Vodun in the U.S. Virgin Islands.

40. Mills, "Immigration Patterns."

41. Pauline Adema, *Folklife of the East Indian Community: St. Thomas, Virgin Islands* (St. Thomas, V.I.: Division of Libraries, Archives and Museums, 1994), chaps. 2 and 3.

42. The Nisky Moravian Church on St. Thomas, for example, supports a private Christian school with two campuses on St. Thomas.

43. The usual saying, as Agnes Nicholas, one of my U.V.I. students, further noted, is something like this, "Of course there is also a bar on every corner." Nicholas, personal interview with the author, 30 October 2001.

44. Lawrence Baschulte, "America's Paradise, or Illusion?" *Virgin Islands Daily News*, 6 July 2002, 18.

45. Ibid.

46. Pastor Leayle Benjamin, interview with the author, 5 December 2001.

47. Simon Peter Opira, interview with the author, 11 November 2001.

48. Church of the Holy Family bulletin: "Twenty-Third Sunday in Ordinary Time," 11 November 2001. Missionaries and evangelists still come here from Europe and the United States, but in past 15 years there has also been a steady flow of West African Catholic missionary priests. Pastors from Virgin Islands Christian churches now often make evangelistic and missionary journeys themselves, to the United States, Africa, Australia—all over the rest of the world. The "Faith and Values" weekly Saturday section of the V.I. daily newspaper, the *Daily News*, chronicles this fact. See, for example, the article on Pastor George Phillips for St. Thomas Assembly of God: "Besides Caribbean countries, Phillips has served in England, Poland and Bulgaria, but serving on the African continent is his passion. . . . He says, 'I am committed to training, motivating and investing in younger ministers on the African continent'" (6 October 2001, p. 24).

49. The bulletin cited previously was for the Dominica independence celebration at Holy Family Church on November 11, 2001. It included the lyrics to 22 songs. Two additional pages had been inserted into the back of program, each containing the lyrics to one additional song.

50. Ibid.

51. Msgr. William John-Lewis, interview with the author, 11 November 2001.

52. Agatha Phillips, interview with the author, March 1994.

53. Ibid.

54. Violeta Donovan, interview with the author, 14 November 2001.

55. Quoted in Nicholas Wolterstorff, *Art in Action*, second edition (Grand Rapids, Mich.: Eerdmans, 1996), 187.

56. Ibid., 188.

57. One dramatic example of such artwork is featured on the cover of Covenant Christian Center's Sunday Bulletin for Sunday, February 21, 1999. In this replica of the original, bold red script proclaims, "It's the Anointing That Destroyed the Yoke." Directly below the first half of the message and above the second half, the artist has placed two dark brown, muscular arms raised so that a sharp, two-edged sword surrounded by flame can break the chains encircling their wrists. Both the words and the visual image contain a vivid link to John-Lewis's sermon at the Dominica Independence Day celebration described earlier in this chapter and to the English Creole song included in the Program for that service.

The artwork adorning Holy Family Catholic Church includes an original painting above the altar of the Last Supper showing Christ and his apostles as Black men. A stained-glass window above the painting, however, represents the Holy Family—Mary, Joseph, and the Christ child—with very pale skin and light hair.

58. Glenwood Pierre, *Anointed Worship* (St. Thomas, V.I.: Lifeline Studio, 2001); Bernard Smith, *Going God's Way* (St. Croix, V.I.: Back Yard Studio, 2001).

59. Wolterstorff, *Art in Action*, 213.

60. Ibid, 169.

61. Brown et al., "Introduction," *Voice Prints*, 3.

62. Viola Clarke, untitled essay, University of the Virgin Islands, March 1995.

63. *Lighten Up* radio broadcast, WSTA 1340, 28 March 2000. "Anointed" music,

sung under the quickening and inspiration of the Holy Spirit, seems to be a common feature of African, African-American, and Afro-Caribbean Christian music. See especially Glenn Hinson, *Fire in My Bones: Transcendence and the Holy Spirit in African American Gospel* (Philadelphia: University of Pennsylvania Press, 2000).

64. Tyson and Highfield, "Introduction," *Kamina Folk*, xv.

65. Bernard Smith, interview with the author, 6 April 2001.

66. Brown et al., *Voice Print*, 3.

67. Sprauve, untitled essay, 5.

68. Brown et al., *Voice Print*, 21.

69. Lester Lewis, interview with the author, March 1994.

70. Brathwaite, *History of the Voice*, 41.

71. Brown et al., *Voice Print*, 17.

72. Ibid., 18.

73. Bernard Smith, interview with the author, 6 April 2001.

74. Glenworth Pierre, "Vision and Testimony," unpublished, undated manuscript in the author's possession.

75. Pierre, interview with the author, 12 July 2002.

76. Glenworth Pierre, "Man's Reject Is God's Best," unpublished, undated manuscript, chap. 2.

77. Pierre, "Vision and Testimony."

78. Pierre, interview with the author, 3 September 2001.

79. Pierre, "Vision and Testimony."

80. Glenworth Pierre, *Virtuous Woman* (St. Martin: Liberty Music, 1997), back cover note.

81. Pierre, "Vision and Testimony."

82. Pierre, interview with the author, 19 March 1994.

83. See it on www.caribbeanmusic.com.

84. Pierre, interview with the author, 23 March 1994.

85. Pierre, interview with the author, 3 March 2001.

86. Sanneh, interviewed in *Christianity Today*, 10 April 2000, 42–43. See also the account of Bernard Smith's life and ministry, which is rich with lessons learned and promises yet to be fulfilled, included on his release, *Going God's Way* (St. Croix: Back Yard Studio, 2001).

87. A song title from a CD release of Glenworth Pierre, *Winners* (St. Martin: Alvin Lawrence Studio, 1999).

88. Lamin Sanneh, concluding remarks, Christianity as a World Religion Conference, Calvin College, Grand Rapids, Mich., 28 April 2001.

2

Culture, Christianity, and Witchcraft in a West African Context

Todd M. Vanden Berg

The original intention for this chapter was to present in clear relief how traditional Longuda beliefs in witchcraft have merged with beliefs about the devil within the Lutheran Church of Christ in Nigeria (LCCN). It was to show how in this meeting a unique understanding of the nature of evil in the world has come about for the Longuda people of Nigeria who are Lutheran Christians. Such an integration speaks directly to important theological questions on the nature and origin of evil in an African context. However, research in the literature on the integration of traditional religious beliefs and Christianity within the context of what one might call orthodox mission churches[1] made the dearth of material on the subject quickly apparent. Little research of any depth had been published concerning orthodox mission churches on issues that speak to their integration of traditional religious beliefs. The first half of this chapter explains some possible reasons for this neglect by scholars in both theology and anthropology. The second half explains, through a case study of the LCCN, how this sort of integration is occurring at a grassroots level within an orthodox mission church. It focuses on Longunda Lutherans' beliefs in witchcraft, the devil, and notions of the nature of evil in the world.

The Theological Call for Africanization

Coinciding with the advent of national independence in Africa during the 1950s and 1960s, African theologians and religious studies scholars began to argue that Africa had a form of Christianity that was not distinctly African but rather Eurocentric. There was a general discomfiture with the form Christianity had taken in Africa, and the call went out for an "Africanization" of Christianity.[2] Various concepts such as indigenization, adaptation, contextualization, incarnation, and inculturation have since been used in this discussion. Underscoring the universality of Christianity, scholars such as C. G. Baeta[3] and John Mbiti[4] have argued that nevertheless there are uniquely African expressions of Christianity. As Luke Mbefo has put it in an article about Nigeria, the advocates of African contextual theology argue that if the African church could reclaim a "cultural originality," it could "develop within its structural outlines a theology that is authentically Christian and equally authentically Nigerian. The justification for this is grounded on natural theology: God had spoken to our ancestors before the arrival of Christianity; our ancestors had responded to God's address before the arrival of Christianity."[5]

Their point is well taken. As Lamin Sanneh has argued, what is remarkable about Christianity is that it finds a position of resonance within many cultural contexts; it is eminently translatable.[6] The question needs to be addressed, however: By what means does this Africanization of Christianity occur or has it been perceived to occur?

Top-Down Versus Grounded Africanization of Christianity

In calling for Africanization of Christianity, many theologians have made two faulty assumptions. First is the assumption that the incorporation of African forms of Christianity should come from the top down. That is to say, African scholars, theologians, and other members of the church hierarchy, as well as European and North American missionaries, are expected to lead the masses through the process of the Africanization of Christianity. The assumption seems to be that Africanization is a dogmatic endeavor. This endeavor often seems detached from the grounded reality of the people in churches. This kind of approach seems largely an attempt to create a uniquely African form of Christianity on a metaphysical level. Such efforts may have very little value for those at the grassroots level.[7]

An example of the top-down orientation may be helpful. In his essay "The Africanization of Missionary Christianity: History and Typology," missiologist Steven Kaplin develops a tentative typology for various forms of Africanization as seen through a historical context.[8] His typology is based on missionary activities and attitudes and assumes only a passive involvement on the part of African Christians, as opposed to the active involvement of missionaries. The six-category typology involves mission actions, not indigenous actions, and thus exemplifies a top-down perspective. Kaplin makes an admirable attempt to show that missionary approaches to the Africanization of Christianity varied historically far more than is usually assumed. But he deals solely with the missions' perceptions of the cultural interchange rather than the actual, grassroots beliefs of the indigenous people involved and the process whereby those beliefs are integrated. Africanization for Kaplin comes from the top down and is specifically derived from missionary efforts.

Religious studies scholar Birgit Meyer contrasts this approach with a grassroots approach that we might call "grounded" integration. *Grounded integration* refers to ordinary church members' efforts to integrate the two separate yet intertwined circumstances of being African and being Christian. Such efforts are not dependent on church officials but rather are predicated on day-to-day living grounded within a specific cultural context. This form of integration may well be the most productive; it certainly is the most utilized.

The second assumption that African scholars and theologians make when calling for the Africanization of Christianity is that such Africanization needs to be jump-started by theologians. This, I believe, is a false assumption that shows a lack of understanding of what has happened and continues to happen at the grassroots level of orthodox mission churches. Andre Droogers speaks to the general tendency for religious scholars to concentrate on the hierarchical upper echelons at the expense of the general religious populace when he states that "Students of religion . . . may develop a blind spot for the practical and the popular in a religion. Their main interest then is to systematize the cerebral side of religion, often presented as the only side or the representative side. The popular side—though majoritarian—is viewed as a less interesting deviation from it."[9]

Not only does this side seem less interesting and less important to many theologians but also, it may be a more uncomfortable topic for them to consider because it often is manifested in unexpected ways. At the grounded level, the spirit moves in mysterious ways—apparently too mysterious for some theologians. Not only may theologians' discomfort reflect the unusual nature and character of the specific areas of integration that occur at a grassroots level but also it may reflect the challenge they may feel on issues of identity, power, and authority within African churches. For the most part, it appears that theologians feel free and comfortable to call for the Africanization of Christianity when such calls are focused on peripheral religious beliefs that do not speak to the core of what it means to be a Christian. Theologians are relatively comfortable in discussing, for example, liturgical forms such as dancing and drumming. But when the topic moves more into core religious beliefs, there is little discussion. Mission theologian Robert Schreiter observes that in discussing the relationship of anthropology to Christian missions, "liturgical accouterments and religious rites may be adjusted in light of anthropological data, but the question of the existence of a spirit world and the need for performing exorcisms may be deftly avoided by those same Christian adapters."[10]

Even more pertinent to the case study that follows, religious studies scholar

Matthew Schoffeleers argues that African theology does not mention the matter of spirits and witches. "African theology owes part of its attractiveness—particularly in the eyes of Westerners—to the fact that it carefully avoids these issues. The price African theology had to pay for this is that it has been unable to develop a theory of sin and evil."[11] Schoffeleers may be correct that theologians have not developed a theory of sin and evil, but grassroots Christians in Africa are already living from day to day with a conception of the nature and origin of sin and evil, as the ensuing case study of Lutheran Longuda believers will show.[12]

Anthropologists and Mission Church Acculturation/Syncretism

When moving from theological to religious studies and anthropological literature, it quickly becomes apparent that few anthropologists have considered mainline orthodox mission churches as venues in which to study the synthesis of religious systems in cultural contexts.[13] For various reasons, it seems, anthropologists have preferred to study other religious phenomena pertaining to the broad anthropological issue of cultural change. In Africa, anthropologists have focused on traditional religious systems or recent religious movements including African Independent Churches, such as the Aladura in Nigeria; Kimbanguism in Zaire; Zion Church in South Africa; and the Legio Maria in western Kenya.[14] Of the few anthropological studies of mission churches that have been done, most have concentrated on the missionaries' involvement rather than on the indigenous members of the churches.[15]

There may be some specific reasons for the dearth of anthropological studies of orthodox mission churches. One is that indigenous religious systems and religious movements may attract anthropological study simply through their more "exotic" nature. Many anthropologists become at least initially interested in the field because they are attracted to the Other. Orthodox mission churches simply do not have an exotic feel.

A second reason may be the historical rift between anthropologists and missionaries. To study a mainline orthodox mission church may bring an anthropologist too close to the missionaries who started the church.[16] Claude Stipe suggests two presuppositions held by many anthropologists that may lead them to hold negative attitudes toward missionaries.[17] The first is that primitive cultures are characterized by organic unity, and therefore any external impingement on the system (e.g., mission efforts) is harmful. The second is the common assumption that religious beliefs themselves are meaningless and that their rituals actually point to other cultural meanings and realities. Frank Salamone suggests, with some irony, that anthropologists' and missionaries' similarities may be the source of this tension. Both believe they have the truth, protect those with whom they work, and oppose that which is defined as evil.[18]

James Peacock puts anthropological biases against mission work in a larger context:

> It is part of a larger bias by many anthropologists and by the intel-
> lectual posture of the discipline and perhaps by academia generally.
> This posture is anti-power; it is critical of the military, of govern-
> ment generally, of capitalism, and of any commitment to a positive
> credo. Within this general attitude, however, anthropologists are par-
> ticularly critical of what we might term hegemonic religions within
> their own society.[19]

A third reason for the lack of anthropological study of mission-founded churches may be the unconscious belief that they have nothing to offer to the discussion of the integration and synthesis of religious systems. Anthropolgists may believe that all of the integration and synthesis is going on in newer religious movements, not in the more ordinary mission-founded churches.[20] Anthropologist Johannes Fabian suggests that

> the claim of the mission church to represent a unified system of be-
> lief and action is often too easily accepted. Perhaps the most serious
> gap, however, is that we know almost nothing about the faith of or-
> thodox mission Christians, and I strongly suspect that improved in-
> formation on that point would make any statements about the "devi-
> ance" of "sects" and "separatist movements" look rather simplistic.[21]

To sum up, on the one hand there are theologians who assume that the Africanization of Christianity has not yet occurred in orthodox mission churches and who call for the Africanization of Christianity from the top down. On the other hand, there are missiologists, religious studies scholars, and anthropologists alike who prefer to study more "exotic" religious movements rather than studying orthodox mission churches. The result is very little concerted study of any kind on the topic of an African integration of Christianity at the grassroots level in orthodox mission churches. The aim of this chapter is to begin to remedy this shortage.[22]

What follows is a brief case study of grassroots integration of religious beliefs within a mainline orthodox mission church context, particularly concerning notions of the origin and nature of evil in the world. The case study focuses on the witchcraft beliefs of members of the Lutheran Church of Christ in Nigeria (LCCN). It demonstrates that the Christianity found in African orthodox churches today is already a uniquely African form. It is a product of grassroots integration of traditional African elements and Christianity as introduced by missionaries. I pay close attention not to missionaries or African academic theologians but to ordinary African Christians, who are synthesizing Christianity and Longuda religious beliefs.

The Lutherans and the Longuda

This case study is based on fieldwork conducted with the Longuda of Adamawa State, Nigeria (figure 2.1), in 1995. It focuses on beliefs held by Longuda LCCN members. The Longuda are a culture group of approximately 40,000 who have had contact with various Christian denominations going back almost to the turn of the twentieth century. Today, Pentecostal, Baptist, Catholic, American Mission Church (AMC), and Lutheran denominations all have congregations in Guyuk, the largest of the Longuda villages and the local government head-quarters. The most common church membership among the Longuda is with LCCN. Lutheran mission contact began in Adamawa State (formerly Gongola State) in 1911 with the Danish branch of the Sudan United Mission

FIGURE 2.I. Nigeria

(DSUM). In 1960, LCCN was established as an independent Nigerian denomination.[23]

Unfortunately, the majority of church records from the early mission period have not been translated from Danish into English. One such text from this early time period, written by the DSUM's first missionary to Adamawa State, Dr. Niels Brønnum, was called "Under Daemoners Aag" ("Under the Yoke of Demons").[24] Such a title provides us with a sense of the attitudes these early missionaries held toward their potential converts' indigenous religious belief systems. The stance of the DSUM—as was the case with most mission churches—denied the existence of witches (Swanya, sing.; Swanba, pl.). The LCCN has generally maintained this stance. The commonly held stance of missions such as the DSUM was that beliefs in witchcraft were holdovers from traditional beliefs that would eventually fade out once Christianity became more incorporated into the African belief system. When it became apparent after a number of years that such beliefs were not fading, the church hierarchy's perspective toward these beliefs changed.

Longuda Witchcraft Beliefs

Where witchcraft beliefs exist, the specific understandings vary only slightly from one culture to the next. Typically, a witch is believed to be an individual who is born with a supernatural ability that others do not have. This ability is used exclusively for evil ends. Witches are understood to be exclusively evil and out to subvert society. They are commonly believed to kidnap children, murder, and participate in cannibalism and vampirism. Witches are thought to have the ability to fly at incredible speeds; shape-shift (including the ability to be invisible); have familiars such as a cat, bat, owl, and hyena; meet regularly with other witches (the sabbath); participate in deviant sexual acts; be active at night; and spread illness, disease, and death. In all these ways, witches are understood to be the embodiment of societal evil. Belief in witches is not universal, but such beliefs can be found all over the world.

Where witchcraft beliefs are maintained, the beliefs are not usually meted out in direct accusations; they tend to remain within the confines of suspicions. Only when a culture is under severe sociocultural stress will accusations become common. When accusations do occur, there is a structure whereby a witch can be cured and made a functioning member of the society.

Following the initial anthropological studies of witchcraft beliefs, anthropologists have often taken a functional approach. Witchcraft beliefs may function to help explain why bad events happen. Such beliefs may also help to define correct social behavior, reinforce authority, define social values, afford human intervention, relieve personal guilt, and create social cohesion.[25] As with many African cultures, Longuda hold strong beliefs in witchcraft. These beliefs play a role in day-to-day activities and contribute to a specific understanding of the way the world operates.[26] For the Longuda, witchcraft beliefs are firmly integrated into a modern context. We need to see how, in fact, Longuda witchcraft beliefs have been incorporated into their contemporary setting, especially within a Christianized view of reality.

Survey Summary

During my fieldwork in 1995, I conducted a survey in two Longuda villages. Although it was not meant to be a representative sample of Longuda, the survey does serve to highlight the strength of Longuda beliefs in witchcraft. In one of the questions, respondents were asked to agree or disagree with the statement, "Witches exist." A full 88.9 percent of those surveyed agreed; 11.1 percent answered "disagree" (table 3.1). Those who believed that witches exist were also asked to respond "yes" or "no" to the statement, "Could a witch ever harm you?" Those who answered "yes" made up 91.8 percent (201), and 8.2 percent (18) stated "no" (table 3.2). Such responses underscore the very strong belief in the existence of witches, as well as the belief that witches are very influential in the world.

As the survey responses show (table 3.3), the belief that witches exist and

TABLE 3.1. Survey Response to the Statement "Witches Exist."

Response	Count	Cumulative Count	Percent	Cumulative Percent
Agree	224	224	88.9	88.9
Disagree	28	252	11.1	100.0

TABLE 3.2. Survey Response to the Question "Could a Witch Ever Harm You?"

Response	Count	Cumulative Count	Percent	Cumulative Percent
Yes	201	201	91.8	91.8
No	18	219	8.2	100.0

TABLE 3.3. Survey Percent Response of Christians and Traditional Believers to the Statement "Witches Exist."

Response	Christian (Percent/Count)	Traditional (Percent/Count)
Agree	83.2 (119)	100 (89)
Disagree	16.8 (24)	0 (0)
Total	100 (143)	100 (89)

that they are influential in the world are opinions that are held not only by those who adhere to the traditional Longuda religious system but also by Longuda Christians. Although 100 percent of those respondents who claimed a traditional religious affiliation believed in the existence of witches, fully 83.2 percent of those respondents who considered themselves to be Christians also believed in witches. Of those who stated that their religious affiliation is Christian, 78.4 percent belonged to the LCCN.

Clearly, both traditional religious believers and Longuda Lutheran believers hold strong beliefs in witchcraft. It is to the Longuda members of the LCCN that I now turn, with a focus on the nature of witchcraft acquisition and the typology of potential witchcraft victims. The aim is to better understand the form and perhaps the function of these beliefs within a Christian setting.

Integration: Witchcraft Acquisition

In more traditional Longuda beliefs in how witches, or *Swanba,* acquire their abilities, the motivations and deeds of *Swanba* are combined into a single package: a person is born with the desire, as well as the supernatural ability, to be an evil *Swanya.* In a contemporary understanding, motivations and deeds can be and are separated. The deeds of *Swanba* in a contemporary understanding are similar to traditional beliefs, but not their motivations. In the traditional belief system, it is believed that *Swanba* are born with evil intent. In the contemporary perception, the possibility that coercion exists is gaining ground on the belief in the inborn desire to do evil.

One of the purposes that the belief in external coercion serves is to reduce personal responsibility for witchcraft. Yet in some ways, the introduction of the possibility of coercion does not make sense. In the traditional context, even if one were accused of being a *Swanya* (this very rarely occurs), different methods could be used to cure a person of witchcraft. These methods include not only stripping a *Swanya* of his or her powers but also stripping the *Swanya* of the desire to do evil. Such a person would then be accepted back into the community as an active and full member. So why is there a need to alter beliefs in the method of acquisition, placing the blame on external impingement, when in the more traditional sense of inherited witchcraft, once a *Swanya* is cured, the individual is accepted back into the community?

This switch may be related to the tendency of witchcraft to be associated, with the devil. Through this association witchcraft has taken on an entirely new dimension involving the juxtaposition of God (good) and the devil (evil). Although the Lutheran leaders' tendency is toward ignoring the witchcraft issue, this has not meant that witchcraft is never discussed within the church. Pastors argue that witchcraft beliefs and accusations are evil and, in so doing, associate witchcraft with the devil.[27] Both missionaries and Nigerian pastors have associated witchcraft beliefs with the work of the devil.

With the association of witchcraft with the devil, the belief that witchcraft can be inherited puts too much of an association with the devil on the individual or family. If, on the other hand, witchcraft acquisition is coercive, then the responsibility and the originator of evil are external to the individual and family. The devil is not within, but rather outside the family—in some other realm of existence. When traditional beliefs in witchcraft and a Christian perspective on the devil interact, it becomes difficult to associate witchcraft with innate abilities and desires. If a person is born a *Swanya* and if a *Swanya* is of the devil, then is that person of the devil? This dilemma is eased if coercion rather than heredity is stressed as the method of becoming a *Swanya*. A *Swanya* can be understood to be a basically good person, a baptized Christian who has been coerced. Despite the teaching of Lutheran missionaries and pastors, witchcraft beliefs have persisted, yet they clearly have been modified to accommodate Christian beliefs.

Integration: Whom Witches Can Harm

There has also been an alteration in Longuda beliefs concerning whom *Swanba* can harm. In a contemporary setting, it is popularly believed that *Swanba* can harm members of their matrilineage as well as Longuda outside the matrilineage. These beliefs are probably part of traditional beliefs concerning witchcraft. In a contemporary setting, it is also believed that *Swanba* can harm anyone, whether kin or not, who has had contact with a *Swanya*. This includes non-Longuda people. Elderly informants stated that the belief that Longuda *Swanba* can harm non-Longuda people is not traditional; rather, it is a more recent development.[28]

The entire Adamawa area in which the Longuda live is one of the most diverse culture group regions in all of Africa.[29] The Longuda have traditionally had extended contact with many culture groups, but it is a relatively recent development that traditionally Longuda villages have had large numbers of non-Longuda people moving in. Today it is common for a Longuda village to have Hausa, Fulani, Lala, Kanabari, Waja, Bara, Tera, Kanuri, Kanakuru, and Bwaza all living within a "Longuda" village. With such extended and intimate contact comes added stress. Witchcraft accusations may be a product of that situation.[30]

A witchcraft accusation that reveals such a stress occurred while I was doing fieldwork. A rumor of witches quickly spread through Guyuk upon the sudden death of a young woman living in Guyuk. I became aware of the woman's death when one of our employees told us that she would have to be dismissed from work early so that she could attend a funeral of one of her neighbors. The woman who died had been in good health just prior to her death. The previous year she had graduated from a technical secondary school located in Guyuk. She became ill on a Thursday or Friday and died early in the morning on the following Monday. It was very difficult to get enough details of the symptoms of the illness, and any information that could be gained from an autopsy would never be gathered because Longuda bury their deceased very quickly after death.

A very popular and fast-spreading rumor that circulated throughout Guyuk gave a firm verdict of the cause: it was witchcraft. According to town gossip, the woman had become good friends with a Muslim woman. The father of this Muslim woman—a non-Longuda man—began to feel that his daughter was becoming too influenced by her Christian Longuda friend. He, being a witch, decided to rid his daughter of this bad influence by killing his daughter's friend. So the story went that the young Longuda Christian woman was killed by a Muslim witch whose daughter he did not want influenced by this woman.

Christian-Muslim tensions are severe in the northern part of Nigeria. In Kano, a large city northwest of Guyuk, a large riot was attributed to these tensions when I was in the field. In fact, just prior to my entering the field in 1994, the beheading of a Christian in Kano had incited a riot and was a common topic of discussion for people. The bishop in Guyuk, in whose compound we lived, was part of an intrastate committee made up of both Christians and Muslims who were attempting to forge bonds of cooperation and understanding. Without a doubt, there was Christian-Muslim tension present in this area of Nigeria, so any witchcraft accusations toward a Muslim man may be understood to be a reflection of the tensions between Christians and Muslims in the area that have been present for decades.[31]

The expansion of potential victims of witchcraft may also be due to a wider understanding of bad occurrences derived from a Christian context. Through the introduction of Christianity, the Longuda associate adverse occurrences with a larger and more pervasive manifestation of evil, the devil. Furthermore, in the Christian scheme, evil is understood in a broader context. It extends to contexts and communities that go beyond the Longuda. Widening the category of those whom Swanba can harm beyond the matrilineage or even beyond the Longuda community allows for the continuation of the traditional explanation for bad occurrences or evil by means of witchcraft. At the same time that villagers develop an awareness of wider networks and relationships beyond the Longuda community, their Christian view of evil's range and agents also expands the range of occurrences of evil that still can be attributed to Swanba.

The manner by which witchcraft is acquired and the type of people who can be harmed by witchcraft thus have been subtly altered in recent times. This is due, at least in part, to an interaction of traditional religious beliefs and Christian beliefs. The introduction of Christianity has altered traditional beliefs about witchcraft and evil; at the same time, these traditional beliefs about witchcraft, which are not accepted by the mission church hierarchy, certainly have been incorporated by the mission church's parishioners. The devil is understood to be actively involved in using witchcraft as a tool for evil ends. Such beliefs in the devil were not taught by the Danish Lutheran mission or by the LCCN church leaders; they have developed out of a grassroots integration of traditional and Christian beliefs by Longuda Lutherans. The result is a new synthesis of religious beliefs.

For Longuda Christians, the newly developed understandings of *Swanba* serve some potentially positive functions. From a practical perspective, LCCN pastors and fellow church members are believed to have the power to alter the effects of *Swanya*. *Kumebe*—traditional healers—are no longer the only practitioners to turn to when witchcraft occurs. In a broader and more significant sense, the revised witchcraft beliefs function as an explanatory model for why bad or evil things happen, and they place these occurrences within a particular Christian-shaped frame of meaning. They are no longer the products of random chance. For many LCCN members, such witchcraft beliefs can function seamlessly within a Christian context.

Integration: Longuda Cosmology of Evil and Original Sin

Efforts to expunge witchcraft beliefs by denying their validity failed. Indigenous pastors (some of whom held such beliefs) saw that the beliefs in witchcraft continued, and they attempted to combat them by arguing that Jesus' power was stronger than witchcraft. This tactic of tacitly acknowledging the possibility of witchcraft, and then quickly following with an argument that Jesus' power is stronger, also failed to diminish belief in the power of witchcraft. This belief in witchcraft continues and, as the survey responses show, a large proportion of LCCN Christians believe not only that witches exist but also that witchcraft can harm even Christians. These beliefs need some unpacking. To what extent do they reflect a Christian worldview or a traditional Longuda one?

Longuda have fairly standard traditional beliefs similar to those found widely across West Africa regarding the origin of bad and evil occurrences. Evil is not something that is inherent in all things but rather is manifest within particular beings. Death is not a natural occurrence but rather is a product of ill intent, usually originated by a witch. Bad occurrences are either explained through witchcraft (*Swanba*), *Swanmbraha* (evil bush spirits), or other gods and spirits such as *Kwandalha*.[32] Traditional witchcraft beliefs, which argue that some Longuda are born witches, support this external notion of evil. The occurrence of witchcraft is not the result of an individual's innate evil, but rather is the result of matrilineal circumstance, something that can be remedied. Evil is understood within the context of witchcraft rather than within the context of an individual's nature. Witchcraft is like a benign growth that can be excised. A person can be "cured" of witchcraft and then lead a productive life, being completely accepted by the community as whole and good.

The traditional Christian perception of good and evil is very different than that of traditional Longuda. The Christian concept of original sin—we are all born sinful—assumes an internal basis for evil that cannot be extricated from people. Although it acknowledges external evil, as witnessed in beliefs concerning the devil, Christianity also holds to the belief that all people contain the potential for evil, an innate propensity toward sin.

The belief held by Longuda LCCN Christians that *Swanba* can harm them suggests that traditional conceptions of good and evil are still firmly held within a Christian context. Such beliefs show that evil and bad occurrences are still understood to be externally based, aberrant intrusions on good lives. Longuda see bad things occur every day, and these occurrences are explained in a traditional context—usually centering around witchcraft. This conceptualization of evil persists among Longuda Christians to the extent that the Christian perception that evil occurs as a natural result of the fall is not stressed or acted out in a day-to-day basis. Beliefs in witches and their power and propensity to harm are evidence of a strongly persistent traditional cosmology of evil.

Various scholars have noted a lack of acceptance for personal sin within the African Christian context. This may be due to a fundamental difference between Christianity and traditional African religious systems. Christianity acknowledges personal responsibility for sin, whereas traditional African beliefs externalize the origin of bad occurrences. Mission theologian M. C. Kirwen disagrees. He believes that African traditional religious systems maintain personal responsibility for immoral or evil activities, stating "there is no 'devil made me do it' excuse in the African world."[33] He goes on to state that in an African context everyone is potentially a witch, which can be understood to mean "you-who-are-immoral." Kirwen's argument weakens, however, when one recalls the nature of witchcraft abilities. In a traditional context, a person is born with the ability, and a contemporary context allows also for diabolic coercion. Either way, the abilities and desires of witchcraft can be separated from the witch. The person is then free to deflect the personal responsibility of witchcraft. Contrary to Kirwen's argument, both traditional and Christianized views of witchcraft externalize evil and deflect personal responsibility.

For the Longuda to maintain the traditional ideology concerning evil, witchcraft beliefs must continue, since witches are the main purveyors of bad occurrences and evil. In this sense, witchcraft beliefs reveal the persistence of traditional Longuda orientations toward evil, even within the Christian context.

The reason stated for Christian immunity to witchcraft among the minority of Longuda survey respondents who believed it is that Jesus is stronger than witches and protects Christians. A problem arises, however, when a Longuda Christian is believed to be harmed by witchcraft. The standard response to such a situation is that the person's faith must be weak, and thus the protective power of Jesus is not fully realized. By including the "faith factor" as a component of witchcraft protection, the synthesis of traditional and Western Christian systems can be maintained. Jesus is understood to be stronger than witch-craft, while witchcraft beliefs are also held. The stress, however, is still on the traditional understanding of evil: bad occurrences are an impingement from an external source.[34] The argument that Jesus is stronger than witches was used by pastors and missionaries in the hopes of eradicating witchcraft beliefs. The faith factor conserved the belief that Jesus is stronger than witches. It acknowledged the superiority of Jesus while allowing maintenance in beliefs concerning the influence of witches. The faith factor was needed because, in point of fact, witches are stronger than Jesus' protection in Longuda belief. I mean by this that the belief in witches as the distributors of evil and the rep-resentatives of a Longuda traditional ideological understanding of good and evil is more strongly held than the Lutheran Christian cosmological under-standing of good and evil. For most Longuda LCCN Christians, the traditional ideology still holds sway.

How can it be that the traditional ideology that explains evil in the world can be held by Christians who acknowledge the redemptive power of Jesus Christ? There may be an explanation why two seemingly different ideologies can exist together. For the Longuda Christian, it may be that Jesus is of central importance for matters concerning the afterlife, whereas more traditional un-derstandings hold sway for everyday experiences. Phillips Stevens elaborates on this possibility in his chart of the horizontal and vertical dimensions of religious experience.[35] The horizontal dimension contains beings that are con-cerned with everyday occurrences, and the vertical dimension has beings that are significant to events not of this world, such as the afterlife. Such an un-derstanding may serve to reveal how such divergent cosmological beliefs of good and evil can be integrated in a Christian Longuda context. John Peel uses the terms *other-worldly* and *this-worldly* in describing the difference in ideolo-gies. Peel argues that modern European Christianity is other-worldly, focusing on the supreme God and that which is to come, and that traditional religious beliefs are this-worldly, focusing on this earthly plane of existence. According to Peel, the two are not in conflict with each other.[36] Others may disagree, but that discussion can wait for another day.

When it comes to the cosmological beliefs in the origin of evil, Longuda Lutheran Christians have maintained the traditional conceptions of good and evil and have integrated those beliefs to stand side by side with the Christian message of salvation. Witchcraft beliefs have remained strong largely because such beliefs are central to the understanding of the origin of bad or evil oc-currences from a traditional perspective. The net result is that witchcraft beliefs are maintained. These beliefs have surely been altered by the introduction and acceptance of Christianity, but they are nonetheless maintained. Bad occur-rences, traditionally viewed from a Christian perspective as regrettable results of the fall, for the Longuda Christians are for all practical purposes dealt with in the context of traditional beliefs. A synthesis between traditional and Christian beliefs concerning good and evil takes place. This synthesis is neither completely "traditional" nor "Christian."

Looking back, it becomes clear that the Christianity that Longuda people practice within the LCCN is a particularly African expression. This integration or Africanization of Christianity has been worked out at the grassroots, grounded level within a mainline orthodox mission church. This particular area of research has been lacking in the past and needs to be studied by theologians as well as anthropologists. The dearth of previous scholarship along the lines of grassroots integration of religious beliefs within mainline orthodox mission churches in no way reflects the potential significance of such research nor, more important, the significance of the resulting beliefs for those Christians who participate in them.

For African theologians within mainline orthodox mission churches, there is a twofold challenge in indigenizing Christianity in Africa. The two challenges really concern the same issue. Put simply, the issue is the sort of questions that are to be asked by African theologians and thus the direction that African theology will take. The first challenge is for African theologians to remain true to the concerns of grassroots African Christians. This is where African Christianity is played out and where the pressing issues of indigenization are found. The questions that African theologians are to consider must be based on issues that are cogent and immediate to African Christians, such as witchcraft and the meaning of evil occurrences. The voices that need to be heard on these issues of witchcraft and the nature of good and evil are those of African theologians, but their voices will be lost in the swirling of the harmattan if they do not remain intimately in contact with questions about African Christianity that are pertinent to grassroots Christians in Africa.

The second challenge to be met by African theologians is to break the intellectual and theological tie to the West. Western worldviews and the theological concerns arising from them may be largely void of value in an African context. Western-trained African theologians must overcome centuries of Western theological interests and begin to set the direction of theology that is derived from a specifically African worldview and cultural context.

The lack of African theological concern on the abiding grassroots issue of the nature of evil in the world, specifically as it relates to witchcraft in Africa, reveals that somewhere along the line, African theologians have fallen short of at least one of these two challenges. Until these challenges are met by African theologians, the contribution African Christians can make to glimpsing the face of God from a new perspective will be missing for Christians around the world. The cutting-edge field for theological inquiry today is not in the West but rather in places such as Africa. The impact will be great only if such leadership is grounded in, true to, and informed by these particular cultural contexts.

NOTES

1. Those African churches that resulted generally from nineteenth- and twentieth-century missionaries' efforts and became independent in the mid to late twentieth century.

2. For example, see C. G. Baeta, ed., *Christianity in Tropical Africa: Studies Presented and Discussed at the Seventh International African Seminar, University of Ghana, April 1965* (London: Oxford University Press for the International African Institute, 1968); A. Shorter, *African Culture and the Christian Church* (London: Edinburgh House Press, 1973); E. Gray Fashole'-Luke, R. Hastings, and A. and G. Tasie, eds., *Christianity in Independent Africa* (London: Rex Collings, 1978).

3. Baeta, *Christianity in Tropical Africa.*

4. John Mbiti, "The Biblical Basis for Present Trends in African Theology," in *African Theology en Route: Papers from the Pan-African Conference of Third World Theologies, December 17–23, 1977, Accra, Ghana,* ed. Kofi Appiah-kubi and Sergio Torres (Maryknoll, N.Y.: Orbis Books, 1979).

5. Luke Mbefo, "Theology and Inculturation: The Nigerian Experience," *Cross Current,* 37 (Winter 1987–1988): 394.

6. Lamin Sanneh, *Translating the Message: The Missionary Impact on Culture* (Maryknoll, N.Y.: Orbis Books, 1998).

7. Ogbu U. Kalu, "The Dilemma of Grassroot Inculturation of the Gospel: A Case Study of a Modern Controversy in Igboland, 1983–1989," *Journal of Religion in Africa,* 25 (1995): 48–72.

8. Steven Kaplin, "The Africanization of Missionary Christianity: History and Typology," *Journal of Religion in Africa,* 16 (1986): 166–86.

9. Andre Droogers, "Syncretism: The Problem of Definition, the Definition of the Problem," in *Dialogue and Syncretism: An Interdisciplinary Approach,* ed. Jerald Gort, Hendrik Vroom, Rein Fernhout, and Anton Wessels (Grand Rapids, Mich.: Eerdmans, 1989), 14.

10. Robert J. Schreiter, "Anthropology and Faith: Challenges to Missiology," *Missiology,* 19 (July 1991): 287.

11. Matthew Schoffeleers, "Black and African Theology in Southern Africa: A Controversy Re-examined," *Journal of Religion in Africa,* 18:2 (1988): 113 (quote), 115.

12. I understand the dilemma of an anthropological study of indigenous religious beliefs. Okot p'Bitek, *African Religions in Western Scholarship* (Kampala, Uganda: East African Literature Bureau, 1970), argues that White anthropologists should not write about African traditional religious systems. Also, Matthew Schoffeleers, in "Black and African Theology," gives voice to the call to have African theology done by Africans. I would question who these Africans should be—the theologians or others?

13. Meyer, "'If You Are a Devil, You Are a Witch and If You Are a Witch, You Are a Devil': The Integration of 'Pagan' Ideas into the Conceptual Universe of Ewe Christians in Southeastern Ghana," *Journal of Religion in Africa,* 22 (1992): 98–132, includes a helpful discussion of this lack of interest. See also Birgit Meyer, "'Delivered from the Powers of Darkness': Confessions of Satanic Riches in Christian Ghana," *Africa,* 65 (1995a): 236–55.

14. H. W. Turner, *A Bibliography of New Religious Movements in Primal Societies,*

Vol. 1 (Boston: G. K. Hall, 1977); George C. Bond, Walter R. Johnson, and Shelia S. Walker, eds., *African Christianity: Patterns of Religious Continuity* (New York: Academic Press, 1979); and see also Rosalind Hackett, *New Religious Movements in Nigeria* (Lewiston, N.Y.: Edwin Mellen, 1987).

15. See Elizabeth Isichei, for example, "Seven Varieties of Ambiguity: Some Patterns of Igbo Response to Christian Missions," *Journal of Religion in Africa*, 3 (1970): 209–27; T. O. Beidelman, *Colonial Evangelism: A Socio-Historical Study of an East African Mission at the Grassroots* (Bloomington: Indiana University Press, 1982); N. Etherinton, "Missionaries and the Intellectual History of Africa," *Itinerario* 7 (1983): 116–43; and John David Yeadon Peel, "The Pastor and the Bablawo: The Interaction of Religions in Nineteenth-Century Yorubaland," *Africa*, 60 (1990): 338–69.

16. My fieldwork experience has shown that often anthropologists have close social contact with missionaries, the very people that they hesitate to include in anthropological study, save for a pointed criticism here and there.

17. C. E. Stipe, "Anthropologists versus Missionaries: The Influence of Presuppositions," *Current Anthropology*, 21 (1980): 165–79.

18. Frank Salamone, "Anthropologists and Missionaries: Competition or Reciprocity?" *Human Organization*, 36 (1977): 407–12.

19. James Peacock, "Anthropology and Missionaries: A Commentary," *Missiology: An International Review*, 24 (April 1996): 164.

20. Rosaland Shaw and Charles Stewart, "Introduction: Problematizing Syncretism," in *Syncretism/Anti-syncretism: The Politics of Religious Synthesis*, ed. Charles Stewart and Rosaland Shaw (London: Routledge, 1994), 1–26. By selectively separating out contributing factors to the syncretic process, Stewart and Shaw suggest that in a postmodern milieu, anthropologists may be participating in a form of imperialism.

21. Johannes Fabian, *Jamaa: A Religious Movement in Katanga* (Evanston, Ill.: Northwestern University Press, 1971), 165.

22. For examples of religious synthesis within an orthodox mission church context, see John David Yeadon Peel, *Aladura: A Religious Movement among the Yoruba* (London: Oxford University Press for the International African Institute, 1968); J. W. Bwiti Fernandez, *An Ethnography of the Religious Imagination in Africa* (Princeton, N.J.: Princeton University Press, 1982); Jean Comaroff, *Body of Power and Spirit of Resistance: The Culture and History of a South African People* (Chicago: University of Chicago Press, 1985); Lesley Stevens, "Religious Change in a Haya Village, Tanzania," *Journal of Religion in Africa*, 21 (1991): 2–25; and Birgit Meyer, "'If You Are a Devil.'"

23. Margaret Nissen, *An African Church Is Born: The Story of the Adamawa and Central Sarduana Provinces in Nigeria* (Viby, Denmark: Purups Gradiske Hus, 1968).

24. Niels H Brønnum, *Under Daemoners Aag* (Kobenharn, Denmark: Dansk Forenet Sudan Mission, 1956).

25. Reo Fortune, *Sorcerers of Dobu* (New York: E. P. Dutton, 1932), is one such pioneering study. For a pioneering work on witchcraft in an African ethnic context, see E. E. Evans-Pritchard, *Witchcraft, Oracle and Magic among the Azande* (London: Oxford University Press, 1937).

26. Todd Vanden Berg, "The Integration of Traditional Religion and Christianity among the Longuda of Adamawa State, Nigeria" (Ph.D. diss., State University of New York at Buffalo, 1996), 101–17.

27. See Meyer, "'If You Are a Devil,'" on this issue with the Ewe of Ghana.

28. Vanden Berg, "Integration," 146.

29. George Peter Murdock, *Africa: Its People and Their Culture History* (New York: McGraw-Hill, 1959), 89–100.

30. Max Marwick describes this social dynamic and argues that witchcraft accusations could be a marker of the greatest social tension or a "social strain gauge"; Marwick, "Witchcraft as a Social Strain Gauge," *Australian Journal of Science*, 26 (1964): 263–68.

31. Vanden Berg, "Integration," 146–48.

32. Ibid., 66–88.

33. M. C. Kirwen, *The Missionary and the Diviner: Contending Theologies of Christian and African Religions* (Maryknoll, N.Y.: Orbis Books, 1987), 53; Vanden Berg, "Integration," 53.

34. Longuda Christians who do not include the caveat of the "faith factor" as a component to a Christian's protection from witchcraft put a strain on the traditional conception of evil. I believe that under these conditions beliefs in witchcraft would gradually fade away, because the threat in witchcraft would be taken away if Jesus were stronger than witches.

35. Phillips Stevens Jr., "Religion," In *Encyclopedia of Cultural Anthropology*, ed. David Levinson and Melvin Embers (New York: Henry Holt, 1996), 1088–1100.

36. Peel, *Aladura*; Robin Horton, "African Conversion," *Africa*, 46 (1971): 86–108. Horton uses the terms *communion* and *explanation-prediction-control* for largely the same ideas and summarizes at length Peel's view in this essay.

3

Shall They Till with Their Own Hoes?: Baptists in Zimbabwe and New Patterns of Interdependence, 1950–2000

Isaac M. T. Mwase

The question posed in the title is not about developing theologies appropriate for the non-Western churches in a postcolonial, postmissionary era. That case has been made, in a sufficiently compelling manner. Theologians in the church's various global contexts are faced with the task of forging a theology sensitive to the factors unique to each context.[1] The question before us is rather about the just allocation of resources, to the end that Christians take their faith's global expression seriously. It calls for a reappraisal of the "three-self" philosophy of missions, especially the idea assumed by many in the modern missionary enterprise that mission field churches must become self-supporting and that these churches should have only those institutions and programs that they are able to purchase and support *exclusively* by themselves.[2]

The case I wish to argue is that world Christianity implies interdependence. Mutual reliance, not unilateralism and isolationism, has to win the day in cross-cultural Christian relations and inform mission policy. I present this case by telling the story of a particular Zimbabwean institution. What one finds on the ground where Christianity is most vibrant requires a rethinking about the allocation of global Christianity's financial resources. Churches in both the developed parts of the world and the developing world need to take seriously Jesus' prayer that they may be one. The metaphor of the church as the Body of Christ must inform missionary philosophy and relationships between missionary and mission churches. True Christian solidarity calls on believers everywhere to cooperate when it comes to financial matters related to the task of building the church.

The following study places in sharp relief the interaction between a missionary enterprise and an emergent national church. The case of the Baptist church in Zimbabwe allows us a glimpse into the workings of the largest denominational missionary-sending agency in the world, the mission board of the U.S.-based Southern Baptist Convention. Southern Baptist mission work in Rhodesia/Zimbabwe was started in the 1950s, when missions in other places already were grappling with postcolonial realities that included the emergence of independent national denominational infrastructures and personnel. The Zimbabwe case thus turns out to be a compressed version of mission–national church relations elsewhere.[3] It should be instructive about mission-founded churches and their postcolonial struggles for sustainable growth and the advancement of their ministries.

Baptists in Zimbabwe

By the 1950s, when Southern Baptists launched their work in the part of southern Africa that later became Zimbabwe, that region already had a significant Christian presence. Christianity established itself in a concerted way simultaneously with the colonial efforts by Cecil John Rhodes, whose Pioneer Column arrived in Harare/Salisbury in 1890. There were pioneering missions in the area several decades earlier, however, notably Robert Moffat's station at Inyati, opened for the London Missionary Society in 1859. After Rhodes's colonization movement, other groups soon established work in various parts of the country. By the 1950s, Roman Catholics, Anglicans, Methodists, Seventh Day Adventists, and other traditions had schools, hospitals, and churches in various parts of the country. Baptists were also among those establishing work, but mostly in the urban areas. British and Australian Baptists worked primarily in the low-density suburbs, the domicile for White settlers. American Southern Baptists would assume the responsibility these White Baptists neglected, to work with the Black population in the high-density suburbs of the major cities and primarily in the north-central rural area of the country (figure 3.1). This region, especially around the Sanyati River, would become their main focus. So it was that White missionaries from the racially segregated American South came to evangelize and disciple an oppressed Black majority in White-controlled Rhodesia.

Southern Baptists thus launched their work in a country experiencing the tensions occasioned by colonialism and then a war of independence. From the

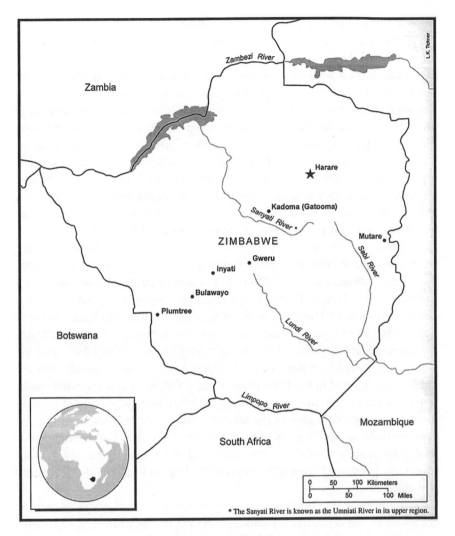

FIGURE 3.1. Zimbabwe

Rhodes Pioneer Column to the Unilateral Declaration of Independence (UDI) by Ian Smith and his Rhodesia Front in 1965, White settlement in the country resulted in the disenfranchisement of the Black majority. Baptist work was planted and grew amid the tensions resulting from the Black struggle for independence from the White minority rule of the Smith regime. A protracted armed struggle eventually forced all parties in the conflict to participate in the Lancaster House peace talks, which led to a general election in 1980. Robert Mugabe won the election and established a government of national reconciliation. The euphoria of independence was certain to contribute to the relationships between missionaries and national church leaders. The struggle for political self-rule naturally fostered nationals' desire for involvement in the governance of the church.

Today, Baptist work in Zimbabwe is the primary responsibility of a spiritually vibrant and yet financially struggling national church, which was first planted by an ambitious missionary agency.[4] What remains on the ground institutionally is a far cry from what prevailed after years of missionary labor. The state of the work that survived is a result of profound shifts in missionary philosophy that are closely related to the dramatic shifts in the theological orientation of the Southern Baptist Convention in the USA (SBC). The Baptist Theological Seminary of Zimbabwe (BTSZ) is a testament of the highs and lows of SBC missionary efforts. Its story no doubt has parallels in many other places touched by missionary-sending agencies in North America.

A good place to start this story is on May 15, 1947, when Clyde T. Dotson, an independent Baptist missionary working in Southern Rhodesia, requested the Foreign Mission Board (FMB) of the Southern Baptist Convention to appoint him and his wife, Hattie, as missionaries. Dotson's request met with a favorable response.[5] The SBC missions in Africa had hitherto been limited to Nigeria, but all of a sudden, the board found itself having to consider "Macedonian calls" not only from Southern Rhodesia but also from Liberia and the Gold Coast (Ghana). It was not until September 14, 1950, however, that the FMB officially voted in the Dotsons as the first SBC missionaries in the southern African region. At the same meeting, the board voted to purchase a mission house in the central region of the country, and it accepted "in fee simple the generous offer of Mr. Connely of Southern Rhodesia, Africa, of 1,000 acres of land to be used by the Foreign Mission Board in the development of mission work in that country."[6] This action marked the beginning of an intricate history of extraversion.[7]

Within the context of this study, *extraversion* is defined narrowly, as what occurs when the economic viability of a project in one country is dependent on funds from a different country. Defining *extraversion* in this way is in keeping with the dictionary definition, which is as follows: "the state of being thrown out or turned outward." In relation to the SBC missionary enterprise in Africa, extraversion involved mainly the funding of mission projects and infrastructure with a budget set and serviced by the FMB in Richmond, Virginia. Initially, support was limited to financial outlays for the living expenses of missionaries and evangelists on contract with the FMB. As the work grew, extraversion became more pronounced, and the labors of missionaries and national leaders resulted in the rapid growth of a Black Baptist national church, a marked increase in the missionary ranks, and the buildup of elaborate ministry infrastructures. At the peak of Baptist work in Zimbabwe, external funding resulted in a budget that supported more than 80 missionaries, the Baptist Publishing House, the Baptist Theological Seminary of Zimbabwe, the Baptist

Camp, Sanyati Baptist Hospital, Sanyati Primary and Secondary Schools, and the Baptist Media Center. After Zimbabwe gained its independence, the government assumed responsibility for the hospital and schools. The Baptist Camp was spun off to become a struggling but self-supporting entity. The only institutions that remain as going concerns for the Baptist Convention of Zimbabwe are the seminary and a scaled-down version of the publishing house. As surely as there was a buildup in missionary hardware paralleled by the increasing numbers of those joining the missionary ranks, when the numbers of missionaries went down, so did support for schools and centers of ministry. The one institution that Baptists in Zimbabwe and their friends have gone to great lengths to sustain is the seminary. A close look at this institution makes for a fascinating study of interdependent relationships.

Extraversional Buildup

Infrastructural extraversion is the term one may use to describe the pattern set in motion by the FMB from the early 1950s, whereby mission work in new areas would be fortified by a massive infusion of dollars to build hospitals, schools, publishing houses, and missionary housing. When the board met at the end of 1950 to survey a half-century of expansion, the area secretary for Europe, Africa, and the Near East, Dr. George Sadler, was the bearer of exciting news about new work.[8] To the 28 established and active mission areas, the board was adding Southern Rhodesia, along with Peru, Ecuador, and Malaya. The report on Southern Rhodesia highlighted the need for more missionary personnel and "funds for capital needs that a well-rounded missionary force would require."[9] In the ensuing years, the FMB funded and sustained an ever-growing infrastructure for Baptist work.

The Dotson Years

Behind the rapid growth of the Baptist church in Zimbabwe were the legendary Clyde T. and Hattie Dotson.[10] Clyde was a master in tapping the resources of the FMB to set in place an elaborate missionary infrastructure. He was to a great extent responsible for a rapid increase in the number of missionaries appointed to central Africa and to then Southern Rhodesia. He also presided over the acquisition of significant real estate holdings and new buildings. Barely a year after official appointment with the FMB, he had a church building halfway completed in Gatooma, and other church buildings were under construction in three of the main population centers of Southern Rhodesia: in Salisbury/Harare, Bulawayo, and Umtali/Mutare. Dotson also acquired a large tract of land at the edge of the Sanyati Reserve with the intention of constructing a missionary compound and several classrooms for an elementary school. This complex at Sanyati became his base of operations. Soon after, the Dotsons traded locations with Ralph and Betty Bowlin, the second couple appointed to Southern Rhodesia, who assumed leadership at the primary school.

A tragic experience that befell Ralph Bowlin prompted a call for resources to establish a hospital. Not too long after the Bowlins were settled in Sanyati, Ralph had to transport a woman facing a complicated childbirth. A recent downpour had left the roads a muddy quagmire. Bowlin attempted to drive the woman to Gatooma but got stuck in the mud about 15 miles from Sanyati and had to send for help from Clyde Dotson. By the time Dotson reached Bowlin two days later, he found the woman had died the previous day in childbirth. They buried her and her baby there by the side of the road. Later Dotson wrote, "We got down on our knees, and prayed the Lord to send us a doctor and to make possible a hospital, so our people would not die like that."[11] The FMB moved without delay in response to Dotson's request for funds to establish a health care facility. Funds were released from the FMB's annual Lottie Moon Christmas offering of 1950 for building and equipping a small hospital on the Sanyati Reserve.[12] By 1953, two physicians, Giles and Wanna Ann Fort, were appointed to direct operations at the 50-bed hospital.

The Rhodesian Baptist Mission

It was not until the end of 1952 that there was a missionary force large enough to relieve Clyde Dotson from the dominant role he played relative to this early missionary infrastructural growth. When the Dotsons went on furlough at the end of that year, 10 new missionaries were in place to continue the work they had pioneered. Clyde reported that there were five organized churches with a membership of 204, 65 baptisms, six schools with 538 pupils, 3 ordained and 17 lay pastors, and 105 members of the women's organization.[13] The remaining missionaries met that year at Sanyati to constitute a formal organization, the Rhodesia Baptist Mission of the Southern Baptist Convention.[14]

One of the important items that came up for discussion at the inaugural mission meeting was a plan for a Bible school. The decision went counter to Clyde Dotson's wish to have a school for ministry near Salisbury/Harare, the major population center in Southern Rhodesia. The new mission scheduled the opening of a Bible school in 1954 at Sanyati.[15] Discussions regarding a school for the training of pastors continued in subsequent mission meetings. Concrete steps were agreed upon for the new African Baptist Seminary at a meeting called in May 1954. The institution would be located at Travellers Rest Farm, about 12^1/$_2$ miles northeast of Gwelo/Gweru. The mission had purchased about a hundred acres of this property. The Bowlins and a newer missionary couple, the Lockards, would share the responsibilities of operating the seminary. Plans were set in motion to begin classes in early 1955.[16] The first class started that February with 11 men.[17]

The growth of SBC work in Southern Rhodesia was a source of much satisfaction for both the missionary force and those funding the enterprise. Clyde Dotson's experience, facility with the indigenous language, and knowledge of the people proved a strong foundation on which many others would build. The work he and Hattie pioneered with national stalwarts that included Joseph Nyati, Abel Nziramasanga (who became first president of the Baptist Convention), and Aaron Ndhlovu later served as a platform for entry into the areas of present-day Zambia and Malawi. Seven years after the Dotsons' appointment, the mission filed the following glowing report:

> seven well-located stations were occupied, with a total staff of 37 missionaries. There were eighteen organized churches, with a total membership of 1,531. Fifteen African pastors served the churches and 66 additional preaching points. Nineteen elementary schools had an aggregate enrollment of 2,555. A theological seminary had forty Africans in training for places of responsibility.[18]

Early Missionary and National Relationships

The growth of Baptist work in Southern Rhodesia was stimulated and promoted by a growing cadre of African men who entered the ministry to serve as pastors and evangelists. These work of these men became an occasion for another kind of interdependence, the mission's direct financial support of nationals serving the churches. Missionaries worked out a system for subsidizing the salaries and allowances of pastors and evangelists.[19]

The emergence of this missionary organization stimulated desire among national pastors to have a role in the governance of the church. Beginning in 1957, it became a mission practice to have two pastors attend the annual mission meeting as representatives of national Baptist clergy. The initial invitation stipulated that these pastors could attend "certain sessions" of the annual meeting.[20] In 1961, African pastors specifically asked for full delegate status and the right to attend all sessions of the annual meeting. Mounting tensions between missionaries and African leaders apparently were diffused by a move to establish a national convention. What emerged in 1963 was the Baptist Convention of Central Africa, whose existence prompted the area secretary at the time, Cornell Goerner, to observe that the Baptist Mission of Central Africa was "deliberately fading into the background."[21] The intention was for the new convention to assume those duties and responsibilities that were hitherto the sole concern of the mission. This hope prompted the following assessment: "In a significant step towards full self-support, all Rhodesian pastors were made directly responsible to a local congregation, and any financial assistance on pastor's salaries granted from mission funds will be channeled through the local church, rather than being paid directly to the pastor.[22]

The desire to make pastoral support a matter of local responsibility was expressed in a 10-year plan in 1960 by the evangelistic workers' committee of the mission. This plan sought to assign the full responsibility for each pastor's salary to every organized church by the end of the period. There were glitches in the implementation of this plan. A 1965 report had this to say: "A plan of subsidy reduction within the churches moved into its *second year* [my emphasis]. Under this plan, financial assistance from the mission will be gradually reduced until all churches become entirely responsible for local expenses including the pastor's salary, within a ten-year period."[23]

African leaders were not happy. Abel Nziramasanga, the first president of the convention, expressed his bitter disappointment at the mission's decision by declaring, "whereas we have had showers of blessing in the past, today we are having showers of stones."[24] African leaders were concerned that missionaries were making such decisions unilaterally. In an effort to defuse tensions, the 1966 slate of officers for the convention called on the missionaries to plan "with them and not for them."[25] One of the by-products of these attempts at a scale-down of external support was a resolution by pastors in the main urban centers for missionaries to direct their efforts to rural areas. The pull of the city was so strong on the missionaries, however, that new ministries sprang up, which ensured that personnel would continue residing in the main urban centers. The consequent development of a radio ministry, a bookstore ministry, and a publishing house all but assured massive infusions of funds and staffing from the FMB. This mission infrastructure ensured robust extraversion well into the 1980s.

Institutional Extraversion: Focus on the Seminary

A full account of the buildup in missionary infrastructure would trace the development of primary and secondary schools, Sanyati Hospital (1953) and outlying clinics, the Media Studio (1967), Baptist bookstores (Gwelo/Gweru, 1963; Plumtree, 1967), the publishing house (1967), the Baptist Camp, and the seminary. Because all of these institutions no longer are an integral part of the ministry of the convention or, in the case of the camp, no longer dependent on foreign funds to thrive, it makes sense to devote attention to the one that still does. The seminary is now, in principle, the responsibility of the convention. The seminary is in fact a fascinating focal point for viewing new forms of interdependence. When one examines the situation closely, one soon discovers that this institution owes whatever well-being it enjoys mostly to the creative fund-raising efforts of its leaders, to those with intimate historical ties to it, and to new friends who are persuaded to support it as a necessary institution for developing a mature local theology and a robust local church.

The Baptist Theological Seminary of Zimbabwe (BTSZ) has survived formidable challenges since its inaugural class met in January 1955. The most trying times in the early years of its existence came when the mission sought to wean African pastors and their churches from the subsidies made available from FMB funds. Between 1966 and 1968, hardly any citizens of Rhodesia chose to study at the seminary. The institution managed to stay afloat because of funds allocated to it by the FMB. Such was the case even after independence in 1980, when Rhodesia became Zimbabwe. The year of independence is when I enrolled as a student at the seminary. I came to a beautiful campus with instructional buildings sitting at the foot of a hill oriented to the west. Sitting at a slightly higher level on the hill were four spacious, modern structures that served as residences for the missionary staff. Modest units nestled to the south of the hill provided accommodation for the national teacher and the students. Even though the war of liberation caused seminary operations to be moved temporarily to the city of Gwelo/Gweru, none of the physical infrastructure of the seminary fell victim to the war. More residential buildings were added to the campus to accommodate a bigger national staff and student body after my graduation in 1983. Ten years later, the buildup had reached its high point. Additions and improvements made to the physical plant and facilities included the following:

1. Water supply system improvements involved the addition of two new water wells, a storage tank, and a pressure pump.
2. The electrical system was upgraded and the supply increased.
3. The following buildings were constructed:
   a. Two staff houses
   b. Three three-bedroom student houses
   c. An office and classroom block
   d. A child care center
4. Two dormitories and most of the single-family student houses were remodeled and refurnished.[26]

Concurrent with the buildup were aggressive efforts to afford the school as much financial self-sufficiency as possible. The 1993 report opens with a section titled "Reviewing Achievements of the Past Decade 1984–1993." The seminary had adopted a nationalization plan, extending from 1990 to 2025. It was subsequently revised to extend from 1990 to 2015. These plans were part of the overall FMB commitment aimed at making Zimbabwean Baptist institutions the sole responsibility of the BCZ. The seminary plan led to dramatic efforts to secure endowment funds for the key areas of seminary life. The seminary, as long as it exists, owes a debt of gratitude to the visionary leadership of Dr Hugh and Mrs Rebecca McKinley. They were responsible for mobilizing friends of the seminary to canvass for endowment funds. The McKinleys tried as best they could to situate BTSZ in such a financial state that when a national staff assumed leadership, it would have the wherewithal to run the school. In 1983, the seminary had no endowment funds. In a dramatic turnaround, the 1993 report shows that the school had total endowment funds of Z$346,971.97 to support three areas as follows:

Student scholarships, national staff salaries, seminary operations	Z$271,880.57
Student support	Z$62,538.01
Distance Christian leadership education (DCLE)	Z$12,553.39

It is difficult to develop a detailed portrait of the seminary's finances from annual reports covering the years 1983 to 1994 and the audit reports for 1994–2000, but they do show the changing financial situation at the seminary. The reports reveal that the seminary owed its financial health primarily to the infusion of funds from the FMB, with tuition revenues and support from the national convention providing significant but much smaller portions. The Zimbabwean Baptist convention has not been able to make significant contributions to the operating budget of the school. This inability I judge to be due to the economies of poverty that prevail in Zimbabwe. As the FMB has reduced its contributions to the seminary operating budget, the national convention has valiantly attempted to increase its own contribution, but its efforts fell far short of the amounts lost due to FMB reductions. The FMB support accounted for about 85 percent of the campus income in 1982, but in 1991 it had dropped to 72 percent. Moreover, in 1992 the FMB announced a plan that called for its annual support for the seminary to decrease from about $15,000 in 1992 to $10,000 in 2005, and to zero after 2015.[27] If the seminary was to survive, its leaders would be forced to find other sources of funding. One might guess that the downturn in support from the FMB resulted from a decrease in mission giving or some other financial straitening back in the United States. In fact, the Southern Baptist mission effort has never been larger, nor its giving more robust. The forces behind the policy change were ideological, not economic.

The Foreign Mission Board and Extraversion

The Foreign Missions Board of the Southern Baptist Convention is the largest denominational mission-sending agency in the world. It now goes by a new name; in 1997, it became the International Mission Board (IMB). In existence since 1845, the board was formed along with the Domestic Mission Board (now North American Mission Board) in the aftermath of a controversy between Northern and Southern Baptists over the appointment of slave owners as missionaries.[28] Well over 14,000 men and women have served under the board's appointment, and more than a third of those appointed since its founding—5,186 to be exact—currently serve, on every continent. In his assessment of the IMB, missiologist Alan Neely identifies several factors that enable this juggernaut of missionary agencies to provide immense resources to mission fields.[29] The IMB enjoys a robust reputation among its constituents, based on a long history, the pride of place in being the largest agency in number of missionaries on the field, and the most effective mission-funding mechanism in history, which enables missionaries to work with adequate support and with minimal financial anxiety. The cooperative program, which came into operation in 1925, allows Southern Baptist churches, from the largest to the smallest, to participate in worldwide missions. Every month, millions of dollars come into the coffers to support mission by way of this cooperative mechanism. Additional funds for supporting the IMB come from special offerings. The Lottie Moon Christmas Offering for foreign missions, as well as its counterpart, the Annie Armstrong Easter Offering for the support of home missions, are annual extravaganzas with a huge budgetary impact. In 2003, the Lottie Moon Christmas offering totalled $136 million, and for 2004 the IMB's total budget was set at $259 million.[30] Scarcity of funds obviously is not the issue behind the funding cuts for the Baptist Theological Seminary in Zimbabwe.

Missionary strategies and values are changing at the IMB, with resulting shifts from career to volunteer and short-term workers and to a revised approach to mission work as well. Traditionally, Southern Baptists took a holistic approach to missions. The proclamation of the gospel and the founding of local churches were accompanied by efforts to meet human needs related to health, education, and general psychosocial well-being. The institutional buildup and scale-down in Zimbabwe is very arguably a case in point for Neely's observation that "the Board has steadily moved to focus more on evangelism and church growth and less on educational, medical, and agricultural missions. The institutions Southern Baptist missionaries established have not all been abandoned, but the subsidies once generously provided have been eliminated or curtailed drastically"[31]

The IMB proclaims that it has chosen to strike out in a new direction.[32] The direction seems not to include works already established but emphasizes what one IMB missiologist calls "church planting movements" (hereafter CPMs). This shift in perspective has many positive factors, but it also is part of a seismic shift in the official theology and agenda of the Southern Baptist Convention, a shift prompted by its takeover by fundamentalist leaders. The IMB, like many other SBC institutions, has experienced a shake-up, and the new leaders want to focus more narrowly on evangelization and organizing new churches. As is evident from the literature on CPMs, SBC mission leaders are not much interested in the continuing development and support of the institutions and infrastructure their predecessors built, such as church buildings, schools, hospitals, Bible colleges, and seminaries. The CPMs missiology insists that evangelization and church planting are the foremost and virtually the only priorities of foreign missions, and it seems to reflect a fear that mission-founded Baptist churches are overly dependent on the IMB.[33]

Such fears do not seem to acknowledge that we now live in a world where interdependence is a fact of life. What world Christianity has to figure out is how to have interdependent relationships that are healthy and mutually rewarding. The teaching of Jesus provides sufficient principles to ensure such healthy relationships. Christians everywhere are supposed to be united. Jesus prayed that his followers be one. He envisioned a movement marked by the most profound kind of solidarity. Love for God and for fellow Christians would produce a healthy and vibrant church. It is dubious that these healthy relationships will emerge when those who receive the gospel are illiterate and poor in health and when those who convey it do not understand the interdependent nature of world Christianity and of the current world economy. Extraversion is the order of the day. The sooner this fact is acknowledged, the better that reflective Christians will be able to manage it in a way that empowers rather than demeans.

The IMB and other American mission boards should not delude themselves into believing that CPMs will flourish solely on the efforts of their career, short-term, and volunteer missionaries. As in the past, it is the national evangelists, pastors, and lay leaders who will do the lion's share of the work. And as was true in the past, the resources that accompany the foreign missionaries are still indispensable, for the churches they help to plant will have collective ventures to pursue and leaders to be equipped for the work. Unless the economies of poverty in the global South change dramatically in the future, Christian solidarity would seem to demand external support. What is needed is not self-sufficiency among the poor, but a way of partnering across cultural and economic differences that affirms Christian solidarity, the interdependency of the Body of Christ.

But back to our story. An interesting twist in the plot has occurred at the Baptist Theological Seminary of Zimbabwe over the past decade that underscores both the enduring need for interdependence and the resourcefulness of a new generation of African church leaders.

When Their Hoes Won't Get the Job Done

The scale-down in FMB funds in Zimbabwe occurred simultaneously with a momentous passing of the torch at BTSZ. Dr. Hugh McKinley and his wife, Rebecca, laid the mantle of leadership on Dr. Henry Mugabe and his wife, Hermina. Mugabe assumed leadership at a time when the IMB's reorientation meant that its funds would no longer be available for operating institutions such as the seminary. Interviews with Mugabe reveal, however, that as IMB funds are being scaled back, the seminary has tapped other sources of funds.[34] During the early years of Mugabe's tenure, which began in 1994, a significant percentage of the seminary's operating budget was picked up by the Alliance of Baptists, a group of "moderate" dissenters in the SBC. The Lott Carey Baptist

Mission Convention, an old and distinguished African American missionary agency, has become a primary financial supporter of the seminary as well. A friendship struck up while Mugabe and Dr. David Goatley, the executive secretary-treasurer of the Lott Carey Mission, were in seminary together, has provided an important trust factor on which to build this supportive relationship. Even before Goatley joined Lott Carey, he had taken a personal interest in the seminary and its financial woes. He was the one who proposed some of the livestock and agricultural projects that Mugabe set in place at the seminary.[35]

Mugabe's main job as principal of the seminary, he believes, is to ensure a viable future for an institution that is strategic to national Christians' witness in Zimbabwe. Baptist leaders there feel they need to train a cadre of men and women who will serve as leaders for church and society.[36] Mugabe has had to be creative in identifying and tapping sources of funding, both for his own family's welfare and for the viability of the institution under his charge. Because his seminary income in 1994 was the equivalent of U.S.$340, he arranged a visiting professorship with the Baptist seminary in Richmond. By teaching during the January term, he has been able to generate funds sufficient to take care of his family from year to year. Of the 42 students enrolled at the seminary in 2001, almost all are receiving some form of financial aid. To provide them with employment and sustainable sources of food, Mugabe has on staff a local farmer, who oversees a commercial vegetable garden and cattle and goat farming. Funds to purchase livestock were provided by the Virginia chapter of the Alliance of Baptists.

Such arrangements and the constant burden of fund-raising have their costs. The Mugabe family has to function for long periods without a husband for Hermina and a father to help three children negotiate the teenage years. Mugabe's health has suffered as well. Hermina noted that despite having a seminary master's degree that qualifies her to help in the instruction at the seminary, she is glad that the family made a decision for her to resume her occupation as a nurse. Because of her job, the family can afford to live in a southern suburb of Zimbabwe's third largest city, Gweru. Living some 15 or so miles from the seminary campus has allowed the overworked principal a place of respite from the pressures and problems associated with overseeing a seminary.[37]

Mugabe's leadership, hard work and resourcefulness have preserved what has become a strategic institution for African Christianity. Several graduates of the seminary now serve on the faculty. Mugabe observed with obvious satisfaction that a number of its graduates occupied top-level leadership positions in several southern African countries. Several alumni are serving as general secretaries of their national Baptist conventions: Mazvigadza for Zimbabwe, Akim Chirwa for Malawi, and Geronimo Cisito for Angola. Other alumni who have become important regional leaders are Jose Chama, president of the Baptist Convention of Angola, and David Nkosi, head of the Bible Society in Angola.

When asked about the importance of the seminary to the work and ministries of the Baptist Convention of Zimbabwe, a variety of Zimbabweans were ready with an answer. Reverend Musiyiwa, a pastor serving in the convention for several decades, noted, "The school is ours. It serves a vital purpose because it is the source of those who lead in the churches."[38] David Chiusaru, chairman of the seminary board at the time of writing, insisted that "a high caliber faculty at the seminary is necessary to train the kind of leader able to function in a modern Zimbabwe."[39] Chamunorwa Chiromo expressed a further hope, that the seminary would evolve into a Baptist university in the fashion of the Methodists' Africa University in Mutare.[40]

Already BTSZ is reforming its curriculum to respond to the needs of contemporary Zimbabwe. The Diploma in Religious Studies offered by the seminary under the auspices of the University of Zimbabwe is the flagship program that is the main draw to students. With this diploma, graduates can pastor and serve as teachers in Zimbabwe's schools. Given the economies of poverty that still prevail in Zimbabwe, such training allows graduates the option of serving in bivocational capacities, which may be the answer to the chronic lack of support available from local churches. Having a pastor who is not dependent on the local church for full support releases local church funds for local ministry and national cooperative ventures. With such an outcome in mind, Mugabe is leading the seminary to shift the training of ministers toward bivocationalism. Even though self-sufficiency is the goal, seminary leadership recognizes that local giving is not equal to the task facing the churches.

The reality on the ground in Zimbabwe is of a church that is alive with excitement and growth and yet lacking the financial resources to minister as it desires. Ingenuity and creativity have led its leaders to pursue interdependent relationships that allow them a healthy measure of autonomy in the projects they pursue and in forging a theology relevant to the contextual realities of a postcolonial Zimbabwe. Could it be that what is happening in Zimbabwe is inevitable for the church? Does the situation in world Christianity demand a modified missionary philosophy? When Christians sing, "We are one in the Spirit, we are one in the Lord," do their words not declare a solidarity that requires financial and relational interdependence?

Appendix

Explanation and Proposed Amendments to "Nationalization Plan"

The "Nationalization Plan, 1991–2025, for Baptist Theological Seminary of Zimbabwe" which the BTSZ Board of Directors approved in 1989 needs to be amended in order to deal with the following facts:

1. BTSZ has been informed by the Baptist Mission in Zimbabwe that Foreign Mission Board funds for the operation of the institution will cease at the end of 2015 instead of 2025.
2. The "Nationalization Plan Schedule for Decreasing Support of the Foreign Mission Board for Operating BTSZ" stated that the exchange rate for converting U.S. dollars to ZIM dollars was to be the 1990 rate of .50 cents. Instead the current rates have been used.

In 1990 BTSZ received from FMB U.S.$19,212.05 for the operation of the institution. (This amount does not include funds received for operation of the Portuguese programme.)

In 1991 BTSZ received from FMB U.S.$14,553.02 for operation of the institution. This is a 24.25% annual decrease in operating funds received from the FMB.

The decrease is likely to be even greater in 1992 thereby forcing the institution to close. At the present rate of exchange (.20) there will be another 35.80% reduction in 1992. The seminary cannot survive these large reductions in buying power.

Therefore we recommend:

1. That the "Nationalization Plan Schedule for Decreasing Support of FMB for Operating BTSZ" be stated in U.S. dollars. (See attached schedule.)
2. That U.S.$15,000 be the base for the "Nationalization Plan Schedule for Decreasing Support of FMB for Operating BTSZ." (See attached schedule.)
3. That BTSZ request U.S.$14,850 from the FMB toward operation of the institution in 1992. (See attached schedule.)
4. That BTSZ request U.S.$14,700 from FMB toward operation of the institution in 1993. (See attached schedule.)
5. That BTSZ request the Baptist Convention of Zimbabwe to provide the remaining funds for the 1992 and 1993 operating budgets (minus the funds generated by BTSZ).

Note: The above recommendations have been approved by the BTSZ Board of Directors, the ASD and the Executive Committee of BCZ.

NOTES

1. Among the more notable ones who have made this case are the Japanese theologian Kosuke Koyama and the Ghanaian Kwame Bediako: Kwame Bediako, *Christianity in Africa: The Renewal of a Non-Western Religion* (Edinburgh: Edinburgh University Press, 1995); Kosuke Koyama, *Waterbuffalo Theology* (Maryknoll, N.Y.: Orbis Books, 1974) and *Mount Fuji and Mount Sinai: A Critique of Idols* (Maryknoll, N.Y.: Orbis Books, 1984). The question derives from a study by the Zimbabwean Christian

leader Henry Mugabe, who also insisted on a postmissionary theology but went on to put that theology to work. See Henry Mugabe, "Tilling with Our Own Hoes: Shona Religious Metaphor for an African Christian Theology," Ph.D. dissertation, the Southern Baptist Theological Seminary, Louisville, Ky., 1993.

2. The three-self formula—that churches should be self-governing, self-supporting, and self-propagating—is credited to Rufus Anderson and Henry Venn, who, respectively, were secretary of the American Board of Commissioners for Foreign Missions and secretary of the Church Missionary Society, about 140 years ago. Winston Crawley, *Global Mission: A Story to Tell, an Interpretation of Southern Baptist Foreign Missions* (Nashville: Broadman Press, 1985) 197–215, summarizes this view.

In recent years, missiologist Glenn Schwartz has published many zealous attacks on dependency on mission fields. See his "From Dependency to Fulfillment," *Evangelical Missions Quarterly* 27 (July 1991): 238–41; and "It is Time to Get Serious about the Cycle of Dependence in Africa," *Evangelical Missions Quarterly* 29 (April 1993): 126–30. These and related articles can be accessed readily at the website of Schwartz's World Mission Associates: http://wmausa.org/artmain.htm.

3. For an analogous story in Central America, see Karla Ann Koll, "Presbyterians, the United States, and Central America: Background of the 1980s Debate," *Journal of Presbyterian History* 78:1 (Spring 2000): 87–102.

4. The Baptist work that I discuss in this chapter is not inclusive of all such work by Baptists. I am focusing on that work that was related to the missionary efforts of the Southern Baptist Convention (SBC) through its Foreign Mission Board (FMB).

5. FMB Minutes, May 15, 1947.

6. FMB Minutes, Sept. 14, 1950.

7. *Extraversion* is a term employed by Paul Gifford to signify cultural and economic dependency in non-Western churches that resulted from the missionary enterprise during the twentieth century. In Steve Brouwer, Paul Gifford, and Susan D. Rose, *Exporting the American Gospel: Global Christian Fundamentalism* (New York: Routledge, 1996), Gifford portrays this syndrome in nearly conspiratorial colors, as part of the imperial designs of capitalism. He presents a more nuanced version in Paul Gifford, *African Christianity: Its Public Role* (Bloomington: Indiana University Press, 1998). Extraversion is inevitable. What must concern those who appreciate the global nature of Christianity and the shift in its numerical center of gravity is how to nurture and manage a healthy form of what we should properly dub interdependence.

8. FMB Minutes, Dec. 7, 1950.

9. Ibid.

10. The main source for this account is Davis Lee Saunders, "A History of Baptists in East and Central Africa," Ph.D. dissertation, the Southern Baptist Theological Seminary, Louisville, Ky. 1973, 73–119.

11. Dotson, Letter of June 24, 1971; *SBC Annual*, 1953, 114.

12. Foreign Mission Board press release, Feb. 15, 1952.

13. *SBC Annual*, 1953, 182–86.

14. *SBS Annual*, 1954, 115.

15. Saunders, 84.

16. Ibid., 86.

17. Commission, XVIII: 6 June 1955, 16–17, 32.

18. 1958, Special Central Africa Report.

19. Rhodesia, Mission Minutes, Dec. 12–14, 1954.

20. Saunders, 94.

21. Commission, XXV: 9 Sept. 1962, 32.

22. *SBC Annual*, 1963, 144.

23. *SBC Annual*, 1965, 143–44.

24. Commission, XXVII: 9 Sept. 1964, 31.

25. Saunders, 100.

26. This and following paragraphs are beneficiaries of the information contained in the 1993 annual report of the Baptist Theological Seminary of Zimbabwe.

27. See Appendix A, "Explanations and Proposed Amendments to 'Nationalization Plan,'" document in the files of the Board of Directors, Baptist Theological Seminary of Zimbabwe, circa 1992.

28. For a brief history of the FMB/IMB see *www.imb.org/core/aboutus.asp*: see also Alan Neely, *A New Call to Mission: Help for Perplexed Churches* (Macon, Ga.: Smyth & Helwys, 2000), 37–54.

29. Neely, 38–42.

30. Source: *www.imb.org/core/fastfacts.asp*.

31. Neely, 41.

32. *Something New under the Sun: New Directions at the International Mission Board* (Richmond, Va.: Office of Overseas Operations, 1999). See also Jerry Rankin, *Mobilizing for Missions in the New Millenium: A Great Commission Vision for Southern Baptists in the 21st Century* (Richmond, Va.: IMB, n.d.).

33. David Garrison, *Church Planting Movements* (Richmond, Va.: Office of Overseas Operations, n.d.).

34. Interviews with Mugabe, July 31–Aug. 3, 2001, at Gweru, Zimbawe, inform this and following paragraphs.

35. Mugabe and Goatley went through the Ph.D. program at the Southern Baptist Theological Seminary about the same time.

36. Reverend Chasara, pastor of Harare Baptist Chuch, is one of the many Zimbabweans who expressed their concern that the seminary become a viable institution that trains leadership for church and society. He noted, "I have several young people who feel a call to service in the church. It is important that our seminary be in a position to give them quality training. Quality training assumes quality trainers." Interview, Aug. 5, 2001, Harare Baptist Church, Harare, Zimbabwe.

37. Interview with Hermina Mugabe, Aug. 2, 2001, Gweru, Zimbabwe.

38. In the same interview, this pastor noted that some churches have seen a marked increase in the number of educated laity. In his eyes, this development calls for a better educated pastor. Interview with Rev. Musiyiwa, Aug. 1, 2001, Baptist Conference Center, Gweru, Zimbabwe.

39. Interview, Aug. 5, 2001, Harare Baptist Church, Harare, Zimbabwe.

40. Interview with Rev. Chiromo, Aug. 7, 2001, Harare, Zimbabwe.

4

A View of Ghana's
New Christianity

Paul Gifford

There is enormous vitality and creativity within African Christianity, as any visitor to any part of the continent will quickly recognize. New forms are proliferating, significantly different from mission-founded Protestantism, Roman Catholicism, and the classical forms of African Independent (or Instituted) Churches. These developments are undoubtedly part of a global phenomenon but equally unique to their African context. Their implications are profound. The new developments are altering the outlook and orientation of older forms and are also being exported to the global North. But these new forms need to be located and examined locally and in detail. This chapter attempts to contribute to this, by examining the burgeoning new churches in one particular area.

To explore this phenomenon, I have concentrated on Ghana, specifically the Greater Accra Region, which contains perhaps about 5 million of Ghana's 18 million inhabitants (figure 4.1). To obtain my data, I spent nearly 21 months between June 2000 and January 2003 in the area. During this time, I attended as many church functions as I could, spoke to innumerable church leaders and members, and steeped myself in the churches' media output—their broadcasts, tapes, videos, and literature. The following is an interpretation of what I encountered.[1]

I do not argue here that Ghana is somehow representative of Africa. Ghana has its own unique history. Ghana was the first African colony to become independent, under Kwame Nkrumah in 1957, in the euphoria and optimism that greeted the dismantling of the European empires. However, before too long, things turned

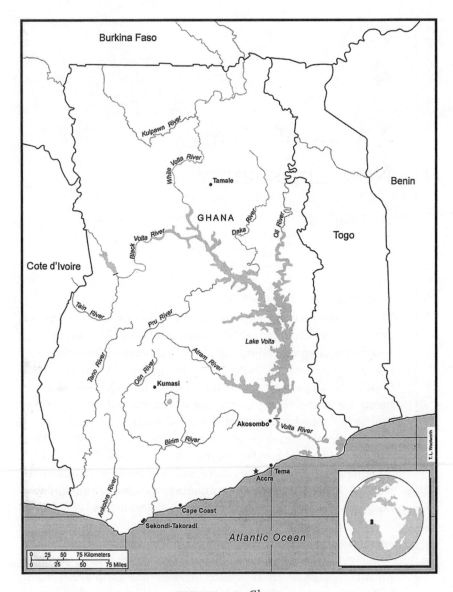

FIGURE 4.1. Ghana

sour. The increasingly despotic Nkrumah was overthrown in a coup in 1966; a period of military rule was followed by the short-lived Second Republic (1969–72), which was ended by another military takeover. The ensuing military regimes were corrupt and economically disastrous, and they brought Ghana to its knees. This was the context for the takeover of Flight Lieutenant Jerry Rawlings in 1979. After a few months of "house cleansing," during which he publicly executed three former heads of state, Rawlings was persuaded to cede power after scheduled elections, but he stepped in again to overthrow this Third Republic (1979–81) on 31 December 1981. Although initially professing socialist goals and an admiration for Gaddafi and Castro, Ghana's economic collapse forced him in 1983 to change tack entirely and to turn to the IMF and World Bank to rebuild Ghana. Under pressure from Western donors, Rawlings returned to constitutional rule in 1992, winning presidential elections in that year and in 1996.

For the elections of 2000, he was constitutionally required to stand down, and the presidency was won by the opposition candidate, John Kufuor. Although Ghana has remained relatively stable in comparison with many of its West African neighbors, and although it is sometimes hailed as a World Bank economic reconstruction success, nothing can disguise the fact that Ghanaians are probably poorer now than they were at independence nearly half a century ago, with a per capita yearly income of less than $400. The nation's enormous economic hardship cannot be overlooked in studying the changing face of Ghana's Christianity.

More than 60 percent of Ghanaians claim to be Christian. Up until about 1980, there were four recognizable strands within Ghanaian Christianity: first, the Catholics, the single biggest church; second, the Protestant mission churches, including the Methodists, two Presbyterian (from the Bremen and Basel Missions) churches, and the much smaller Anglican communion; third, the established Pentecostals (the Apostolic Church, the Church of Pentecost, the Christ Apostolic Church, and the Assemblies of God); and fourth, the African Independent Churches.[2] The mainline churches have been of considerable significance in building the modern nation—to a degree probably unparalleled in Africa—particularly through their schools, which have created Ghana's elite for more than a century. Yet no one can doubt that since about 1980 the whole profile of Ghanaian Christianity has changed, with the established churches in many respects eclipsed by something quite new. Few people in Ghana could be unaware of this shift. There are charismatic prayer centers, all-night services, conventions, crusades and Bible schools, new buildings, bumper stickers and banners, and particularly, the posters that everywhere advertise an enormous range of forthcoming activities. No one with a radio or television can avoid the media productions. Above all, everyone knows of the new religious superstars, Bishop Nicholas Duncan-Williams, Pastor Mensa Otabil, Bishop Charles Agyin Asare, and Bishop Dag Heward-Mills. If these are the most prominent or the household names, it is just as obvious that they are merely (to borrow a metaphor from English football) the premier division in a multidivisional national league. No one who reads the tabloid press can be unaware of the burgeoning crop of new "prophets," for they are featured prominently. Also prominent on the landscape are local branches of religious multinationals (often from Nigeria) like Winners' Chapel and the Synagogue Church of All Nations springing up all over.

These churches are not all the same, something that makes describing Ghana's new Christianity a rather daunting task. Even in Accra, there is such a range of these new churches that exceptions can be found to every rule. Besides this variation, change is both considerable and rapid. Even among the first division, it would be a mistake to gloss over the differences. Briefly, Duncan-Williams's Action Chapel International, founded in 1979 and the pioneer in Ghana, is most obviously a "faith movement" church (to be explained later), even if the American faith origins were mediated through Nigeria's flamboyant Benson Idahosa. Agyin Asare's Word Miracle Church International emphasizes evangelistic and healing crusades, and although the diseases cured at these crusades would certainly be understood in terms of demonic causality, that case is not nearly so developed as in the churches founded by Ghana's new "prophets." Heward-Mills's Lighthouse Chapel International is characterized by a stress on church planting and lay leadership. Mensa Otabil, the founder of the International Central Gospel Church, is almost exclusively a teacher, with no emphasis on healing, relatively little on evangelizing, and hardly ever a mention of demons. All these strands, with their different although normally compatible emphases, are part of the new flowering of churches I label "charismatic," even while illustrating the considerable range involved and the difficulty in talking about "charismatic Christianity" tout court.

Nor do these churches attract the same class of people. It is possible to devise an admittedly blunt grading system, based on things like the kind of cars in the parking lots, the hairstyles and haircoverings of the women, the number of men in formal traditional clothes, the use of English, and the obtrusiveness of mobile phones. A very rough guide to class (understood very loosely) is that if the affluent Catholic Parish of Christ the King (President Kufuor's church) rates a 10, these new churches rate as follows: Otabil's ICGC gets a 9, Duncan-Williams's ACI receives a 7.5, Agyin Asare's WMCI merits a 5.5, Heward-Mills's LCI gets a 5, and the prophetic churches rate a mere 1.

Nor has Ghana's charismatic Christianity remained static. We can visualize developments in terms of waves. If for convenience we can date the beginning of Accra's charismatic Christianity to around 1979, with Duncan-Williams leading the first faith gospel wave, we can distinguish three further waves. The second is the teaching wave in which expository preaching is the most salient characteristic; this is best illustrated by Otabil. The third is the miracle healing introduced by Agyin Asare, where services and crusades often are dominated by this practice. Fourth and last is the prophetic, where the seer's gifts of a particular "anointed man of God" assume much greater salience. What complicates matters is that each succeeding wave has tended to affect all existing churches, so "pure" or "nonhybrid" types are hard to find. For example, Duncan-Williams's ACI is still best seen as a faith gospel church, but even it had to advertise its 2000 annual convention as a "prophetic" convention—by 2000 almost *everything* had to be prophetic. All churches have not been influenced to the same degree, but the tendency is there.

Nevertheless, despite these provisos, some generalizations can be made. First, this Christianity is about success. A Christian is a success; if not, something is very wrong. The success emphasis is seen in the names of churches (Victory Bible Church, Winners' Chapel), and for these churches, size and numbers and expansion are tangible signs of success, hence the words *global*, *world*, or *international* in the title of so many. Illustrating the same thinking, Lighthouse Chapel International calls itself simply "the Megachurch." Success is evident in members' bumper stickers so favored by Ghanaians ("Unstoppable Achievers," "I Am a Stranger to Failure," "The Struggle Is Over"), in the labels given to years ("2001, My Year of Double Blessing," "2000, My Year of Enlargement," "2000, My Year of Fulfillment"), in the themes of conventions ("Winning Ways," "Highway to Success," "Taking Your Possessions"), and in their hymns ("Jesus Is a Winner Man," "Abraham's Blessings Are Mine"). In just talking to these Christians or studying their sermons, testimonies, and literature, certain words recur. The key words are *progress, prosperity, break-through, success, achievement, destiny, favor, dominion, blessing, excellence, plenty, open doors, elevation, promotion, increase, fullness, expansion, triumph, finances, overflow, abundance, newness, fulfillment, victory, power, possession, comfort, move-ment, exports, exams, visas,* and *travel.* Conversely, the negative things to leave behind are closed doors, poverty, sickness, setback, hunger, joblessness, disadvantage, misfortune, stagnation, negativities, sadness, limitation, suffering, inadequacy, nonachievement, darkness, blockages, lack, want, slavery, sweat, and shame. These realities are understood in a fairly commonsense way.

I could go on. I have not skewed the data by omitting bumper stickers reading "Blessed Are the Poor in Spirit," "Take Up Your Cross Daily, and Follow Me," "My Year of Self-Denial," or "My Year of Abnegation." Such stickers do not exist and are unthinkable in this Christianity.

Success is to be experienced in every area of life, but it primarily relates to financial or material matters—to prosperity. Sometimes prosperity obviously means sufficiency or adequate wealth, such as "It's his will that you prosper—not a million cedis in the bank, but my needs are being met, that's prosperity."[3] Says Otabil: "Prosperity is not the same for everyone . . . a bicycle for one who walks, that's prosperity" (18 August 2002). But more often, by far, it seems to mean abundant wealth. Ebenezer Markwei: "I hear the sounds of cars, new cars, luxury cars" (7 November 2000). A visiting Nigerian: "Get ready to prosper: you haven't seen anything yet" (27 October 2000). Even Otabil, whom we have just quoted about bicycles to show that prosperity may mean sufficiency, more often intends it in a stronger sense: "God desires to bless you beyond your wildest dreams and wildest expectations" (27 August 2002). And the Prophet Salifu of Alive Chapel International: "Child of God, your Father in heaven wants you to have all the wealth you could possibly get." The head pastor at Winners': "Before the year comes to an end, there are people here who will be counting millions of dollars in their accounts . . . the money is already there in my account now, millions of dollars. You are that person, in the name of Jesus" (11 June 2000). Also at Winners': "Between now and next December, some people here will own their own aircraft" (13 May 2001). Probably the biggest word in this Christianity is *breakthrough*, which I think means, in another key phrase, "uncommon favor."

All these churches make much of being "biblical," and their use of the Bible is along these lines. The Bible functions primarily as a repository of narratives. The stories are overwhelmingly narratives of the miraculous about (in what appears to me their order of importance) Abraham, Joseph, Elijah and/or Elisha, David, Daniel, Joshua, Moses, and Job. The crucial thing is not the miraculous in itself but that the narratives illustrate God's desire and ability to intervene to prosper his chosen followers. Thus the Bible is no mere historical record. It is addressed to *me* and to me *now*. As Agyin Asare has said: "If we come as they did in Bible days, we will receive as they did" (28 April 2001). These biblical personages are used to illustrate points like the following. Abraham illustrates a vision or promise fulfilled, a covenant observed, and faith rewarded with wealth. Joseph illustrates the need for a vision, but particularly the rapid transformation of fortune, that in 24 hours one can go from being a nobody to a somebody—even ("from prison to palace" is the stock phrase) to number two in the country. Elijah and Elisha routed enemies and performed spectacular miracles. David overcame odds, most spectacularly against Goliath, and was raised from shepherd boy to king. Daniel remained faithful through all trials and was brought safely to glory. Joshua miraculously crossed the Jordan, which was barring his progress, brought down the walls of Jericho, and took possession of the Promised Land. Moses confounded Pharaoh and destroyed his persecutors at the Red Sea. Job, despite trials, remained faithful and therefore was doubly rewarded.

That these figures come predominantly from the Old Testament is obvious. When the New Testament is used, there are some miracles of Jesus that are particularly apposite, but probably more important than the Gospels is the Acts of the Apostles, with Peter's deliverance from prison (Acts 12) and the freeing of Paul and Silas (Acts 16) particularly significant. The person or teaching of Jesus is not particularly prominent in this Christianity, but one thing is certain: he is not understood to have been poor. As Agyin Asare has expressed it, alluding to the wise men bearing gifts: "Joseph and Mary may have been poor, but as soon as Jesus came into their lives money started coming in."[4] And another preacher: "Archaeologists say Jesus came from Nazareth, a town of one street and 11 houses. Look where he is now. That's what I call winning" (6 March 2001).

There are nonnarrative passages that recur, too, and equally they stress the victory or success motif. There are texts of encouragement; others stress the need to look to the future, not the past; others, the power and will of God to intervene; still others, his covenant promises.

It is this stress today on success that is characteristic in these charismatic churches, and it is an emphasis that has displaced their earlier focus on healing. Bengt Sundkler, the Swedish missionary to South Africa and the first to take African Independent Churches seriously, once wrote of one of the subdivisions of these churches that what the sacraments are for Catholics and the Word for Protestants, healing is for Zionists.[5] But healing, although naturally an integral part of general success and well-being, is no longer prominent. This fact is significant because it is sometimes said that the years that have seen these churches proliferate are the years when user charges imposed by the World Bank and the IMF put the Western health care of clinics and hospitals out of the reach of many, so these churches arose to meet that need.[6] That does not seem to be the case; these new churches are meeting other needs.

This Christianity is not distinguished by any millennialism, nor is it about an afterlife in any sense. It is this life that is the focus. Sometimes one of these Christians refers to "these end times," but this is more likely to be understood in a restorationist sense; namely, these are special times in which all the miraculous activity recorded in the Bible is to be made evident again.

So this Christianity is about plenty, victory, success. How it brings these about is understood in different ways. The means are several, and the balance between them has changed over recent years. One is "Success through a Positive Mental Attitude" (to use the theme of a book by the Reformed clergyman Norman Vincent Peale, who was influential in the United States in the 1950s and 1960s and is found widely in Ghana in pirated Nigerian editions).[7] So these churches encourage and motivate, to such an extent that sometimes this is taken to be their prime function. Many of these Christians describe what ambitious steps they have taken, which they would not have without the self-belief fostered in these churches. Biblical figures are often used as examples of confidence; for example, David is used to show that we should not be daunted by seemingly overwhelming odds. It is a frequently heard motif that David, loading his sling for the encounter with the giant Goliath, was not overcome with fear; on the contrary, he said to himself: "This guy is so big I can't miss." Nonbiblical examples are nearly as useful for motivation. Thomas Edison is a staple; he had little education but went on to invent the light bulb. I remember watching some Ghanaian TV sermon while my wife was doing something in the background. At the end she observed: "Did you realize that in that whole sermon Jesus was not mentioned but Bill Gates was mentioned twice?" In fact, I had not noticed it because that is quite unremarkable.

More significant than motivation in bringing about success is a theology that is called the faith gospel, or the health and wealth gospel, or the gospel of prosperity, according to which a Christian (through Christ's sacrifice on the cross) is already healthy and wealthy, and all he or she must do to take possession of health and wealth is to claim possession. Hence, it is sometimes dismissed as the "name it and claim it" gospel. That is the teaching behind that quote from Winners' mentioned earlier: "Before the year comes to an end, there are people here who will be counting millions of dollars in their accounts. . . . The money is already there in my account now." Although in theory a clear distinction can be made between Pentecostalism and the faith gospel, and indeed in some countries there is considerable tension between Pentecostal churches who reject it and others that espouse it,[8] in Ghana it is clear that virtually all the new churches are marked by the faith gospel, although not all to the same extent.

In the United States, where the faith gospel originated and was made popular in the 1970s by Oral Roberts and other leading Pentecostals, succeeding through faith came to be closely linked to giving to God, utilizing particularly the biblical image of sowing and reaping.[9] Giving to God normally means giving to his representative. In Ghana, this development has been crucial. The faith gospel is not just characteristic of these new churches in the sense of serving to distinguish them from other forms of Christianity, but it is pervasive in and indispensable to these churches. It is pervasive and indispensable because their new church facilities, staff cars, musical equipment, crusades and conventions, all their foreign travel, and indeed the whole new class of religious professionals have to be paid for, and in a fragile economy. The faith gospel, with its idea of seed faith (or giving in order to receive), has proved a very fruitful way of raising the necessary funds to make it all possible. This faith gospel is not an incidental; it is a motor that has driven Ghana's Christian expansion. Yet it is possible to read articles on these churches that hardly mention the faith gospel, or only as an aside. A common view is that there is in Ghana a great Christian revival going on, which unfortunately in a few cases is blemished by this faith gospel. That does not capture the full dynamic, nor do the frequent allusions to the greed of pastors. That is not the significant point, although everyone can point to pastors who have done very well out of their new churches. The point is much more general; the faith gospel is pervasive because without it none of this expansion of charismatic churches, in such a depressed economic situation, would have been possible.

The second characteristic of Ghana's new Christianity, after success, became particularly evident in the early 1990s, when this faith gospel came to be so explicitly linked with a "deliverance" theology, probably because the faith gospel was not achieving all it promised. Wealth and success are still the right of the Christian, but now these blessings were proclaimed to have been blocked by demonic influence. Remove this blockage, and the success and wealth naturally ensue. Charismatic Christianity is normally marked by the worldview in which spiritual forces are pervasive and dominant. Thus, according to many charismatic teachers, it is spiritual forces that are holding me back from the victory and success and wealth that as a Christian are my right. Here we must draw attention to the continuities between this new Christianity and the world-view of pre-Christian African religion. We can generalize about the orientation and ritual process characteristic of Ghana's pre-Christian religion by noting that it was concerned with this-worldly realities: flocks, crops, fertility, animals, wives, children. Religious professionals were expected to procure these, and rituals were designed to ensure them. Here we have an explanation for the ready reception of the faith gospel, which likewise bears so decidedly on the here and now. It is just as important, though, that in traditional African religion the physical realm and the realm of the spirit are not separate from each other. They are bound up in one totality, for there is nothing that is purely matter. Spirit infuses everything. Although natural causality is not entirely disregarded, causality is to be discerned primarily in the spiritual realm. There is no matter or event that might not be influenced by the gods, ancestors, spirits, or witches. Any enemy could use spirits to bring misfortune into a person's life. A spirit acting negatively may affect the whole family, clan, or state. Religious rituals exist to preserve the proper relationship with these spirits.[10]

This spiritual worldview is common to, even characteristic of, the majority of these new churches. I think this is a key reason for their proliferation; this Christianity not only claims to have the answer to the poverty and marginalization of Ghanaians but also expresses those answers in an idiom that so many Ghanaians naturally respond to, yet an idiom of which the historic churches always disapproved.

In the early 1990s, it was often prayer camps where the evil spirits were diagnosed (often through extensive questionnaires) and exorcised.[11] The prayer camp phenomenon peaked about 1995. In the late 1990s, this practice of deliverance took on a slightly new form. A prophet or an "anointed man of God" could release your blockage. He did not need a questionnaire. He often did not require you to tell him your problem; both the problem and the remedy are either evident to him because of his gifts or are revealed to him. In the last few years, this anointed man of God, or prophet, has become the standard means of deliverance. Often before the suppliant speaks (often before one knows one is a suppliant), the prophet can tell the spiritual cause of "stagnation" and effect the deliverance right there.

One of the most prominent of these new churches in Accra is the Nigerian multinational Winners' Chapel, founded in Lagos in 1983; by 2000 it had 400 branches in Nigeria and was in 38 African countries. Here again, size is important, and Winners' boasts in Lagos the biggest auditorium in the world, seating 50,400.[12] Winners' came to Accra in 1997, and by the end of 2001 attracted about 16,000 on a Sunday morning. Here the success message is relentless. At Winners' Chapel, success is promised "now," "today," or "this morning." It is normal to hear statements like the following: "Many of you are beautiful, but no man has asked to marry you. Today, after the anointing, ten people will rush to you" (18 February 2001). Again, "As you depart from here today, you will be receiving phone calls, for a new job, a new business, new opportunity" (11 June 2000). "Within 30 days from today, your life will be dramatically changed. By the end of this week your crisis will be gone" (1 April 2001). All these churches welcome newcomers, but Winners' makes a great fuss over its newcomers, of whom there are about 300 a week, about half of whom reportedly stay. First-time attendees are told: "If you don't see a miracle in two weeks, you can go back [to your previous church]." At Winners', it is obvious that although the success promised embraces all areas of life, it is material success that is paramount, and healings are very subsidiary.

Often in the last few years, rituals have become associated with one's "breakthrough." At Winners', for example, a white handkerchief is called a mantle. In many services, each person waves one, and it is given a double anointing (a reference to Elisha in 2 Kings 2:9) by the prophet leading the service. Members of the congregation bring their "instruments of destiny"— scissors (dressmakers?), pens (teachers or office workers?), pliers (electricians?)—and wave their mantles over them. Winners' conducts a special washing of the feet, building on Jesus' example at the Last Supper, when he washed his disciples' feet, but even more so on Joshua 14:9: "Whatsoever your feet tread upon shall be given unto you for a possession." After the foot washing, you are exhorted to step onto the land or into the car or house you desire, which will then become your possession. Another ritual is called the covenant handshake. As the head pastor says: "It looks like the hand of man, but as I shake your hand the right hand of God will find you and give you your miracle" (18 February 2001). It can take hours for more than 10,000 people to come forward to shake the hand of the anointed man of God. Winners' most characteristic ritual involves oil. In the service, after rubbing oil over head, hair, face, and arms, while the man of God shouts "Receive husband! Receive baby! Receive car!" and so on, the congregation cries: "I receive it!" All these rituals are very new in this form of Christianity, which is normally considered something quintessentially Protestant and hence averse to liturgy and ritual.[13] They also bear witness to the increasing emphasis on the gifts of the specially anointed man of God in achieving the success this Christianity proclaims. After *miracle* and *breakthrough*, these Christians' most important word now is probably *anointing*. This shift to the special gifts of the individual is relatively new; even in 1995, the word *prophet* was not widely used. By 2002, many of the new pastors were styling themselves prophets.

Our discussion of these new churches would be incomplete without reference to their media. In fact, if success is the first characteristic and the worldview of ubiquitous spiritual forces is the second, the third characteristic could be their intensive media involvement. Accra has three TV channels, and religious programs (all from these new churches; the historic churches do not feature at all) are as much a staple as European football and Latin American soap operas. But even more significant is FM radio. Accra has seen the proliferation of FM radio stations in the last few years. In 2002, there were 15. Although both the Rawlings and lately the Kufuor governments have refused to license purely religious radio stations, some are religious in all but name. On many of the other stations also, Christian programs of this new type abound. It costs nothing to have pastors provide tapes of their sermons or come into the studio to pray for people who phone in with their problems to free them of their blockages. Many phone in to testify to the transformation of their circumstances through the gifts of the anointed man of God. Testimonies over these radio stations provide better advertising, virtually free, than these churches could purchase.

These testimonies are an important aid in our task of establishing what this new Christianity is about. Besides the continual stream of testimonies over the airwaves and the readily proffered testimonies of Christians, a good many of these churches have time within services for testimonies from members. Winners' always has seven or eight; some prophetic churches have up to 30 or 40 much briefer ones. Many regard these testimonies not as optional extras but as something necessary. In the words of Agyin Asare: "You must testify. If you don't, you won't keep your healing" (28 April 2001). It is sometimes presumed that these testimonies center round deliverance from sin and vice. That is not my experience. The testimonies almost invariably focus on the material realm, on finances, marriage, children, visas, jobs, promotion, or travel. Only a small fraction, perhaps 10 percent, refer to moral reform or deliverance from laziness or drink. Testimonies support the contention that these churches are about success in the way described previously.

Finally, complicating all this is the fact of rapid change. I have argued that the most obvious characteristics of these churches are, first, the stress on success and, second, the explanation through spiritual forces. Yet, if the overwhelming majority give great importance to spiritual forces, there is also a different approach to this issue. The leader of these new churches with the highest profile in Ghana is Mensa Otabil. His Christianity, too, is about success and wealth. But he is clear that one's success is not thwarted by demons or witches, nor are they responsible for poverty. His position is well caught here: "You want to be a success, with families, houses, jobs, education, finances, wealth. . . . You don't become a failure through witches, wizards or juju. You become a failure because of choices made by you or on your behalf. We must take full responsibility for how our lives turn out" (6 August 2001). He does not directly attack the worldview that sees spirits as pervasive. I have heard him a few times say: "Maybe there are witches. Maybe there are even some here today to hear me preach. In that case, welcome! You are most welcome!" but then he just moves to a level of explanation where witches simply have no place. The spiritual forces invoked so often in these churches he almost discounts.

Nor does Otabil espouse any form of the faith gospel, although he recognizably emerged from that stable. His message is still one of success and motivation, but poverty is not overcome nor success achieved through faith or his gifts, his "anointing," miracles, rituals, or deliverance. Success is achieved by work, through education (a particular concern), and through national political reform.[14]

Ghana's new Christianity is therefore notably difficult to characterize simply. For the most part, it promises this-worldly blessings and perpetuates the spiritual worldview characteristic of Ghana's pre-Christian religion, and it has been suggested that herein lies the secret of its wide appeal. But the diversity is enormous, and this brief mention of Otabil reveals the variety and thus shows how difficult it is to generalize about this Christianity, not least about its public effects. Many claims have been made for this new Christianity, several of them quite positive: these churches will create a new work ethic,[15] they will transform political culture, and they will foster democratic virtue.[16] In Ghana, however, the phenomenon has generated great suspicion, and many Ghanaians who are not participants in it feel that much of the new Christianity is extremely dysfunctional. Newspapers trumpet alleged abuses of pastors and prophets. Many go further and argue that, regardless of specific abuses of individuals, this form of Christianity itself is unhelpful. The stress on witchcraft is socially disruptive; one commentator deplores the injustice done by "pastors and priests who have turned into witch hunters. Indeed they have, by their false doctrines, destroyed many homes after declaring either a mother, wife or an in-law a witch."[17] Many think the faith gospel is dubious: "This country produces more priests now than doctors because the priestly profession is now an avenue to quick money. This is what our Christian society has become today."[18] Others fear that the insistence on miraculous divine provision militates against development; in the words of one politician, "Promising people to reap where they have not sown not only encourages them to be corrupt but also lazy. Until the various religious bodies redefine their doctrines on miracles and urge the people to work diligently, the government's quest to increase productivity in the country [will] never materialize."[19] Others deplore the increasing tendency to explain everything in terms of spiritual forces. An editorial in Ghana's biggest circulation newspaper laments: "It seems our society is gradually being swallowed by superstition. The numerous churches that dot the various residential areas daily attribute all the afflictions of the individual to the devil and his or her prosperity to the divine. Once a society is built on such a mystical foundation, hard work and perseverance fail to take hold."[20] These churches are also widely considered to be of little help in combating the threat of an AIDS epidemic: "Preachers of the gospel are now preachers of prosperity and instant miracles with little or no reference to morality in their messages."[21]

In the more directly political sphere, doubts remain, too. The hopes that they will be cradles of democracy may be unfounded. One must bear in mind that many of these churches are not really communities or fellowships at all. Some are, and many more began like that, but just as many now are composed of clients of a particular "man of God." Certainly the famed cell groups often taken as almost characteristic of these churches have become far less significant in the last decade.[22] More significant, it is widely admitted that there has been a move away from egalitarian tendencies to a more authoritarian ethos. What may have begun as fellowships in the early 1980s became churches and even denominations. The leaders, originally called simply "Brother" (or, more rarely, "Sister"), became "General Overseer," then perhaps "Bishop" or "Archbishop"—a noticeboard at LCI proclaims Heward-Mills as "the Megabishop." Many church leaders have acquired honorary doctorates; titles are as important here as in society at large. Many leaders move around with bodyguards, a symbol of status in Ghana. The prophetic phenomenon has brought this trajectory to its culmination. Prophets are persons of a totally different order from their congregations, with special gifts—and even here we have seen the rise of "Major Prophet" and "Mega Prophet." And during the Rawlings years, few of the charismatic churches posed any challenge to the political culture; on the contrary, many were easily co-opted into cheerleading, especially through the annual thanksgiving service, which became virtually a service in support of Rawlings.[23]

Nevertheless, Mensa Otabil has remained immune from much of this suspicion. Although virtually unique in both message and approach, through addressing social ills in his radio and television broadcasts and through his public calls for hard work, planning, vision, and reform, he has established impeccable credentials. In 1998, he established Ghana's first private university. Because he managed to avoid co-optation, he emerged from the Rawlings years with his status enormously enhanced. As possibly the most "successful" church leader in the country, he has attracted considerable imitation by Ghana's new pastors. Consequently, some observers have claimed that the public issues he has raised and the socially aware approach he has adopted bid fair to become more prominent; in this sense, one Ghanaian academic mentioned to me a possible "Otabilisation" of Ghana's new Christianity. However, the future of this Christianity is far from certain. It not only affects society but also is affected by society. What strands prevail and what effects they have will be affected by Ghana's fortunes more generally—on factors like economic progress, political stability, and poverty reduction. None of these is assured.

The developments we have sketched here are of concern not solely to Africa. They impinge on the West, too. In London, the majority of practicing Christians are now Black or Asian. The largest church in London now (members claim it is the largest since Charles Spurgeon preached in the 1860s) is Kingsway International Christian Centre, founded by the Nigerian Matthew Ashimolowo. In November 2002, this church was taken over by Britain's Charity Commissioners, because its administration was allegedly in breach of its charitable status. Ashimolowo himself was reported to make around a million pounds a year from his church. Even if, as was protested, he did not take all he was entitled to, it remains the case that there seemed no clear line between the church's income and the pastor's.[24] More generally, the faith gospel, so pervasive in many immigrant churches, has become such a concern that Britain's Evangelical Alliance in March 2003 published an analysis titled *Faith, Health and Prosperity*, which, despite its irenic tone, could not disguise its misgivings.[25] What it revealed was obviously so new in Britain's established Christian circles that the *Times* of London carried a discussion of the report entitled: "Poor Christians Are Deluded by 'Grab It' Gospel." The tone of the *Times* report was one of incredulity at such a distortion of "true" Christianity.[26] One of the conclusions of historian Philip Jenkins's *The Next Christendom* is that the Christianity emerging in the Third World will strike the Christians of the old world with its strangeness, to such an extent that the North may well come to define itself against Christianity.[27] It appears that part of this prediction is already coming to pass.

NOTES

1. For an extended treatment of all the issues raised here, see Paul Gifford, *Ghana's New Christianity: Pentecostalism in a Globalising African Economy* (London: Hurst, 2003).

2. On the first two strands, the literature is considerable. Only recently have scholars done justice to the third; see E. Kingsley Larbi, *Pentecostalism: The Eddies of Ghanaian Christianity* (Accra: Centre for Pentecostal and Charismatic Studies, 2001); and Kwabena Asamoah Gyadu, *Renewal in Contemporary Ghanaian Christianity* (Leiden: E. J. Brill, forthcoming). The standard work on the fourth category is still Christian G. Baeta, *Prophetism in Ghana* (London: SCM, 1962).

3. Said by a visiting pastor at Duncan-Williams's ACI on 26 November 2000. For other quotations used in this essay, I simply add a date in the text immediately following the quote. Roman type indicates it was heard at a service on that day; italics indicate it was heard via a media broadcast on that day.

4. Charles Agyin Asare, *Rooted and Built Up in Him*, 2nd ed. (Accra: Miracle Publications, 1999), 406.

5. Bengt Sundkler, *Bantu Prophets in South Africa*, 2nd ed. (Oxford: Oxford University Press, 1961), 220; see also 231–37.

6. Discussed in J. N. Tetteh, "The Dynamic of Prayer Camps and the Management of Women's Problems: A Case Study of Three Camps in the Eastern Region of Ghana," M.Phil. thesis, University of Ghana, Legon, 1999.

7. Norman Vincent Peale, *The Power of Positive Thinking* (Lagos: Blessed Family Publishing Ministry, n.d.).

8. Simon Coleman, *The Globalisation of Charismatic Christianity: Spreading the Gospel of Prosperity* (Cambridge: Cambridge University Press, 2000).

9. See David Edwin Harrell, *Oral Roberts: An American Life* (Bloomington: Indiana University Press, 1985).

10. For studies in the religion of southern Ghana, see M. J. Field, *Religion and Medicine of the Ga People* (London: Oxford University Press, 1937); M. V. Gilbert, "Rituals of Kingship in a Ghanaian State," Ph.D. dissertation, University of London, 1981; R. S. Ratray et al., *Religion and Art in Ashanati* (Oxford: Clarendon Press, 1927); Abamfo Ofori Atiemo, "Mmusuyi and Deliverance: A Study of Conflict and Consensus in the Encounter between African Traditional Religion and Christianity," M.Phil. thesis, University of Ghana, Legon, 1995; S. G. Williamson, *Akan Religion and the Christian Faith* (Accra: Ghana Universities Press, 1974).

11. For a fuller discussion, see Paul Gifford, *African Christianity: Its Public Role* (London: Hurst and Bloomington: Indiana University Press, 1998), 90–102.

12. See the claim in their *Winners' World*, February 2002, 20.

13. Although from a perspective such as Berger's these new churches with their "mystery, miracle, and magic" constitute the functional equivalent of Catholicism. Peter Berger, *The Sacred Canopy: Elements of a Sociological Theory of Religion* (New York: Anchor Books, 1990), 111.

14. For another discussion of Otabil's Christianity from a different perspective, see a paper by Christian van Gorder, "Beyond the Rivers of Ethiopia: the Afrocentric Pentecostalism of Mensa Otabil," presented at the conference "Christianity as a World Religion," Calvin College, Grand Rapids, Mich., 26–28 April 2001.

15. Bernice Martin, "New Mutations of the Protestant Ethic among Latin American Pentecostals," *Religion* 25 (1995): 101–17; Bernice Martin, "From Pre- to Postmodernity in Latin America: The Case of Pentecostalism," in *Religion, Modernity and Postmodernity*, ed. Paul Heelas, with David Martin and Paul Morris (Oxford: Blackwell, 1998), 102–146.

16. David Martin, *Tongues of Fire* (Oxford: Blackwell, 1990); David Martin, *Pentecostalism: The World Their Parish* (Oxford: Blackwell, 2002), especially the section titled "Africa," 132–52.

17. Tina Aforo-Yeboah, "Murder in the Name of Witchcraft," Accra *Spectator*, 28 April 2001, 13.

18. Accra *Chronicle*, 5 September 2002, 3.

19. Accra *Graphic*, 6 July 2001, 11.

20. Accra *Graphic*, 16 September 2002, 7.

21. Eunice Menka, "Condoms, the Church and HIV/AIDS," Accra *Times*, 28 June 2000, 6.

22. In the late 1980s, most of Ghana's major charismatic churches started to establish local branches in residential suburbs, because transport to the central church was both difficult and expensive and because they were all beginning to lose members to new churches arising in the suburbs. With this proliferation of branch churches, the rationale for cell groups was less convincing, even though all pastors I spoke to insisted on the crucial role they still played. Even Winners', which as set policy has one large church per city and no branches, has only "109 fellowships of between 7 and 15 members each" (interview, assistant pastor, 7 May 2001), which at the most generous calculation comes to a grand tally of 1,635 members involved; this is only about 15 percent of its weekly attendance.

23. See Gifford, *African Christianity*, 86–87.

24. *Ghanaian Chronicle*, 6 December 2002, 1; London *Times*, 17 Mar. 2003, 17.

25. Andrew Perriman, ed., *Faith, Health and Prosperity: A Report on "Word of Faith" and "Positive Confession" Theologies by the Evangelical Alliance (UK) Commission on Unity and Truth among Evangelicals* (London: Paternoster Press, 2003).

26. Ruth Gledhill, "Poor Christians Are Deluded by 'Grab It' Gospel" London *Times*, 17 March 2003.

27. Philip Jenkins, *The Next Christendom: The Coming of Global Christianity* (Oxford: Oxford University Press, 2002), 161–62.

5

The Role of Churches in the Peace Process in Africa: The Case of Mozambique Compared

G. Jan van Butselaar

The new world order that emerged at the end of the twentieth century had a large impact in many countries in Africa, including the role of churches on that continent. That became clear in the beginning of the 1990s, when the All Africa Conference of Churches (AACC) organized a symposium in Mombassa, Kenya, under the title "Problems and Promises for the Mission of the Church in Africa."[1] This conference turned out to be one of the most inspiring meetings that the African ecumenical body had organized in recent years. A great number of veteran church leaders, African scholars in different fields of study, and representatives of a new generation of African Christian leaders gathered there to discuss the situation of the church in the sociopolitical field on the continent, for much had changed in several African countries.

In the years since independence, a strong relationship had developed between church and state in Africa. Many African churches had gained African leadership long before that was the case in the political arena of their countries. That development had two important consequences. First, the church had become a learning place for democracy, at a time when there were no other places to express political opinions. So the church became, to a certain level, the cradle of the new, postcolonial Africa. That gave the church an important role in public life in Africa—almost at the same time as it lost that role in Europe. Second, when the newly independent countries were looking for well-educated leadership that was up to the new political responsibilities, it was clear where they could find them: in the mission and church schools and universities. Many of the new political leaders had even studied, at least for a time, at theological seminaries for pastors and priests. When they discovered that their vocation lay elsewhere—namely, in the political field—the friendship with their former classmates and future religious leaders did not come to an end; they continued to share a common understanding of life in Africa. When these new leaders were later given the responsibility to develop a new society in their countries, it was obvious that they sought counsel from their friends, many of whom were now bishops and church presidents in offices not far from their own.

In this way, the new leaders instinctively perpetuated an old African tradition. In former times, the religious practitioner of the village was normally one of the most important counselors of the chief. So what developed between church and state in Africa after independence was not a new *corpus christianum* but rather a return to old patterns of society.[2] It gave the church an important role in the newly independent countries. The danger inherent in that situation showed itself only much later, when several of the new African leaders turned into dictators. The church leaders then found it difficult to dissociate themselves from their friends. They tried to redress the situation in a "brotherly" way, by means of confidential admonition. To the public eye, inside and outside Africa, church leaders were seen as the uncritical lackeys of the ruling powers. But that danger was not foreseen in the years of nation building, which were full of hope for a prosperous future.

By the early 1990s, that period had definitely come to an end. The rather positive image of Africa had by then dramatically changed; the political and economic balance sheets after 30 years of independence were quite discouraging. A call for a fundamental renewal of politics in Africa was heard everywhere. Democratization became the new catchword. Sometimes this process went along peacefully; often, however, it resulted in violent clashes between the opposition and the ruling powers. In Zambia, presidential elections were tense but did not produce extreme violence. In Zaire, the opposition was severely persecuted, as was the case in Kenya, where some opposition leaders were assassinated and others treated so badly that they had to go to England for medical treatment.[3] In the small central African country of Burundi, many people disappeared, including potential leaders and critics of the minority regime.[4] But all that could not stop the unraveling of the corrupt systems. Often, it turned out that it was not just the president of a country who was responsible for corruption and exploitation but also a small group of people close to the central power, as was the case in Rwanda. Strategic industries were owned in many African countries by a favored few. High taxes and import duties did not show up in the state accounts, from where they could have benefited the poor and developed the infrastructure of the country. Development money sometimes mysteriously disappeared even before reaching Africa's shores or was appropriated to state industries and institutions that did not make the most efficient use of it, to say the least. Political and judicial authorities cooperated to silence any critique about these procedures; victims of the system were prevented from airing their protests.

Another feature that was brought to the fore in these years was the role tribalism and nepotism played in many African societies. Those who attained some substantial station in life felt deep communal obligations to help their kinfolk. Moreover, to maintain their power, authorities had to assure the help of persons and groups that could be counted on as absolutely reliable. Both needs were met by appointing members of one's own ethnic group or even one's own family to important functions, regardless of whether they were qualified for the job. The result was that many well-educated Africans, who could have played an important role in the development of their nation, were sidetracked.[5] These practices also strengthened the already existing tensions between the different tribal or regional groups. For a long time, nepotism was defended by leaders who stressed the importance of traditional African group and family solidarity. But the rampant corruption that resulted from this behavior once the traditional custom was integrated in modern society made this excuse invalid in the eyes of many, especially the new urban middle class. "No more nepotism," was the outcry; "no more tribalism. We need a new society." Churches had to find out what their role could be in this new situation and how to answer the call for change. That was especially the case in those situations where the tense situation had developed into bloody conflict or even full-fledged civil war, as was the case in Mozambique. In that country, churches eventually intervened and served powerfully in the ministry of peace and reconciliation. We will study their role more closely in this chapter and compare it with the work of churches for peace in some other African countries.

To understand the churches' role in bringing peace and reconciliation to Mozambique (figure 5.1), it is important, first off, to see how this land received Christianity and how it became a fundamental force among the people. In fact, this story starts with the expeditions of Prince Henry the Navigator (1394–1460), who was inspired by a double vocation in his adventures: to develop the commercial interests of his country, Portugal, which recently had been liberated from Muslim power, and the propagation of the Christian faith. For him, these two aims of his travels were not opposed to each other; according to the *corpus christianum* idea of his days, church and state shared a common interest. Defending the well-being of the nation logically included defending and furthering the (Christian) truth.[6] That principle also held in the foreign exploits of the nation. In the case of Africa, the missionary motive was strengthened by the old and influential myth of the Middle Ages that a Christian kingdom ruled by Prester ("priest") John existed somewhere on the continent. To discover this kingdom and to strengthen the Christian faith in Africa were important incentives for these early European explorers. At the end of the fifteenth

FIGURE 5.1. Mozambique

century, Henry arrived at Delagoa Bay in Mozambique. It took several more years, though, before the first missionary entered the country, the Jesuit Gonçalo da Silveira (1560). His mission first saw great success, especially at the court of King Mutapa Nogomo. But soon, for a number of reasons, the climate for Christian mission changed. Missionaries at the court were murdered, and Portugal decided to send in a punitive expedition against the murderers.[7] From then on, Catholic missions in Mozambique declined. The fact that some missionaries became engaged in commercial enterprises, slave trading not excluded, provides some explanation for the mission's demise. When in the course of the seventeenth century the Portuguese developed *prazos de corôa*, semi-independent colonial domains in which cruel regimes oppressed the local population, Catholic missions came almost to a standstill.[8] In the nineteenth century, the Roman Catholic missions had almost ceased to exist in the country. The few foreign missionaries who were still at work were not seen as very effective, either by the colonists or by the local population.

Toward the end of that century, the arrival of Protestant missionaries of several denominations, societies, and nationalities brought about a new impetus for the propagation of the gospel. The first of them was the American Board of Commissioners for Foreign Missions, which sent a delegation in 1879 directed by E. H. Pinkerton and, after his untimely death, by E. H. Richards to King Muzila in the east of the country. But they had little success. Only one mission station in Inhambane, on the coast, resulted from these actions. More successful was the missionary action of quite a different group of "missionaries," formed by Mozambicans who came home after a period of work or refuge in South Africa. There they had discovered the power of the gospel through the work of European missionary societies. From the end of the nineteenth century onward, these returning nationals started spontaneously proclaiming their new found inspiration and were eagerly listened to by the local population, their leaders included. Yosepha Mhalamhala, Lois Xintomane, and Robert Mashaba are the names of some of these pioneers.[9] At the end of the nineteenth century and especially the early twentieth century, they were followed by foreign missionaries, who joined them to strengthen their work. That could not undo the most important feature of the work of these Mozambican evangelists; that is, they gave Protestantism in Mozambique a definite African character over against the Portuguese colonial context of the country and its Catholic churches. That characteristic also was to be seen in later times: when in the first half of the twentieth century there was no room for civil education for Mozambicans under colonial rule, churches filled that gap and provided leadership training through youth groups.[10] These and similar actions gave the Protestant churches, although small minorities in Mozambique, a strong starting point to act for peace and reconciliation in the country in later years. They were experienced participants in the struggle for the well-being of the nation.

These churches had to deal also with a more difficult heritage that rendered their work for peace rather complicated: the relationship between church and state. In Mozambique, that relationship had passed through different periods. The effective presence from the end of the nineteenth century on of Protestant missions in Mozambique had an awakening effect on Catholic missionary action in the country. This Catholic revival was most welcome for the Portuguese colonial authorities. Their hold on the enormous piece of land that Mozambique is was far from effective. Several more important European powers tried to prove that they had more right to be called masters of Mozambique than the not so efficient Portuguese administration. So when Protestant missionaries came in, they were viewed by the Portuguese as agents of foreign powers who were competing for possession of the colony, or at least as possible witnesses for the very partial de facto rule of Portugal in Mozambique. It caused the colonial state to start protecting and furthering the interests of Catholic missions, not out of religious zeal but for political reasons.[11]

In 1910, an important change took place in metropolitan Portugal. The monarchy came to an end and was replaced by a republic. This republic was strongly anticlerical, in line with liberal ideas that were dominant in Europe during those days. For Mozambique, it meant that privileges for Catholic missions over against the Protestant ones came to an abrupt end. But in fact, neither group was very popular with the new authorities. That attitude changed once more when o estado novo of Salazar was proclaimed (1926). From then on, the Catholic Church and the state became a unity in Mozambique. Their relationship became so close that it was often difficult to know who was the real power in the country, the governor-general or the Catholic archbishop of Lourenço Marques, as Maputo was then called. For the Protestant missions, it was a difficult time. Although the foreign missionaries did their utmost to please the colonial authorities and were even sometimes recognized by them for the quality of their "civilizing work," they were always considered a possible danger to Portuguese rule in Mozambique. For the local population, the Protestant churches became centers of independence. The first president of the liberation movement Frelimo, Eduardo Mondlane, had been raised in the (Protestant) Swiss Mission Church.[12]

When the struggle for independence started in Mozambique in 1964, the Catholic Church was perceived by the freedom fighters as a close ally of the Portuguese colonial establishment. That does not mean that all Catholics were supportive of the colonial state's cruel suppression of the longing for independence among the population. There were noteworthy exceptions, especially in the northern parts of the country. The murder of the local population of Wiriyamu by the Portuguese army was made public by the White Fathers (who eventually left the country in protest) and caused an international outcry against Portuguese colonialism.[13] The Portuguese bishop of Nampula, Don Manuel Vieira Pinto, was expelled from the colony in 1974 for his critique against the warfare of his fellow countrymen. But this could not remove the impression that, on the whole, the Catholic Church of Mozambique was an ally of the Portuguese oppressor.[14]

For the Protestant churches, the case was different. Suspicions of the Portuguese colonial power against these "foreign agents" were fueled by the revelation that not only had several leaders of the liberation movement that fought the Portuguese come from the Protestant churches but also that the freedom fighters marched to songs and tunes from the Protestant hymnbook. The Presbyterian Church (Swiss Mission) suffered more than others from these allegations. In 1972, the president of that church, Zedequias Manganhela, and several senior pastors were arrested. Manganhela died in his prison cell.[15] During those years, the Programme to Combat Racism (PCR) of the World Council of Churches decided to give humanitarian support to Frelimo, the liberation movement. That decision only strengthened the Portuguese colonial power in its conviction that Protestants were on the side of the freedom fighters and made relationships even tenser.

There were exceptions to this image of a rift between Protestant churches and the colonial authorities in Mozambique. Several Protestant groups that were inspired by conservative religious organizations mainly originating from South Africa, where the apartheid government was the strongest ally of Portugal in Africa, were considered harmless by the authorities. The fact that the Anglican Church in Mozambique still received a Portuguese bishop, a close friend of the Portuguese prime minister, in 1967, when the struggle for independence was running high, took away any doubt about the political direction of the leaders of that community.[16]

When in 1975 Frelimo finally came to power in the country, it was no surprise that its leaders criticized the country's Catholic leadership.[17] But the new government went further, inspired by the ideas of European Marxist philosophers: religion was the opium of the people, and churches were run by foreign agents and ruled from outside the country, from Rome or Geneva or Johannesburg. That was the accusation Samora Machel made in his maiden speech as president of the newly independent country. He also prophesied that in five years' time nobody in Mozambique would even need a church.[18] So, Protestant and Catholic churches alike were labeled antirevolutionary forces and therefore to be excluded from public life as much as possible. It was a bitter moment for the churches, especially for all those in Catholic and Protestant circles who had defended and supported the liberation struggle. Neither did such unfounded accusations help the Frelimo government gain international recognition. With this attack on religious freedom, the government gave opponents easy arguments to depict them as disrespectful of fundamental human rights.[19]

The new political situation was a heavy setback for the churches in the country. Many church members left their communities and followed the leadership of Frelimo. Many foreign missionaries went home. Those who stayed did not receive posts in the nationalized schools and health services. Local churches were closed; church work, even its social service, was hindered or forbidden. In these first years, there were great expectations that Frelimo would bring the country to a level of development that matched neighboring countries, notably South Africa. At first, the fierce antireligious propaganda of the regime, combined with the reputation of the largest Christian denomination,

the Roman Catholic Church, as a collaborator in Portuguese colonial oppression, seemed to bear fruit: large sections of the population turned away from
the church. The end of Christian presence in the country seemed near. Even
the moral role of the churches in society was no longer recognized. People
were hesitant: whom to follow? The attractive promises of the victorious new
government or the old teaching of the churches? It was a time of trial for the
churches in Mozambique.

In this complicated situation, these churches received little support from
their international relations. Rome thought it better to keep quiet, given the
colonial history of the Catholic Church in Mozambique, and it quickly ordained
some African bishops—the first in Mozambique's history. The ecumenical
movement around the World Council of Churches would hear no evil spoken
of the Frelimo government. Had they not supported them through the PCR
when Frelimo was still a liberation movement? So the request to channel
church aid funds through government offices rather than through local
churches was met with sympathy in ecumenical circles. Inside the country,
Protestant churches applied "silent diplomacy," much in the same way as was
the case in European Marxist countries: no open critique, certainly not outside
the borders of the country, but clear stances in private discussions or symbolic
actions. In this context, the president of the Presbyterian Church in Mozambique, the Rev. Isaias Funzamo, once asked the appropriate ministry for a travel
permit to visit a remote village. Because he was a well-known public figure,
government officials wanted to be informed quickly about the possible reason
for his trip. When they heard that in that particular village the local church had
been closed without a valid reason, they ordered it to be reopened before the
church president arrived. Sometimes, silent diplomacy worked out well.[20]

This story shows also some difference between the position of churches
living under a Marxist system in Europe and those living under the same
condition in Africa. In Eastern Europe, churches were sidetracked in all possible ways and could hardly act independently from or over against the government. African churches, although reluctant to criticize their governments
openly, whether Marxist or not, still found ways to influence the authorities in
a more confidential or nonverbal way. In the case of the Frelimo government,
there even existed some duplicity in the attitude toward the churches. Officials
publicly condemned the churches as relics of the colonial past, but informally
they respected these communities as expressions of African faith, of African
people.

Frelimo's claim that paradise was just around the corner for independent
Mozambique, once an uncompromising Marxism was applied, was not fulfilled. On the contrary, economic and political problems gave people serious
doubts about the effectiveness of the Marxist system for a quick and healthy
development. The situation in education and health care became so dramatically adverse that people started longing for the time when church and mission

were responsible for those fields. The food rationing that soon had to be put in place in the cities gave further proof that the Marxist system was not working in Mozambique. Politically, several leaders became disappointed in the political direction that the Frelimo government took. Personal clashes caused further divisions.

Eventually, a civil war broke out. Opposition forces united in a new movement, Renamo,[21] which started attacking the country's borders in the early 1980s, mostly against civilians who could not defend themselves. It was the beginning of a very cruel period in the history of the country. However, it was no longer the foreign colonialists who did the mischief but Mozambicans fighting fellow Mozambicans in an unimaginable way.[22] Both sides were adamant in condemning the other for the cruelties. Both sides were interested only in a final and total victory, no matter what the cost. Churches called for peace and preached against cruelty, but their voices were hardly heard. What did impress the people, though, was the concrete help and shelter the churches provided to those in need: internal refugees, orphans, and others. After many years of stagnant existence, that *diakonia* built once more a measure of trust between church and society.

To save the country and the population, it was clear that peace talks had to be started, and the sooner the better. But how to organize peace talks between parties that did not want to see eye to eye and were describing each other as armed bandits? It turned out that, for various reasons, the churches had an important role to play in this respect. First, churches had been witnessing the suffering of the grassroots population in the country, whether in Frelimo- or in Renamo-held territory. They had seen the rampant famine of those who fled the countryside and came to the cities, especially to Maputo. Second, the churches seemed to be well placed vis-à-vis the warring parties. Protestant churches, on the one hand, were considered to have a relatively close relationship with the Frelimo government; the Catholic Church, the strongest religious group in the center and north of the country, had personal relations with some leaders of Renamo. So, when the time came to pass on from accusations to negotiations, churches could play their role. Already in 1984, the (Protestant) Mozambican Christian Council (CCM) set up a Peace and Reconciliation Commission to further dialogue between the different groups. The commission consulted first with the Frelimo government but initially could not gain its permission to start talks with Renamo. The Catholic bishops of the country also became active for peace. They had started contacts with Renamo in 1982. Shortly after, they urged both the Frelimo government and Renamo to pick up contact and start a dialogue for peace.[23]

Only after the death of President Machel in 1986 did the efforts of the churches to mediate in the peace process really start to bear fruit. After some preliminary contacts and with the help of the All Africa Conference of Churches (AACC) and the World Council of Churches (WCC),[24] the Mozambican Christian Council held meetings with the Renamo leader Dhlakama in Nairobi. Catholics were also invited for these talks. Kenya's assistant minister of foreign affairs at the time and former WCC staff member, Bethuel Kiplagat, facilitated those meetings. As he would state later: "In Africa, condemning each other for cruelties does not bring peace. The only way is to sit and talk to each other."[25] In spite of this positive attitude, the meetings in Nairobi did not bring the parties closer together. Instead, mutual accusations were repeated, and animosity seemed to set the agenda rather than growing trust in each other. According to some, the WCC was not very helpful in this part of the process.

But then a new mediator came to the fore: the (Catholic) Community of Sant'Egidio, headquartered in Rome.[26] The involvement of this group in Mozambican affairs was long-standing, dating from the 1970s. They were, in the late 1980s, contacted by Bishop Jaime Gonçalves of the Catholic diocese of Beira, who had personal contacts with the Renamo, powerfully present in his diocese. That condition was a good start for winning the confidence of the Renamo leaders for new peace talks, scheduled to take place in Rome. Sant'Egidio managed to make a link with the Frelimo government through the intervention of the leader of the Italian Communist Party, Enrico Berlinguer, who was fully trusted by the Frelimo leadership. Further, with the help of Professor Ricardi and Don Matteo Zuppi, leaders of the Sant'Egidio Community, contacts were made with Italian and Vatican diplomatic circles. Both groups were willing to support the peace efforts of Sant'Egidio, morally as well as financially. According to Zuppi, at that time there were three important conditions for fruitful negotiations between the warring parties: there was a neutral mediator (Sant'Egidio), a guarantee for the Renamo (Bishop Gonçalves) and a guarantee for Frelimo (the Italian state).[27] In July 1990, the first round of talks was held; in August 1992, the twelfth and last round ended in the signing of a joint declaration of intent to agree to a cease-fire in October of that year. The whole process has been amply described. Here, it is important to see how the churches, together with Sant'Egidio, were able to operate effectively in this situation and be brokers of peace, where other (secular) parties had failed.

Zuppi, who was present from the beginning to the end in this peace process, stressed the crucial function of "church space" as neutral ground, where negotiators could speak freely, without fear of diplomatic backfiring. That neutrality did not mean that the church as mediator had no political vision. On the contrary, the push was strong toward bending the minds of the different parties to think peace instead of (devastating) war. The big difference with other negotiators, though, was that the church as such did not aim for political power. That was clear from the beginning and created the much-needed trust for the painful process of giving up dear political principles that lay ahead of the two warring parties involved. In that sense, Sant'Egidio provided an atmosphere where confidentiality was guaranteed, where new understanding and new relationships could be developed, and where the impartiality of the mediator was undisputed.

A second condition for successful peace talks, claimed Zuppi, was the choice of the method to be followed in the negotiating process. There, it was important to start first with identifying the points that the parties agreed on before entering the talks. In that way, mutual recognition could be established, and some feeling of unity could be experienced. In the course of the following discussions, new points could be added to the initial list of shared visions, shared analyses, and possible solutions. After this exercise, differences between the parties had to be formulated. These two categories were fundamental for making up an effective agenda for the peace talks. Once the points of agreement and disagreement were formulated, both parties could identify with the process, and each of them could be convinced that their particular points of view had been taken into account.

Finally, hard work was needed to find effective and realistic solutions to the problems that divided the parties. In the case of Mozambique, an important issue was the role of some state agencies that Renamo experienced as threatening: the secret service, the state police, and the army. After several rounds of discussion in the following years, on each of these points clear definitions on the role and the size of these instruments of power in society were formulated and agreed on. So an opening was made to organize and monitor together these and other instruments of state.[28] It was these three conditions—impartial but engaged mediator, effective methodology, and solution-oriented approach—that brought tangible results in the Mozambican peace talks.

According to Zuppi, it was remarkable that where the church, represented by Sant'Egidio, was able to bring parties together, the generally indicated actor for organizing peace guarantees, going by the name of "the international community," failed to function in the case of Mozambique. This failure was caused by the lack of a proper framework for peace talks. Sant'Egidio was able to provide a framework that put both parties at ease. And so the church, as church, could pursue one of its important missions according to the Gospel of Matthew (5:9), as a peacemaker.

After the formal peace agreements were signed, the churches continued to further the cause of peace and stability in the country. Sometimes this was done in a very concrete way. For example, the Christian Council of Mozambique in Zambezia province, with the help of UNICEF and some Dutch development agencies, started a project called Tranformação de Armas em Enxadas: beating swords into plowshares (Micah 4:3). That project sought to take away one of the great dangers for lasting peace: the enormous number of weapons that were circulating in society. Therefore, churches offered to trade arms for utensils that were more for the new time that had arrived: sewing machines, bicycles, corrugated iron, concrete, and domestic appliances. The arms were professionally dealt with by a specialized institute. Within a year, an enormous amount of weaponry was offered for destruction traded for "plow-shares." It was one of the most successful actions of the Christian Council in recent years.

The most powerful contribution toward enduring peace the churches gave after the signing of the agreements was to provide in their weekly worship a platform to reconcile with one another. There, victims and tormentors—and for many their roles had changed several times during the civil war—met each other, confessed their guilt to each other, and together prepared the way toward a new future. Churches in Mozambique thus were able to fulfill their mission of peace and reconciliation in society. Since the beginning of the civil war, their role in society had only grown. Many started to look at the churches as the new center of public life, the new center of moral structure, the new center for personal and cultural development.[29]

A formal recognition of this successful mission came at the sixth assembly of the AACC in Harare, 1992. There, the new AACC Peace Award was awarded to two Mozambican bishops, the Anglican Denis Sengulane and the Catholic Jaime Gonçalves.[30] It was an important witness to the representatives of the African churches from all over the continent present at that meeting that peace is possible—and that churches and Christians have a role to play in such pro-cesses, sometimes even as crucial a role as in the case of Mozambique.

Mozambique is certainly not the only country in Africa where churches and Christians were brokers of peace. Many other situations in many other countries can be quoted where they were active in this respect, sometimes with a visible positive result. Not always, though, did these actions for peace from the side of the "church" take the same form. That can be seen once the process described in this chapter is compared with what went on in other African countries that were suffering from internal strife or even from civil war. Briefly, here is what was going on in South Africa and Rwanda, both countries where atrocities took place on their soil between rival political and ethnic par-ties.

The case of South Africa is colored by the word *apartheid*. This political system was developed to safeguard the privileges of a minority White com-munity against the Black majority in the country. Officially, it was developed for the benefit of all "nations" that inhabited the country; effectively, it meant a cruel oppression and exploitation of the one group by the other. This injustice existed for hundreds of years in the country, although apartheid as government policy was formulated only in the middle of the last century. It was especially hard to endure for many because it was said to be based on "Christian" prin-ciples.[31] The Boer government that came into power in 1948 was composed of members of the Boer churches in the country; they were asking to be supported by their churches in developing a theological justification for a lasting segre-gation and racial hierarchy in the country. They were not disappointed. The

Boer churches provided this theological basis for the new racist policy. It took them almost 40 years to discover their sinful behavior and to repent openly from their mistakes.

When the struggle of the oppressed majority against apartheid took violent forms and the country became internationally isolated, the churches as organizations had difficulty functioning as brokers of peace: were they not part of the problem? Only some ecumenical bodies such as the South African Council of Churches and the Institute for Contextual Theology were able to make a contribution to a process of awareness building in the country. But because they were experienced as "foreign agents"[32] their protests were often not heard as clearly inside the country as they were applauded outside. Even the Black churches in the country had difficulty in acting openly against the racist apartheid system and exposing the nonsense of its "theological" foundation. Some Black churches were financially dependent on their White "mother churches"; some others had difficulty seeing how they could combine their spiritual character with political action.

Did this mean that the church in South Africa was ineffective in the struggle for peace in the country? In looking at the church as institution, that was true to a high degree. But "church" is not just institution or organization. It is foremost the community of believers, the community of those who have put their faith in Jesus Christ. Once we look to the church from that point of view, the role of that church in the struggle for peace and the victory over racial injustice in South Africa cannot be denied. It was strongly taken up, not so much by church organizations, as by charismatic church leaders, from the 1960s until the victory over apartheid in the 1990s. It is important to note that not only Black church leaders assumed that role but also White ones, both often to their personal danger. Many names come to the fore, when we study the struggle for peace in South Africa. One of the first was Beyers Naudé, who gave up his high position in his Boer church rather than to deny his conviction that apartheid was a sin.[33] Later, Black church leaders became powerful spokespeople for the case of a South Africa free for all. The most famous became Desmond Tutu, ecumenical thinker, archbishop of his church, political strategist.[34] He gave such powerful leadership that the festschrift published at the occasion of his honorary doctorate in theology from Pretoria University (once a stronghold of apartheid theology!) rightly concentrates on the principles and dynamics of leadership.[35] These two names were certainly not the only ones of church leaders that can be quoted who opposed injustice and oppression in their country and prevented by their action a full-fledged civil war. Many more could be added. Together, they formed a modern "school of prophets" that spoke the word of God, the word of peace, in a society divided by racism, ethnic hatred, and violence. The church in South Africa acted for peace, be it through the instrument of these charismatic church leaders.

Quite different was the situation in Rwanda. This small country in central

Africa hit the news desks of Western media in the 1960s, when its struggle for independence was marked by ethnic clashes between the majority group of the formerly oppressed Hutu and the minority group of the formerly governing Tutsi.[36] But since then, little was heard from that corner of the world. The first republic under President Kayibanda strongly identified, as can be understood, with the Hutu majority in the country. After a revolution in the aftermath of new ethnic clashes in the country (1973), a second republic was created under the leadership of President Habyarimana. He tried to be more balanced in the division of power and opportunities between the different ethnic groups in the country. Whether he succeeded in this objective is interpreted differently by historians, according to their political preference.[37] At least for almost two decades, a situation of no large-scale conflict was maintained in the country that benefited all. When, in 1980, an extremist Hutu lobby tried to impose their racist views on government policy, president Habyarimana came down heavily on them; many were imprisoned. During those years, the churches supported their government wholeheartedly. They were convinced that the status of relative peace in the country was the best condition for the development of the society and for the well-being of the people. At the end of the 1980s and in the early 1990s, that relatively peaceful situation changed dramatically, under the pressure of worldwide economic decline and local overpopulation. The ruling group became greedy, far greedier than acceptable. Tensions rose high in the country and often expressed themselves in actions of in ethnic hatred. Things got even more complicated. In those critical moments of Rwandese history, the children and grandchildren of the Tutsi refugees from the 1960s asked permission to return to what they considered their home country.[38] That was refused, arguing that the country was already overpopulated. Shortly after, a civil war broke out in 1990, by which the refugees tried to get in anyway. Their invading army, the military wing of their political movement, Rwanda Patriotic Front (RPF), occupied northern parts of the country and behaved cruelly in those areas. In that situation, churches were calling for peace, but their voice was hardly heard, either by the government or by the invaders. Internationally backed peace talks in Arusha, Tanzania, in 1993 seemed at first to produce some results and create a way to peace and reconciliation. But then a year later, the plane of the president of the country was shot down, and he and his Burundese counterpart were killed in the attack. That triggered an atrocious retaliation against the presumed perpetrators of the attack, the Tutsi and their alleged allies from Hutu circles.[39] Western media largely monitored the horrible genocide that followed. They even stayed on in the country when UN troops and the military of other Western powers that could have prevented the large-scale killings withdrew like dogs with their tails between their legs. The loss of life was heavy: between half a million and a million Rwandese died in a horrible way. Millions of others had to flee the country. Once the genocidal government was kicked out, the new party in power, the RPF, was not behaving with great justice or mercy over against alleged perpetrators of genocide, to say the least. Many died in prison, in internal refugee camps, or in refugee camps in Zaire/Congo, regularly attacked by the army of the new government.

The world was horrified by the stories and the images from Rwanda in 1994. How could this happen? Many commentators remembered bitterly that the country had the highest percentage of Christians in Africa; what happened to their faith? What happened to their Christian morals? What did the churches do?

These questions received at first a negative response. Churches, as church institutions, did little or nothing to prevent the killings. They clearly had taken the side of the ruling majority government and were reluctant to protest openly against human rights abuses by this government. When protests came, they often were too late and too weak. Neither were church leaders heard speaking with a prophetic voice, as was the case in South Africa. They identified too much with the ruling classes, before but also after 1994. Under pressure of the new RPF government, all church leaders were replaced by persons sympathetic to their cause; they did not dare to open their mouths other than in support of the new authorities. In Rwanda, church leaders were unable to come out openly on the side of justice and peace for all.[40] Was this the absolute downfall of Christianity in Rwanda, the final failure of a Christian faith that is concerned with justice and peace? Some parties in Rwanda, too anxious to do away with the leading role of churches in society, were quick to advertise this conclusion and to strengthen it with stories of clergy that took part in the genocide.[41] Therefore, today it has become almost impossible to analyze to what extent clergy were involved in the genocide. Perhaps the best account can be found in the story of Bishop Sibomana, who was not afraid to describe the wrongful attitude of both parties in the conflict.[42]

But not all was bad in the case of Rwanda, in spite of the image created. In fact, churches did not betray their calling for peace, as often has been suggested—that is, when not only the role of the official churches, international ecumenical institutions, and church leaders is considered but also the role of the laity, the "people of God." Touching stories have been told about individual Christians who, at the risk of their own lives, saved the lives of the persecuted men and women.[43] Even more important were the initiatives of laypeople after the annus horribilis of 1994. One of them came from a group of Rwandese refugees of different ethnic backgrounds. They met in Detmold, Germany, and mutually confessed their guilt. They even developed a plan for reconciliation (1998).[44] Delegations from this group visited the morally devastated country and tried to convince churches and Christians to take the road of forgiveness and reconciliation. Another example is a group of Rwandese that met in Machakos, Kenya (1999). They tried to put the conflict in the context of the region, including the situation in neighboring Burundi and Congo, also the scene of bloody civil war. It was out of their faith conviction that they urged governments and rebellious groups to come together and work for peace.[45] Other groups, such as the Groupes Bibliques Universitaire, an evangelical student movement, developed educational programs for peace and reconciliation.[46] In fact, churches, represented by their members, were calling for peace and working effectively for reconciliation when the political actors in the country were still talking war and preparing for retaliation. Churches, even those in Rwanda, played a role in building peace, inside and outside the country, through the faith commitment of their "people in the pew."

When we compare the role of churches in South Africa and Rwanda with what was realized in Mozambique, it is clear that the formally instituted churches in those two countries were curtailed dramatically in their abilities to put the call of the gospel for peace and justice into action. They were unable to do so for different reasons. But that did not mean that the "church" was absent from the scene of peacemakers. Individual Christians and nonecclesial Christian groups who had understood the words of their Lord took up the task of building bridges of hope, of developing ways of cohabitation, of installing and strengthening the longing for shalom. Mozambique was a clear case of denominations working for peace. But also elsewhere in Africa, churches and Christians overcame structural obstacles to follow their Lord and give voice to his call for justice and peace for all living creatures, even at the cost of their own lives.

NOTES

1. André Karamaga, ed., *Problems and Promises of Africa: Towards and Beyond the Year 2000: A Summary of the Proceedings of the Symposium Convened by the AACC in Mombasa in November, 1991: A Proposal for Reflection* (Nairobi: All-Africa Conference of Churches, 1993). See also G. Jan van Butselaar, *De Tweede Bevrijding. Problemen en Beloften voor Kerk en Samenleving in Afrika* (Amsterdam: NZR, 1992).

2. Stanley Mogoba, "The Role of the Church in the Formation of Democratic Assumptions and Behaviour," in *A Democratic Vision for South Africa: Political Realism and Christian Responsibility*, ed. Klaus Nürnberger (Pietermaritzburg, South Africa: Encounter Publications, 1991), 567–71; Caesar Molebatsi, "The Role of the Church in the Formation of Democratic Assumptions and Behaviour," in *A Democratic Vision for South Africa*, 572–79.

3. David N. Gitari, *Let the Bishop Speak* (Nairobi: Uzima Press, 1988); H. Okullu, *Quest for Justice* (Kisumu, Kenya: Shalom, 1997).

4. Filip Reyntjes, *L'Afrique des Grands Lacs en Crise. Rwanda, Burundi: 1988–1994* (Paris: Karthala, 1994); Joseph Gahama, "Limites et Contradictions du Processus de Démocratisation au Burundi," in *Les Crises Politiques au Burundi et au Rwanda (1993–1994): Analyses, Faits et Documents*, ed. André Guichaoua (Villeneuve d'Ascq Cedex, France: Université de Lille and Paris: Karthala, 1995), 77–88.

5. See the personal story of Antoine Rutayisire in his article "Rwanda: Église et

Génocide," in *Le Tribalisme en Afrique . . . Et Si on en Parlait?* ed. Daniel Bourdanné (Abidjan, Ivory Coast Presses Bibliques Africaines, 2002), 33–35.

6. Fritz Blanke, *Missionsprobleme des Mittelalters und der Neuzeit* (Zürich und Stuttgart: Zwingli Verlag, 1966).

7. Arthur Grandjean, *La Mission Romande. Ses Raciness dans le Sol Suisse Romand. Son Épanouissement dans la Race Thonga* (Lausanne, Switzerland: Bridel et Paris: Fischbacher, 1917), 139.

8. Allen F. Isaacman, *The Africanization of a European Institution: The Zambesi Prazos, 1750–1902* (Madison: University of Wisconsin Press, 1972).

9. G. Jan van Butselaar, *Africains, Missionaries et Colonialists. Les Origins de l'Eglise Presbytérienne du Mozambique (Mission Suisse), 1880–1896,* Studies of Religion in Africa, vol. 5 (Leiden: Brill, 1984), chapters 2 and 4.

10. Teresa M. da Cruz e Silva, "Protestant Churches and the Formation of Political Consciousness in Southern Mozambique (1930–1974): The Case of the Swiss Mission" (Ph.D. thesis, University of Bradford, 1996).

11. Alf Helgesson, *Church, State and People in Mozambique,* Studia Missionalia Upsaliensia 54 (Uppsala, Sweden: Tryck, 1994).

12. Even during the Marxist days of Frelimo rule, the Museum of the Revolution in Maputo showed the personal Bible of Mondlane as one of his favorite objects; the Swiss missionary A. Clerc dedicated the book to him. See Eduardo Mondlane, *The Struggle for Mozambique,* Penguin African Library, vol. 28 (Harmondsworth, England: Penguin Books, 1969). The Swiss Mission Church is officially known as the Presbyterian Church of Mozambique. See G. Jan van Butselaar, *Africans, Missionaries et Colonialists.*

13. Adrian Hastings, *Wiriyamu* (London: Search Press, 1974).

14. The picture of the church-state relation given by Vines and Wilson—that the Catholic Church was less (morally) supporting of the colonial war than generally accepted—seems too rosy to be true. Alex Vines and Ken Wilson, "Churches and the Peace Process in Mozambique" in *The Christian Churches and the Democratisation of Africa,* Studies of Religion in Africa, vol. 12, ed. Paul Gifford (Leiden: Brill, 1995), 130.

15. Adrian Hastings, *The Church in Africa, 1450–1950* (Oxford: Clarendon Press, 1994), 212; Charles Biber, *Cent Ans au Mozambique. Le Parcours d'Une Minorité* (Lausanne, Switzerland: de Soc, 1987), 131.

16. Bengt Sundkler and Christopher Steed, *A History of the Church in Africa* (Cambridge: Cambridge University Press, 2000), 986.

17. See Thomas Henriksen, *Mozambique: A History* (London: Collings and Cape Town: Philip, 1978), part 2.

18. Adrian Hastings, *The History of African Christianity, 1950–1975* (Cambridge: Cambridge University Press, 1979), 213. The visit of a Russian Orthodox bishop some years later in Maputo gave rise to naughty questions from the population, already suffering from lack of food: "How come that in the USSR they still have a church—was their revolution not longer than five years ago?"

19. Freedom of religion is part of the UN Declaration of Human Rights, art. 18; see Jonneke M. M. Naber (ed.), *Freedom of Religion: A Precious Human Right. A Survey of Advantages and Setbacks* (Assen, Netherlands: Van Gorcum, 2000).

20. Information given by Rev. Funzamo in a discussion with the author, Maputo, Feb. 1981.

21. This is not the place to discuss the reasons for the outbreak of the war, the character of Renamo, or the forces behind Renamo. For more information, see Chris Alden and Mark Simpson, "Mozambique: A Delicate Peace," *The Journal of Modern Africa Studies* 31, no. 1 (1993): 109–30.

22. The Dutch novelist Adriaan van Dis wrote a horrifying story of the civil war in Mozambique. Adrian van Dis, *In Afrika* (Amsterdam: Meulenhoff, 1991).

23. Vines and Wilson, "Churches and the Peace Process," 137.

24. The WCC in the end was giving up its stand of uncritical support to the Frelimo government that had characterized its attitude until that moment.

25. Kiplagat, speaking at the seventh general assembly of the AACC, Addis Ababa, Ethiopia, Oct. 1997.

26. For a full description of the peace process in Mozambique and the involvement of Sant'Egidio, see Roberto Morozzo della Rocca, *Moçambique da Guerra à Paz. Historia de Uma Mediaço Insolita* (Maputo, Mozambique: Livraria Universitaria, 1998).

27. Zuppi, interview with van Butselaar, Rome, 12 Sept. 2000.

28. Morozzo della Rocca, *Moçambique da Guerra à Paz*, 227ff.

29. G. Jan van Butselaar, "The Role of Religion in Africa Today: A Report from Mozambique," *Neue Zeitschrift für Missionswissenschaft* 56, no. 3 (2000): 133–40.

30. G. Jan van Butselaar, *Leven in Overvloed. De Zesde Algemene Vergadering van de All Africa Conference of Churches (AACC), Harare, 25–29 Oktober 1992* (NZR 592/92) (report, Netherlands Missionary Council, 1992).

31. See for more information my *Church and Peace in Africa. The Role of the Churches in the Peace Process* (Assen, Netherlands: Van Gorcum, 2001).

32. Their funds came almost totally from donors in countries outside South Africa. Even foreign governments (Scandinavia and the Netherlands) and the (then) European Community expressed their opposition to apartheid by financing their programs.

33. C. F. Beyers Naudé, *My Land of Hope: Autobiography* (Cape Town: Human and Rousseau, 1995).

34. Desmond Tutu, *The Rainbow People of God: The Making of a Peaceful Revolution* (New York: Doubleday, 1994).

35. Dirk J. Human (ed.), *Bridging the Gap: Principles and Dynamics of Leadership. Festschrift for Desmond M. Tutu*, (Verbum et Ecclesia 23/3).
(Pretoria, South Africa: University of Pretoria, 2002).

36. See Cees M. Overdulve, *Rwanda: Un Peuple avec Une Histoire* (Paris et Montréal: Harmattan, 1997).

37. After the revolution of 1960, the history of Rwanda was reviewed in the light of the new freedom. After 1994, that happened once more.

38. That is perfectly understandable, considering the extremely difficult and dangerous situation of refugees in Africa.

39. See, for a personal account of this horrible episode, C. Karemano, *Au-delà des Barrieres. Dans les Méandres du Drame Rwandais* (Paris: Harmattan, 2003).

40. Rutayisire, "Rwanda: Église et Génocide," 22.

41. A famous case was that of the Roman Catholic Bishop Misago, who was acquitted in the end; two Rwandese nuns who were brought before their judges in Belgium under the antigenocide law (since withdrawn) were convicted for helping the genocidal mobs.

42. André Sibomana, *Gardons Espoir pour le Rwanda* (Paris: Desclée de Brouwer, 1997).

43. Mark Deltour, *Dragers van Hoop. Getuigenissen over Dood en Nieuw Leven in Rwanda* (Averbode, Natherlands: Altiora, 1998).

44. Francois Rubayize, *Guérir le Rwanda de la violence. La Confession de Detmold un Premier Pas* (Paris et Montréal: Harmattan, 1998).

45. Ernest Runkangira (ed.), *Actes* du Colloque de Machakos (Brussels, 2001).

46. Abel Ndjeraréou, "Dieu et la Tribu" in Bourdanné, ed., *Le Tribalisme en Afrique*, 109–72.

6

Christian Witness in the Public Sphere: Some Lessons and Residual Challenges from the Recent Political History of Ghana

Kwame Bediako

Ghana in Search of a New Political Culture

In 1992, Ghana adopted a democratic constitution to mark its entry into its Fourth Republic, thus ending 20 years of rule by the military under the leadership of an Air Force officer, Flight Lieutenant Jerry John Rawlings. That year, while retaining his military title, Rawlings presented himself as a presidential candidate on behalf of his own political party, the National Democratic Congress (NDC), and was elected, beating off opposition from the New Patriotic Party (NPP), headed by the eminent retired history university professor, Albert Adu Boahen. The opposition contested that result and described Rawlings's victory as a "stolen verdict."[1]

In 1996, Rawlings secured a second and final presidential four-year term of office, according to the constitution, defeating again the candidate of the NPP, John Agyekum Kuffuor. In the 2000 elections, however, Kuffuor defeated the new NDC candidate, one-time university professor of law and Commissioner of Inland Revenue John Atta Mills. At the inauguration of Kuffuor's presidency on 7 January 2001, Rawlings was present to congratulate the new president.

Occasional interventions by Rawlings into the party political arena since have been of little consequence. All the indications are that Ghana has entered a new era in its political life. It may even be appropriate to speak of a new "political culture," marked by signs of greater transparency of governance and public accountability before an informed and vocal population, served by a diverse and free press and media and undergirded by a mood of national confidence and hope that the nation's residual socioeconomic and other problems can be faced with equanimity. Ghanaians take just pride in the achievement of one of their compatriots, Kofi Annan, the serving General Secretary of the United Nations, who is now a Nobel Peace Laureate. It is yet another "sign of the times" for the nations, many believe.

Christian Presence amid Religious Pluralism in an Age of "Globalization": The Weakness of Some Prevailing Perspectives

It cannot have escaped attention that religion, especially Christianity, has had a significant role in the recent political history of Ghana. Paul Gifford, in his wide-ranging analysis, *African Christianity: Its Public Role*, does, in fact, describe Ghana's national ethos as "recognizably Christian."[2] It would be misleading, however, to conclude that this national "Christian ethos" is producing a Christendom scenario in which all other religious options and alternatives are eliminated or presumed irrelevant. On the contrary, in the religiously pluralistic society of Ghana, "traditional" religion, in its various local forms, continues to make its presence felt, with its periodic prohibitions and taboos placing limits on "Christian freedoms" and moderating any notions of Christian triumphalism.[3] At state and other public events, libation invocations by priests of local shrines, as well as Muslim prayers by imams, continue to be offered alongside Christian prayers by church officials and representatives. President Kuffuor, a practicing Roman Catholic, has as vice president Alhaji Aliu Mahama, a practicing Muslim. On 7 January 2001, the president's oath of office was sworn on the Bible, whereas the vice president's oath was sworn on the Qur'an. Both oaths were administered by Chief Justice Isaac Abban, a Methodist layman.

The religious situation in Ghana, as in many other places in contemporary Africa, shows how a widely accepted significance of Christian faith can exist within the religious pluralism of a non-Western setting, where the Christendom model of Christianity's relation to society generally is not possible. To understand such public manifestations of the faith, some of the prevailing analytical perspectives, especially the dominant West-inspired perspectives, conditioned as they are by an acceptance or a rejection of the Christendom model, may be rather ill suited.[4] Indeed, Paul Gifford's *African Christianity: Its Public Role* falls into this category. For all its rich documentation and judicious commentary in a number of places, Gifford's study is disappointing, precisely because of such a failure in perspective.

One of the more perceptive comments that Gifford makes regarding Christianity in African life is that the religious situation in Africa is one in which "an appeal to a primal imagination . . . does not involve a positive repudiation of Enlightenment rationality in the way that is required in the West."[5] This ought to mean that one should treat more seriously the argument that we now have in Africa the opportunity for exploring new Christian theological discourse and idiom by respecting the continuing primal worldviews of non-Western Christians, in this particular case, of African Christians.[6] Instead, by holding the view that "whatever else it is, Christianity is a cultural product honed in the West over centuries,"[7] Gifford seems to suffer from what appears to be an echo of the Eurocentrism of the past. Consequently, he is unable to follow through his own insight into the modern African situation.

Another survey of the evidence at a more popular level that comes to conclusions similar to Gifford's is Kenneth Woodward's 2001 article in *Newsweek*.[8] After considering the facts of Christianity's changing center of gravity on the threshold of the new century, Woodward could only conclude:

> Although Christianity's future may lie outside the West, Western influence is still decisive wherever the Gospel is preached. In religion, as in other international affairs, globalization means that superpowers remain dominant. For the world's poor, Christianity often appeals just because it is seen as the religion of the most successful superpower, the United States. Nonetheless, as the world's most missionary religion, Christianity has a history of renewing itself, even in the most culturally inhospitable places. That is the hope that hides behind the changing face of the church.[9]

Both these assessments of the evidence regarding the new configuration of the Christian world suffer from the distorting effect of the continuing assumption that "Christianity is essentially a religion of the West," and they exhibit the resultant opinion that the fact that such a high proportion of the world's Christians now are Africans is "almost a nuisance."[10]

Like Gifford, who is puzzled that "Africa is not reacting to globalization by revitalizing African traditional religion" but instead appears to be "opting into exotic religions,"[11] Woodward, too, appears unable to conceive of Christianity in other than Western cultural and geopolitical terms. He is compelled to conclude that the expansion of the Christian faith outside the modern West is simply the expansion of the economic and political influence of the West.

The evident weaknesses in the analyses offered by Gifford and Woodward should prompt us to take to heart the following word of caution regarding much contemporary analysis of religion and religious phenomena:

> Religious activism intrudes upon the post-enlightenment secular world of sociological theorizing as rudely, and with as little compre-

hension, as secularism once intruded upon a world united by belief. One of the paradoxes of the modern sciences that have made much of our world more accessible to human intellect is that it has made this part less so.[12]

In other words, we may be unduly sanguine if we presume that approaches provided by the social sciences are by themselves any more successful in achieving fully nuanced interpretations of Christianity than other traditional theological approaches.[13] Nor may we presume to answer the questions arising from Christianity's interactions with the events and processes taking place in the southern continents before those questions have been adequately formu-lated from within those interactions, or without due regard to the perspectives of the major players or actors themselves.

Ironically, a clue as to what may be required is given in another social science study on African Christianity and on African Christians in the diaspora, published by the Dutch scholar Gerrie ter Haar. Writing on African Christians (mostly Ghanaians) in Europe, with particular reference to the Netherlands, she has shown how "Dutch communities which so far have found it difficult to integrate African Christians in the Netherlands into the wider Christian community . . . put the emphasis on the African rather than the Christian iden-tity of these believers." And thus the Dutch "use 'culture' as a mechanism to demarcate and separate, whereas the African diaspora Christians take the op-posite view and aspire to use their Christian faith as a means of integration into Dutch society."[14]

Ter Haar's insight, which she subsequently refined in a larger publica-tion,[15] is important and points to some specifically "Christian" dimensions of the African participation in globalization that may escape secular-minded ob-servers. She lays stress on the fact that the development of these "African-initiated" churches outside the African continent, propagating a "self-confident Christianity" and "claiming universal qualities for a religious world-view which, as it happens, has important roots in Africa,"[16] is a significant departure that should lead to a renewed appreciation of Africa's role in the modern world.[17] "To call them 'African' churches," ter Haar comments, "implies a lim-itation of their task in Europe. They look at themselves as 'international' churches, expressing their aspiration to be part of the international world in which they believe they have a missionary task."[18] Inasmuch as the "interna-tional" ethos of the diaspora African Christians reflects the attitude of their churches in Africa that send their pastors out as missionaries to the West, this development contributes a useful perspective on the nature of the external relations that link African churches and the outside world, particularly in the West. Gifford, Woodward, and other Western commentators have been pre-vented from seeing that this new trend has occurred, that it is possibly irre-versible, that it offers a new outlook on the relative positions of Christians from the West and Africa, and that it indicates, to an increasing degree, a new self-reflection on the part of African Christianity.

It is perhaps too much to expect that the significance of modern African Christianity should readily find general acceptance, given the history of the interpretation of Africa in Western scholarship, including its missionary wing. Considerable intellectual adjustment may be required before one is able to acknowledge that, at the start of the twenty-first century, Christianity has become the most global of all religions and that its radically changed manifestation in the world has turned it into a predominantly "non-Western religion," to the extent that it has now ceased to be shaped primarily by the events and processes at work in Western culture.[19]

The considerable accession to Christianity in the predominantly religious world of Africa has coincided with an equally marked recession from Christianity in the modern West, a situation that cannot be separated from the rapid erosion of religious outlook, particularly in Western Europe. Paul Gifford, who notes this fact, responds to it by postulating "different Christianities." The one, "supernaturalistic," which emphasizes the "realm of demons, spirits, witches" is the African variant; the other, "supernatural," focuses on the realm of "God, heaven, prayer, the resurrection of Christ, sacraments" being the Western variant! One does not need to pledge unqualified endorsement of all that happens within African Christianity to see that this distinction is dubious. A more helpful approach is to recognize that "the internal transformation within Western Christianity" (that is, in the direction of secularization), which Gifford regards as "a major cultural shift," has a bearing on the recession from Christian faith in the modern West.[20] The essential point is that religious *accession* and religious *recession* both belong within Christian religious history and that the character of Christian impact in the world is not linear and cumulative but rather serial and dialectic. If Karl Rahner was right in his observation that the modern West is "a milieu that has become unchristian,"[21] then this raises the question as to how helpful intellectual categories can be in the interpretation of the Christian presence in the modern world, when they are shaped within, and according to criteria determined by, a de-Christianized "Christian West."

And yet, because the resources for scholarly research remain heavily weighted on the side of the West, it becomes a matter of serious concern in studies of the Christian presence in the world that the decline of Christian profession in modern Western culture seems to carry "at its heart a moral relativism that discounts Christianity's transcendent claims and resists that religion, or any religion for that matter, as a valid source of truth and guidance."[22] It stands to reason, therefore, that an African quest for the social and public significance of "Christianity's transcendent claims" is compelled to look, for its foundations, to the experience of African Christianity.

Africa and Christian Identity in a Pluralist World

Writing on Africa in *A World History of Christianity*, Kevin Ward recognized that "at some point in the twenty-first century, Christians in Africa will become more numerous than Christians in any other single continent and more important than ever before in articulating a global Christian identity in a pluralist world."[23] Elsewhere I have suggested that the lived experience of African Christians, in their total religious, cultural, and sociopolitical contexts, may be one indicator as to how Christians may exist in a post-Christendom pluralist world.[24]

In the present global transformation of Christianity, which has made the designation "universal religion" more accurate than ever before, Christians are also more dispersed than ever before. The notion of territorial Christianity, or Christendom, in the West, supremely the achievement of Charlemagne and which endured until relatively modern times, has effectively collapsed. Indeed, it can be argued that the modern missionary movement from the West played a significant role in bringing about the crumbling of Western Christendom, though this outcome may not have been intended. Be that as it may, the fact now is that virtually all Christians the world over live in plural societies, comprising people of other religious faiths or of none. How persons of diverse religious persuasions may live in harmony has become one of the most crucial questions in any appraisal of the social and public significance of religion.

So far as religious engagement in a pluralist setting is concerned, the modern West has less to offer than may be readily recognized, unless it be the lessons from the disaster that was Christendom. There are two main reasons for this. The prolonged experience of Christendom in the West meant that Western Christian thought lacked the regular challenge to establish its conceptual categories in relation to alternative religious claims, while the secularized environment that followed the Enlightenment has tended to suggest that specifically religious claims are no longer decisive. As a result of this Western handicap, the encounter with religious pluralism may lead to either religious fundamentalism or else the diminishing of religious conviction. It is what Lamin Sanneh describes as "a situation that tolerates people to be religiously informed so long as they are not religious themselves."[25]

In contrast, modern African Christian thought has had to establish its categories in the interface of African Christian confession, on the one hand, and the perennial spiritualities of the primal religious traditions of Africa, on the other.[26] Thus the experience of African Christianity does have some unique contributions to make to the present subject. This is why it must be reckoned as a loss that most studies of interreligious encounter continue to ignore the primal religions, possibly because they were for so long regarded by Western scholars as "primitive," with little or nothing to contribute. Yet the long tradition of hospitality and tolerance that African primal religions have maintained in their meeting with the missionary religions of Christianity and Islam must qualify them to contribute substantially to the quest for interreligious dialogue and harmony.[27] And over and above these practical considerations, the primal religions of the world are eminently qualified for having a unique historical connection with Christianity, especially, because they constitute the religious background of the majority of Christians of all nations so far in all Christian history, including that of Western Christians.[28]

If religious affirmations are what they purport to be, claiming to transcend the human measure by pointing beyond to the divine, religious people cannot be reasonably expected to compromise their religious convictions. Gilbert Murray's observation on the religious outlook comes to mind here: "Religion . . . is all-encompassing and demanding of total allegiance—infinite in its application to life. The man who makes terms with his conscience is essentially nonreligious."[29] And yet it is possible to show that a religious militancy that seeks the enforced elimination of all alternatives need not be intrinsic to the nature of religion itself. One need look no further than the supreme Christian symbol of an innocent crucified redeemer of the world to take cognizance of this. It is here that the Western Christian "ontocracy"[30] that was Christendom, is seen to have been a disaster.

African Christianity, African Politics, and the Challenge of New Public Theologies

The Desacralization of Power

This brings us to the challenge of new public theologies, which now confront African Christians. Modern Christian Africa, for all its missionary inheritance from the West, has avoided replicating Christian ontocracies. The notable exceptions were the older regimes in Ethiopia and apartheid South Africa—both of which have collapsed. But it is undeniable that in many societies of Africa, precolonial political systems tended toward ontocracy, as traditional religious and cultural norms were inclined to sacralize power and authority. It is possible, therefore, to trace the traditional religious roots of some of the problems of postindependence political authoritarianism in Africa.[31] At the same time, the historical role of the religion of the Bible in desacralizing notions of power and rule,[32] and its impact on the modern political environment in Africa have also been noted.[33] One must recognize, therefore, the contribution of African churches to the process of democratization in Africa in the 1980s and 1990s as a genuinely religious achievement, linked with "the mind of Jesus" in the African churches.[34]

This is not the place to fully develop the notion of the political options of Jesus or to expound the concept of "the politics of Jesus." Of course, mainstream Christian theology reads the career of Jesus in religious terms as sacrifice and atonement. However, the "concrete social meaning of the Cross" is no less important.[35] The reported encounter between Pontius Pilate, representing the Roman Empire, and Jesus, the innocent yet nonassertive victim of evil, represents the high point of the desacralizing emphasis in the tradition of the Bible.[36] Pilate's claim to have the "power either to free or to crucify" Jesus shows that he held a conception of power that sacralized the political authority of the empire. By contrast, Jesus' response, "You would have no power over me if it were not given to you from above," shows how Jesus desacralized the empire itself. In theological perspective, Pilate's authority, "like all human authority, is delegated; its source is Divine and therefore it is not arbitrary power, which can be exercised capriciously without moral blame."[37] Therefore, Jesus' willingness to suffer, though guiltless and innocent, becomes the ultimate clue to his mind on issues of power and authority. By his willing acceptance of death on a cross—the ultimate refinement in imperial methods of death by torture—Jesus desacralized all worldly power, relativizing its inherent tendency toward absolutization and its pretensions to ultimacy.

If the "Christ paradigm" has any significance in the public sphere, therefore, however essential it may be that transformation should find expression in sociopolitical institutions and structures, it needs also to find incarnation in personal lives. In this regard, Africa's most important resource for the development of new redemptive public theologies may well reside in its current Christian spiritual vitality, whereas the African churches' greatest challenge lies with their ability to "conscientize" their Christian communities in the direction of the "social" meaning of their religion. Elsewhere I have sought to show that part of the Christian contribution to the struggle for democratic culture in Africa will involve making room in the public sphere for "the mind of Jesus" as a nondominating, non-self-asserting, redemptive mind, as this relates to the issues of power and authority.[38] Without a conception of authority and power such as Jesus held, taught, and demonstrated by his cross informing civil society and becoming rooted in the minds of those who seek political office, the hope of attaining the goal of a genuine democratic culture may prove elusive.

Some Indicators from the Recent Ghanaian Story

One may not belittle, therefore, as Paul Gifford appears to do, efforts aimed at linking the mainsprings of responsible Christian political action with the political vision of the kingdom of God and the political option of Jesus as recorded in the Gospels.[39] Discerning observers of Ghana's presidential and parliamentary elections in 2000 would have noted the extensive involvement of local nongovernmental organizations, including church groups and local FM radio stations, acting as monitoring agencies at polling stations. The Christian Council of Ghana, under the leadership of General Secretary Robert Aboagye-Mensah, had an important role prior to the elections in "conscientizing" Christians in churches on their responsibility in the public political sphere and in ensuring good governance. The conduct of the elections, therefore, depended far less on the role of external, so-called international observers than on the internally generated commitment to ensuring free and fair elections.

Given the perceived formidable obstacles to a free and fair election in the way that incumbency was being used by the ruling party, there was a widespread belief that, should the elections indeed turn out to be free and fair, that would be providential, truly a gift of God. This explains the multitude of prayer vigils that were held in the run-up to the elections and the focusing of regular occasions for prayer in church upon the forthcoming elections. Indeed, the national mood was so much one of expectancy in God that the ruling party tried, rather belatedly, to exploit it to their own advantage. The catchy NPP slogan in the local Twi language, *asee ho*, meaning "down at the bottom," referring to the position of the party's symbol on the ballot paper, was converted by the ruling NDC to *osoro ho*, meaning "up there," as if to say that, because God is in heaven, the electorate should vote for the symbol and candidate at the top of the list! However, this slogan did not catch on. People knew where their hope in God lay, ironically not *osoro ho*, but *asee ho*!

This mood was captured in a local gospel song that became widely popular at the time, *Awurade kasa* ("Lord, speak"), a prayer that took on the political undertones of "Lord, speak through the election results." Following the NPP election victory, NPP supporters put out a 2001 calendar celebrating the result with the caption, "The voice of the people is the voice of the Lord." They were alluding to the gospel song. That this was not mere jingoism is demonstrated in the new government's concern for national reconciliation and consensus building. This is not to say that with this outcome, all sociopolitical issues facing Ghana are resolved. It is simply to say that the religious faith of a good number of the electorate found expression in specific actions that indicated that a wholesome foundation was probably being laid for the future political life of the country. This should be recognized for what it is, nurtured, and built on.

The Historical Significance of the Political Career of William Ofori-Atta ("Paa Willie")

There is a further element in the recent Ghana story that may hold promise for new forms of Christian witness in the distinct direction of a public theology. In 1992, on the threshold of the elections that were to inaugurate the Fourth Republic, the National Association of Evangelicals of Ghana (NAEG), which hitherto had not been noted for its interventions in the public political arena, instituted a series of public lectures in memory of the distinguished Ghanaian politician William Ofori-Atta. It was the NAEG's way of seeking to make a relevant political statement in view of the generally perceived need for good governance in national politics. The choice of William Ofori-Atta was appropriate and, perhaps, even symbolic.

There was probably no single person in Ghana who had quite as wholesome an impact on the country's political life for more than five decades, than "Paa Willie" or William Eugene Amoako-Atta Ofori-Atta, to give his full name. There were not many who, in the course of a long and difficult political career, had endured five arrests and detentions without trial. And yet, William Ofori-Atta survived them all, even to preach a charitable sermon at the memorial service for the police officer who had carried out the order for one of those arrests. Though he belonged to the company of the "Big Six" pioneers of the country's struggle for political independence—a company that included also Kwame Nkrumah (the first president), Obetsebi Lamptey, Ako-Adjei, J. B. Danquah, and Akufo-Addo (president in the Second Republic)—it was, above all, as a Christian politician, statesman, and evangelist that William Ofori-Atta, came to be generally remembered across the country. Equally revealing was the fact that following his death on 14 July 1988, a senior state official involved in planning the state funeral for him was known to have observed, "Paa Willie belonged to all of us." And yet it was well known that in life Paa Willie had held quite clearly defined political views and that his political convictions caused him to be associated with a particular political tradition in the country. Paa Willie was chairman of the Council of State of the Third Republic until the 31 December 1981 revolution that ushered in the government of the Provisional National Defense Council (PNDC) curtailed his active political life. And yet, at his death, the PNDC government paid this tribute to him:

> He brought to politics a new breath of sincerity, modesty and honesty. Such were the qualities of the man that he went through the rough and tumble of party politics with equanimity and a sense of humor. He never abandoned his principles, even in the face of defeat and adversity. Paa Willie's major preoccupation was service to his country and his fellow Ghanaians. . . . He did not use his talents or office for the acquisition of personal wealth, and he worked, lived and died a simple and devoted patriot.[40]

Preeminently a democrat, Paa Willie was open to winning and exercising political power by the ballot box, just as he was open to not winning political power, also through the ballot box. In his long political career, he experienced both. It was the feeling within the NAEG that this demonstration in his life of the possibility both of exercising political power with modesty and without arrogance and of losing political power without losing face was probably the most enduring testimony of his long political career to the country. The lectures were therefore intended to explore how Paa Willie's political testimony pointed to the unique insight offered by the biblical and Christian theology of power, namely, the conception of nondominating power.[41]

In 1985, three years before his death, William Ofori-Atta gave the J. B. Danquah Memorial Lectures of the Ghana Academy of Arts and Sciences on the theme "Ghana: A nation in crisis," which he concluded with a prayer that indicated his own state of mind on the question of a Christian's involvement in politics:

> I pray God that Ghana may be a shining example of a people who love freedom, who allow their own people to enjoy freedom and who inspire other nations in Africa and elsewhere with our practices and with our dedication to the cause of freedom at home and abroad.
>
> I pray God that in freedom our people may come to know the peace and prosperity and happiness which were the dreams of the founding fathers and which all nations under God enjoy as their birthright.
>
> And may this our country be committed to the Almighty God and be governed by upright and God-fearing men, dedicated to the concept of a democratic constitutional government in the name of God and for the welfare of the people and of the dignity of the individual to our God's greater glory.[42]

It was evident that far from regarding politics as a "dirty game," William Ofori-Atta considered the political arena as fit for "godly" men and women. There was a widespread public perception that William Ofori-Atta had been one of them and that his political career showed the relevance of the Christian faith as a significant factor in the transformation of society. We have noted the rather extraordinary fact that, following Ofori-Atta's death, several diverse sections of the community came to believe that Paa Willie "belonged" to them, too: the government, because he was a veteran nationalist politician and statesman; the bar association, because he was a distinguished lawyer who had served as national president of the association; the State Council of Akyem-Abuakwa Traditional Area, because he was a prominent royal; and obviously the Christian community, because he was a much-loved and energetic Christian and Presbyterian layman. The moderator of the PCG preached the sermon at his funeral, and a host of other associations paid tribute to him. Perhaps the most interesting and significant tribute came from the Akyem-Abuakwa Traditional Council—Okyeman Council—in a citation by which it awarded him a posthumous decoration, the traditional state's highest insignia, Okyeman Kanea—the light of Okyeman, the light of Akyem-Abuakwa Kingdom.

Yet the fact was that in the last 24 years of his life, Paa Willie lived as a fervent Christian in a rather distinctive manner. His own understanding of his "evangelical" conversion in 1964, during a period of detention under Kwame

Nkrumah's government, was that the Christian faith, as he knew it, could not merge easily with the religious aspects of traditional life and custom, as he understood them, so keen was his sense of the uniqueness of Christianity in the person of Jesus Christ. In his own words: "Christianity is a person. That person is the Lord Jesus Christ, the Son of God,"[43] so radical was his sense of his Christian identity. Okyeman Council could not have been unaware that it was honoring a Christian, for the citation ended with the words: "Oheneba [Prince] Okyeman Kanea, fare thee well, and may you remain in the gracious keeping of our Lord Jesus Christ."[44]

It is an open question as to how the terms of such a parting citation may be said to relate to the notion that in traditional Akan understanding, the dead—and the prominent dead especially—go to join the ancestors bearing messages from the living. We are left to assume that this particular royal goes to Jesus Christ, for this is what is affirmed by the traditional state that had nurtured him and yet had had no influence on the religious faith in which he died. Okyeman Council's expectation that Paa Willie would rest peacefully "in the gracious keeping of our Lord Jesus Christ" may be yet another indicator of the many-sided and many-layered senses in which African societies continue to appropriate the relevance of Jesus Christ in the public sphere. In Ofori-Atta's case, one may conclude that the impact of Christianity on African life—communal as well as individual—and at the specific level of cultural identity remains complex and yet is perhaps more profound than is realized by those critics who allege that Christianity ought to be felt as culturally alienating for Africans.

Some Residual Challenges

The recent political history of Ghana may be a pointer to the fact that for African nations caught between the legacy of "bad governance" in their immediate postindependence past and the perceived need for change in the direction of a genuine democratic culture, the challenge is not simply to "run a democracy" by the mere adoption of the external trappings of democratic reform, like elections and the institutionalization of parliamentary procedures. If African politics is to take in wider political pluralism and to show a greater tolerance of dissent as the fundamental assumptions of genuine democratic culture, then African societies need to put in place new conceptions of political power and authority. It seems that in this connection, African Christianity may have some distinctive contributions to make.

In the present quest for new political arrangements in Africa, the discussion is often distorted, so that it is made to seem as if the choice is between so-called Western forms of political organization and "indigenous" African systems and patterns. What one needs to realize is that "Western" democracy is not indigenous to the Western world, nor does it belong to the West alone, for it has emerged largely under the impact of *Christian* political ideas. But because many Western nations have lost touch with the Christian faith and become secular, they have also lost touch with the Christian roots of their political institutions. And so it is not sufficiently realized that Christianity has in fact played a key role in the emergence of political freedom in the modern world. One result of this historical amnesia is that in Africa in particular political theorists, historians, and governments, too, have continued to nurse a suspicion of Christianity as somehow alien, alienating, and unhelpful in dealing with the modern questions of African political and cultural renewal and "renaissance." Even the late eminent Ghanaian sociologist, politician, and prime minister in the Second Republic (1969–72) K. A. Busia, a well-known layman of the Methodist Church, may be justly criticized for being suspicious of Christianity in the modern African quest for democracy.[45]

And yet a proper understanding of the issues involved shows that the struggle for true democracy in Africa unavoidably involves making room for the "way of Jesus," the way of nondominating power in the political arrangements by which we relate to one another in our societies and nations. The mind of Jesus, as related to questions of politics and power, is *not* a dominating mind, *not* a self-pleasing or self-asserting mind, but rather a saving mind, a servant mind. "For Christ did not please himself" (Romans 15:3). Jesus' way of dealing with political power represents the perfect desacralization of all worldly power. The recognition that power truly belongs to God, rooted in the Christian understanding of power as nondominating, therefore liberates politicians and rulers to be humans among fellow humans and ennobles politics itself and the business of government into the business of God and the service of God in the service of fellow humans. Here, perhaps, one may see the true significance of the Christian political career of Ofori-Atta: not because he was a born again Christian in politics but because his political thinking and action went along these lines, reflecting the mind of Jesus.

Christian history amply demonstrates that the resacralization of power is ever in danger of reappearing. For in Christian perspective, the goal of human existence is the biblical vision of *shalom*—peace, wholeness, salvation, fullness, in the kingdom of God—and the arrival of democracy is not the coming of the kingdom. This means that the kingdom of God is the only lasting kingdom, and by bearing witness to the kingdom of God, the church of God emerges as the only truly permanent political institution on earth. And so, political rulers, by becoming disciples of Christ, are given the best opportunity to have their political service count beyond themselves. Political leadership—or better still, political service—thus becomes the service of God in the service of others. It is to this end that Christian witness in the public sphere ought to aspire.

Paradoxically, in the contemporary Ghanaian context with its "recognizably Christian" ethos, the need to relate to the continuing presence of other religious options and alternatives may well constitute one of the hopeful signs that such a "public" Christian witness and service can be sustained.

NOTES

1. See the document *A Stolen Verdict*, published by the NPP after the 1992 election results were announced.

2. Paul Gifford, *African Christianity: Its Public Role* (London: Hurst, 1998), 110.

3. Ghana's national newspapers, *Daily Graphic* and The *Ghanaian Times*, have followed closely the attempts to impose "traditional bans" on drumming and noise making during periods for the observance of silence as prescribed by the priests of local shrines.

4. See Andrew F. Walls, "Structural Problems in Mission Studies," in *The Missionary Movement in Christian History: Studies in the Transmission of Faith* (Edinburgh: T. & T. Clark; Maryknoll, N.Y.: Orbis Books, 1996), 146–55.

5. Gifford, *African Christianity*, 333.

6. See Kwame Bediako, *Christianity in Africa: The Renewal of a Non-Western Religion* (Maryknoll, N.Y.: Orbis Books; Edinburgh: University Press, 1995), especially chap. 6, "The Primal Imagination and the Opportunity for a New Theological Idiom," 91–180. What is meant by "continuing primal world views of non-Western Christians" follows the position taken at the World Council of Churches Consultation on "Christian involvement in dialogue with traditional thought-forms," held at Ibadan, Nigeria, in 1973. The consultation stated: "A primal world view operates in varying degrees within the continuing primal religious traditions, within neo-primal forms, within those who have abandoned the primal inheritance of their fathers and found no new faith, and within those who have adopted some form of Christian or any other religion without shedding their own culture." In *Primal World Views, Christian Involvement in Dialogue with Traditional Thought Forms*, ed. J. B. Taylor (Ibadan, Nigeria Daystar Press, 1976), 5.

7. Gifford, *African Christianity*, 322.

8. Kenneth Woodword, "The Changing Face of the Church: How the Explosion of Christianity in Developing Nations is Transforming the World's Largest Religion," *Newsweek*, 16 Apr. 2001, 46–52.

9. Ibid., 52.

10. Andrew F. Walls, "Of Ivory Towers and Ashrams: Some Reflections on Theological Scholarship in Africa," *Journal of African Christian Thought*, 3:1 (June 2000): 1–4, 3 (quote).

11. Gifford, *African Christianity*, 321.

12. M. Fields, "Charismatic Religion as Popular Protest: The Ordinary and the Extraordinary in Social Movements," in *Theory and Society*, 2:1 (1982); quoted in Jibrin Ibrahim, "Ethno-religious Mobilisation and the Sapping of Democracy in Nigeria," in *African Democracy in the Era of Globalization*, ed. Jonathan Hyslop (Johannesburg: Witwatersrand University Press, 1999), 97.

13. See, for example, Paul Gifford, *The New Crusaders: Christianity and the New Right in South Africa* (London and Concord, Mass: Pluto Press, 1991), 83ff.

14. Gerrie ter Haar, "Strangers in the Promised Land: African Christians in Europe," *Exchange* 24 (Feb. 1995), 29.

15. Gerrie ter Haar, *Halfway to Paradise: African Christians in Europe* (Cardiff, Wales: Cardiff Academic Press, 1998).

16. Ibid., 192.

17. See Kwame Bediako, *Christianity in Africa*, especially chap. 14: "The Place of Africa in a Changing World: The Christian Factor," 252–67.

18. Ter Haar, "Strangers," 29.

19. See Kwame Bediako, "The Significance of Modern African Christianity: A Manifesto," *Studies in World Christianity (The Edinburgh Review of Theology and Religion)*, 1:1 (1995): 51–67, states the argument. Kenneth Cragg, *Christianity in World Perspective* (London: Lutterworth Press, 1968), is a sensitive representation of the traditional Western missionary's perspective.

20. Gifford, *African Christianity*, 327.

21. Karl Rahner, *The Shape of the Church to Come* (London: SPCK, 1974), 32.

22. Lamin Sanneh, *Encountering the West, Christianity and the Global Cultural Process: The African Dimension* (Maryknoll, N.Y.: Orbis Books, 1993), 184.

23. Kevin Ward, "Africa," in *A World History of Christianity*, ed. Adrian Hastings (Grand Rapids, Mich.: Eerdmans, 1999), 235.

24. Bediako, "Significance of Modern African Christianity."

25. Lamin Sanneh, *Piety and Power-Muslims and Christians in West Africa* (New York: Orbis Books, 1996), x.

26. See Adrian Hastings, *African Christianity: An Essay in Interpretation* (London: Geoffrey Chapman, 1976); also Kwame Bediako, "African Theology," *The Modern Theologians* (2nd edition), ed. D. Ford (Oxford: Basil Blackwell, 1996) 426–44; and also Kwame Bediako, "African Christian Thought," in *The Oxford Companion to Christian Thought*, ed. A. Hastings (London: Oxford University Press, 2000).

27. For an early example from West Africa, see the very sensitive treatment of Samuel Ajayi Crowther's career in P. R. Mackenzie, *Inter-religious Encounters in West Africa: Samuel Ajayi Crowther's Attitude toward African Traditional Religion and Islam* (Leicester, England: Leicester Studies in Religion, 1976).

28. See Harold W. Turner, "Primal Religions of the World and their Study," in *Australian Essays in World Religions*, ed. Victor C. Hayes (Bedford Park, South Australia: Australian Association for the Study of Religions, 1977) 27–37; also A. F. Walls, "Africa and Christian Identity," in *Mission Focus* 6:7 (Nov. 1978): 11–13.

29. Gilbert Murray, *Five Stages of Greek Religion* (London: Watts, 1935), 6.

30. For this word as denoting the effective union of throne and altar, see Arend T. van Leeuwen, *Christianity in World History* (London: Edinburgh House Press, 1964), 158–73, 274–304.

31. See Bediako, *Christianity in Africa*, 234–51.

32. See van Leeuwen, *Christianity in World History*, 402–3, 417–19.

33. Harold W. Turner, "The Place of Independent Religious Movements in the Modernization of Africa," *Journal of Religion in Africa*, 2:1 (1969): 43–63.

34. See Kenneth R. Ross, "Not Catalyst but Ferment: The Distinctive Contribution of the Churches to the Political Reform in Malawi, 1992–1993," in *The Christian Churches and the Democratization of Africa*, ed. Paul Gifford (Leiden: E. J. Brill, 1995),

98–107. Ross cites J. B. Metz, *Faith in History and Society: Towards a Practical Fundamental Theology* (London: Burns & Oates, 1980), who speaks of the "dangerous memory" or "subversive memory" of Jesus Christ, which the Church carries through history (102). It is rather curious, therefore, that a recently published collection of essays, *African Perspectives on Governance*, ed. Goran Hyden Dele Olowu and Hastings W. O. Okoth Ogendo (Trenton, N.J.: Asmara, Eritrea: Africa World Press, 2000), hardly mentions the Christian churches of Africa as having any role in the promotion of good governance and the sustaining of civil society.

35. See John Howard Yoder, *The Politics of Jesus* (Grand Rapids, Mich.: Eerdmans, 1972), 134.

36. See John 18:28–40. See also the comments on this passage by Barnabas Lindars, *The Gospel according to John* (London: Oliphants, 1972), 568.

37. J. H. Bernard, *The Gospel according to St. John* (Edinburgh: T. & T. Clark, 1928), 619.

38. See Kwame Bediako, "Unmasking the Powers: Christianity, Authority and Desacralization in Modern African Politics," *Christianity and Democracy in Global Context*, ed. John Witte (Boulder, Colo.: Westview Press, 1993), 207–30; See also Bediako, *Christianity in Africa*, 234–51.

39. Gifford, *African Christianity*, 70ff; 340f.

40. "Tribute by the PNDC," in *Tribute to the Late Mr. William Eugene Amoako-Atta Ofori-Atta (Paa Willie), Member of the Big Six* (Accra: n.p., 1988), 21–22.

41. The first series of the William Ofori-Atta Lectures, delivered by Kwame Bediako as "Challenges of Ghana's Fourth Republic: A Christian Perspective," are as yet unpublished.

42. William Ofori-Atta, *Ghana: A Nation in Crisis*, The J. B. Danquah Memorial Lectures, Series 18, Feb. 1985 (Accra: Ghana Academy of Arts Sciences, 1988), 35–36.

43. William Ofori-Atta, "The Uniqueness of Christianity: The Reasons for Our Faith: An Essay by Paa Willie," in *Tribute to the Late Mr. William Eugene Amoako-Atta Ofori-Atta*, 71–75, quote from p. 75.

44. "The Okyeman Citation," in ibid., 31–33, quote on p. 33.

45. See K. A. Busia, *Africa in Search of Democracy* (London: Routledge & Kegan Paul, 1967). For a similar and more recent attitude of suspicion toward Christianity, see the collection of essays from South Africa, *African Renaissance: The New Struggle*, ed. Malegapuru William Makgoba (Cape Town: Mafubel/Tafelberg, 1999). The article by Pitika P. Ntule, "The Missing Link between Culture and Education: Are We Still Chasing Gods that Are Not Our Own?" (184–99) studiously avoids the suggestion that Christian faith is in any real sense an African experience that can have its place in the quest for a comprehensive "renaissance" within Africa.

PART II

Reflex Impact

World Christianity and the West since 1850

7

Interpreting Karen Christianity: The American Baptist Reaction to Asian Christianity in the Nineteenth Century

Jay Riley Case

One day in late April 1828, A-Pyah Thee, a religious leader of a small, obscure village of the Karen tribe in Burma, sent 30 of his villagers to see two white people who had just moved to the city of Tavoy (figure 7.1). After a three-day journey, the entourage appeared at the door of George and Sarah Boardman, American Baptist missionaries. Producing the *Book of Common Prayer*, the Karen delegation explained that 12 years earlier a white man had visited their village, given them the book, and instructed them in certain religious practices and ceremonies. The village had divided over these teachings, with one faction following the lead of A-Pyah Thee, who assumed the position of teacher of the new faith. Although at least one of them could read Burmese and a few more could speak Burmese, none of them could read or speak English. In fact, most of them knew only the Karen language, which at that time had not been reduced to writing. Now A-Pyah Thee had sent this delegation to George Boardman so that the American could explain the contents of the book to them more fully. They also asked him if he would return with them to their village. Boardman explained that he hoped to do so some time in the future and gave them a tract in Burmese for their return trip.[1]

During the next four months, six additional Karen delegations, apparently from different villages, sought out the Boardmans. On at

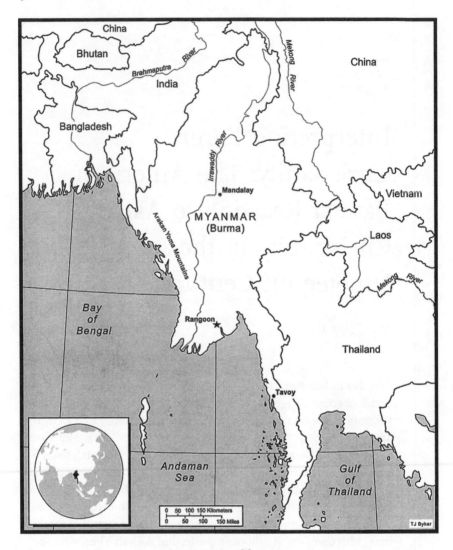

FIGURE 7.1. Myanmar

least five separate occasions, they requested that an American missionary or a
Karen Christian come to teach in their villages. A few Karens asked if they
could stay with the Boardmans for several days to study the religion and languages of the missionary. Three of these Karen guests witnessed the baptism
of Ko Tha Byu, a Karen who had been living with the missionaries for several
years and had recently become the first Karen to convert to Christianity. Immediately after his baptism, Ko Tha Byu set out with the Karens to preach to
the people in their villages, the first of countless evangelistic trips that he would
take over the remaining 12 years of his life. Meanwhile, a Karen delegation

that arrived in Tavoy at the end of June informed Boardman that Karen evangelists had been traveling through the villages, reading from a book and leading villagers to convert to Christianity. Though they had not actually met the evangelists themselves, this group of six Karens decided to take the three-day journey to Tavoy to find out what they could about this religion from Boardman.[2]

The persistent inquiries and active evangelism by these small delegations marked the first stages of a popular movement of Christianity among the Karen people that grew to about 16,000 in the next two decades.[3] Although Karen Christianity ultimately grew only to about one-sixth of the Karen people, its significance can be gauged in several ways. First, Karen Christianity is an example of Christian faith that has been translated from one culture to another, a pattern that Andrew Walls and Lamin Sanneh have identified in other geographic and historic locales.[4] Built upon the foundation of the Karen vernacular, grafted onto Karen oral tradition, and directed by indigenous leadership with minimal missionary oversight, early Karen Christianity proceeded in ways that missionaries often could not anticipate in or fully understand.

Second, as one of the first non-Western Christian movements connected to evangelical missionaries, Karen Christianity had a notable impact on American evangelicalism. In the era when the evangelical missionary movement first began to consider the complexities of its encounters with many cultures around the world, Karen Christianity generated great interest because something in this small region of Asia seemed to work. Throughout the nineteenth century, Karen Christianity hovered right at the surface of American missionary consciousness in general and American Baptist consciousness in particular.[5]

At the same time, Karen Christianity created a range of challenges to American Baptists for the simple reason that it was *not* a Western movement. The rapid growth of Christianity among an "uncivilized" people forced American Baptists to reassess Western conceptions of civilization. The initiative, zeal, and evangelistic success of Karen evangelists compelled missionaries to consider the role of indigenous agency in the absence of missionary oversight. Struggling to make sense of this process in the context of nineteenth-century American culture, Baptist missionary spokespeople ultimately created a somewhat flawed interpretation of Karen Christianity. By explaining the growth of Karen Christianity as part of the "civilizing" process, missionary spokespeople implicitly portrayed Asian Christianity as an extension of Western culture, a portrayal mirrored by other evangelical denominations. Though some missionaries pointed out the inadequacy of this interpretation, its assumptions colored American perceptions of the missionary encounter to the extent that it continues to shape how historians view world Christianity today. At the same time, though, the evangelistic and educational success of Karen Christians compelled Baptists to maintain faith in the capabilities of non-whites at a time when Whites in American culture perceived unbridgeable chasms between themselves and people of other races and cultures.

Karen Christianity

Although our knowledge of early-nineteenth-century Karen culture is limited by a scarcity of sources, existing evidence indicates that Karen Christians adapted Christianity to the specific issues of their time and place. Theirs was not a tranquil situation. A seminomadic, preliterate minority living on the margins of Burmese society, the Karen people faced discrimination and mistreatment by the dominant Burmese, who viewed the Karens as a wild people. Few Karens had adopted the Buddhism of the Burmese, holding instead to tribal religious beliefs. Conflict between the Karen and Burmese, which continues to this day, intensified in the midst of political instability.[6]

Although Karen converts shed some of their tribal religious practices, they did not simply replace one set of cultural and religious beliefs with another. Behind the Karen move to Christianity lay an oral tradition tied to Ywa, the creator god of traditional Karen religion. According to this oral tradition, Ywa had given a book of life to an elder brother, the Karen, but he had lost it. This caused him to lose favor with Ywa, thereby plunging him into ignorance. The youngest brother, the white man, had departed with the book but would return someday to share the book with the elder brother, who would be restored if he obeyed the book. Karen Christians saw the arrival of Baptist missionaries as the fulfillment of this prophecy.[7]

The application of the Karen name for God, Ywa, as the name of the Christian God generated significant theological and cultural dynamics within Karen Christianity. Evidence indicates that Karen converts filtered both the changes and the continuities of the new Christian faith through Karen culture, not Western culture.[8] In their spirituality, Karen Christians drew upon the tradition of Karen teachers called *bukhos*, who had taught that the ways of Ywa differed from those of *nats*, which were seen as evil spirits.[9] Traditional Karen songs extolled Ywa as perfect, omniscient, omnipotent, omnipresent, unchangeable, and eternal, characteristics that fit well with Christian belief. Karen oral traditions included stories of a creation, temptation, fall from God's favor, and future resurrection. Karen religious ethics promoted prayer, honor to parents, and love for one's enemies, while prohibiting theft, murder, idolatry, adultery, deception, and swearing. In fact, these Karen traditions resembled the biblical ideas so closely that several Baptist missionaries speculated that Karen must have derived them from contact with the Old Testament or the Jewish people at some point in ancient history.[10]

Biblical similarities to Karen oral traditions and the Burmese marginalization of the Karen also helps explain why converts took to literacy with such alacrity. Karen evangelists flocked to the missionaries to learn to read. They then promoted literacy and conversion among the Karen villages. American Baptist missionaries eagerly responded to these requests, publishing 21 million pages in the Karen language in the 1830s and 1840s. In 1841, Francis Mason began publishing the *Morning Star*, a Karen religious monthly that became Burma's longest running vernacular newspaper until it was forcibly shut down by the government more than a century later. By 1853, Karen Christians had snapped up all but 74 of the 6,000 copies of the Karen New Testament that the missionaries had published between 1843 and 1851.[11]

In the earliest decades, most of this literature scattered to converts who had never encountered a missionary. Karen evangelists took the initiative in spreading their new faith from the very beginning. Meanwhile, American missionaries scrambled along behind, trying to adapt their missionary machinery to this new situation. George Boardman, who had settled in Tavoy under the firm conviction that he would work among the Buddhist Burmese, did not embark on the first American missionary tour of Karen villages until nine months after A-Pyah Thee's villagers arrived at his door. By that time, at least 12 different delegations of Karen inquirers had visited him, making at least eight separate requests for American missionaries, Burmese Christians, or Karen converts to visit the villages. Ko Tha Byu, who had to convince George Boardman to sanction his evangelical forays to his own people, made at least five tours of Karen villages before Boardman first ventured out to see for himself what he could do among the Karen. Meanwhile, an unknown number of Karens, armed with tracts written in Burmese, had been spreading the message as well.[12]

This pattern continued in the three decades that followed. The ten Baptist missionaries who had learned the Karen language by 1841 simply could not keep pace with four dozen Karen evangelists and thousands of new converts scattered among villages more than several days' journey away. In 1837, when Elisha Abbott first ventured into areas of the Bassein region where no white person had traveled before, he was surprised to discover Karen converts awaiting baptism.[13] Ko Tha Byu seems to be responsible for converting most of the 1,270 Karens who had received baptism by the time he died in 1840. While male and female American missionaries, accompanied by Karen evangelists, occasionally conducted preaching tours through the Karen regions, they spent most of their time at mission stations far from Karen villages, building schools and translating biblical literature. To add to this separation, tensions between the British and the king of southern Burma cut off American missionary presence altogether in southern Burma between 1839 and 1852. Christianity continued to spread among the Karens of that region, though. When American missionaries returned to the area after the Second Anglo-Burmese War, they encountered about 5,000 new Karen Christians.[14] The cultural implications of this situation seem apparent. Even if they had wished to conform to all manners of Western culture or place themselves under the direct authority of a missionary, the first generation of Karen Christians would have found it extremely difficult simply because the vast majority of them had never even met an individual from the West.

Further scholarship should reveal more about how the Karen people as a whole negotiated cultural issues as Christianity spread, but a few patterns can be suggested at this point. Most of the Karen people resisted the Christian message because they did not convert. Those who did convert, though, probably maintained a popular spirituality that differed at several points from official missionary theology, similar to the situation among the Longuda Christians in Nigeria that Todd Vanden Berg describes elsewhere in this volume. A report from a missionary in 1852 indicates that Karen evangelists practiced divine healing and the exorcism of evil spirits. On divine healing, the missionary withheld judgment. However, he found it "almost impossible to show them the absurdity" of the existence of demons. The Karen evangelists perhaps felt themselves to be on solid theological ground, in that they justified their position by employing the impeccably Baptist method of referring to biblical authority.[15] Like many other non-Western Christians, though, the Karen would not be able to find a contingent of American missionaries willing to agree with them on these points until the emergence of the Holiness and Pentecostal movements.

Missionary Reactions

As they scurried to keep up with the Karen evangelists, American Baptist missionaries tried to make sense of the cultural forces unfolding before them. Nineteenth-century anthropology provided only a limited set of intellectual resources. Boasian anthropology had not entered the Western educational system, and the term *ethnocentrism* had not yet been coined as a word. In fact, the word *culture* had not yet been put to use in the English language.[16] Without an established theory of culture to aid their thinking, American Baptist missionaries usually drew upon the intellectual framework of "civilization," a concept that came to dominate nineteenth-century thinking on culture and race in Europe and the United States. *Civilization* carried a wide range of meanings and implications, but almost all concepts of civilization in nineteenth-century America placed "primitive" societies at the bottom end of a cultural ladder and "high" civilizations at the top.

Nineteenth-century American Baptists lived in a society suffused with these hierarchical conceptions of civilization. They lay behind government policies toward Native Americans and the efforts of the American Colonization Society to transport blacks to Africa. Many politicians used more virulent and explicitly racialized notions of civilization to justify Manifest Destiny, Indian removal, and the slave system. The most sophisticated anthropological theories described civilization as the educational, social, technological, and moral triumph of humans over savagery. Even those who worked for the rights and equality of non-whites, such as African American leaders, abolitionists, and Cherokee spokespeople, conceptualized their arguments in a framework of hierarchical civilization. And the most highly educated and influential evangelicals repeatedly proclaimed that the progress of America demonstrated that they lived in the most highly developed form of Christian civilization.[17]

Evangelical theology did not provide much in the way of cross-cultural thinking. Although they always cast their efforts in some sort of Christian framework, early-nineteenth-century missionaries had no theology of mission readily at hand. Many evangelical missionaries read *The Life of David Brainerd* by Jonathan Edwards, but the work functioned more as a devotional meditation on missionary self-sacrifice than a theology for engaging other cultures.[18] For the most practical advice on how to engage Asians, American Baptists turned to the examples set by the William Carey and English Baptists in India. From Carey they gleaned the idea that missionaries needed to train indigenous leaders or a "native ministry" to evangelize and lead local congregations.[19] Even with a paucity of converts, the first generation of American Baptist missionaries in Burma regularly expressed the hope that indigenous Christians would actively evangelize and teach their own people. In this way of thinking, the "native ministry" would also play a key role in promoting civilization among their people.[20]

As products of American culture then, the first generation of Baptist missionaries conceived of Asian people as residing somewhere along a hierarchy of civilization. Descriptions of Burmese and Karen cultures reflected missionary attempts to find the proper place for these people on this conceptual ladder. When Baptist missionaries wrote in an ethnographic mode, Burmese culture fared fairly well in comparison with other Asian cultures, because it displayed quite a few characteristics of the American conception of civilization. Along with the standard litany of characteristics that indicated Asian "heathenism," Baptist missionaries identified positive features of Burmese government, family relations, religious practices, social relations, education, and medicine. Burmese laws, other than those dealing with religious freedom, were "wise, and pregnant with sound morality; and their police is better regulated than in most countries," though the people lacked generosity and hospitality. The Burmese people fell victim to "superstitious" beliefs in evil spirits, ghosts, demon possessions, and charms, but they were "certainly not incapable of strong attachments, or of exercising the social virtues."[21]

This scheme of civilization, however, dictated that the Karen people resided near the bottom of the ladder, well below the Burmese. The earliest missionary ethnography of the Karen people, written by George Boardman in his diary the day that A-Pyah Thee's delegation arrived at his door, categorized the Karens as a primitive people. Boardman explained that the Burmese called the

Karens "wild men" because they "have no written language, no religion, avoid the cities" and "dwell in the wilderness" like Native Americans. Later, he described the Karens as "the simplest children of nature I have ever seen."[22]

The rapid, unmediated growth of Karen Christianity, however, challenged the American Baptist notions of civilization in several ways. Missionaries suddenly found it more difficult to square Karen Christianity with their own assumptions about the close relationship between Christianity and civilization. Many missionaries had assumed their efforts would prove most effective with groups higher on the ladder of civilization. But after several decades of intensive missionary work, very few of the highly "civilized" Burmese converted to Christianity.[23] George Boardman's initial reluctance to turn his attention from the Burmese to the Karen people, despite persistent inquiries by several Karen delegations, may be partly explained by a belief that Christianity faced brighter prospects among the refined Burmese than among the "wild" Karen.

Karen Christianity presented a far more perplexing task than explaining the fundamental differences between Karen and Burmese cultures, though. Baptist missionaries had to explain why Christianity prospered among the Karen Christians, who operated with minimal contact and supervision by missionaries, let alone Western civilization. The Karen skills in evangelism, hunger for literacy, and passion for education compelled missionaries to reassess the relationship between civilization and Christianity. This assessment was hardly uniform and systematic. However, Baptist missionary reactions to Karen Christianity in the 1830s, 1840s, and 1850s can be roughly divided into two impulses. The first approach, exemplified by the efforts of Elisha Abbott, contained features that came the closest to viewing missionary work among the Karen people as a translation movement.

Elisha Abbott's relationship to Karen evangelists, or the "native ministry," convinced him that the Karen people did not need all the accoutrements of Western civilization to maintain a vital Christian faith. In fact, the imperial conflict in Burma and evangelical zeal of Karen Christians actually compelled Abbott to grant authority to Karen leadership before Baptist missionaries had given much thought to the issue. From 1839 to 1852, when American missionaries could not enter south-central Burma, Karen preachers not only evangelized but also established Christian bodies in that region, acting as de facto ministers. As early as May 1840, Abbott observed that "nearly all these assistants are at the head of large Christian congregations, and are, in fact pastors, except in administering the ordinances."[24]

Here, then, lay a nearly intractable problem for Baptist missionary machinery. As unordained pastors, these Karen evangelists could not baptize those they converted. In their desire for baptism, hundreds of Karen converts journeyed to Abbott's base in British-controlled Arracan, a journey that often took 10 to 15 days. Even though he baptized more than 400 Karens who made the trip, Abbott admitted that he had to rely on the judgment of the Karen evangelists for the spiritual examination of the candidates. He also observed that no females made the trip. So in 1843 Abbott made a unilateral decision on a matter of evangelistic policy, a behavior not unknown among Baptist preachers. He asked a body of Karen evangelists to submit the names of several candidates for ordination, whom he then ordained. In the following two years, these two newly ordained pastors, Myat Kyaw and Tway Po, each baptized around 2,000 Karens, more than any American missionary in Burma would baptize in a lifetime.[25]

Once he had promoted two Karen men to the highest position of authority that Baptist polity recognized and unleashed them to regions unsupervised by missionaries, Abbott turned his attentions toward justifying his actions to his supporters in America. "If God has called these men to *preach* the gospel," Abbott reasoned, and they were already leading Christian congregations, "has He not also called them to administer its ordinances?" In Elisha Abbott's writings, the nomadic and barely literate Karen evangelists worked effectively with little supervision by American missionaries, a portrayal that obviously minimized the importance of Western civilization in maintaining the health and vitality of Karen Christianity.[26]

At the same time, though, other missionaries described their work among the Karen people as a custodial enterprise. This impulse fit more easily with civilizing ideas. This approach, which can be found in Francis Mason's writings, grew primarily from concerns over the lack of educational resources available to Karen Christians hungry for education. In an urgent plea for more missionaries, Mason sent a letter to American supporters in 1843 in which he implied that a crisis existed within Karen Christianity. Only two of the native assistants in Mason's region had as much as 12 months' schooling, and most had less than 6. To drive home his point, Mason explained how one of the most effective assistants under his direction, a man who had been baptized more than a decade earlier, had recently asked him, "Paul, Paul, who was Paul? Was he a Christian?"[27]

Mason presented conflicting portrayals of the Karen people as he tried to reconcile this movement with his notions of civilization. At times he praised the capabilities of individual Karen evangelists and, in fact, wrote a laudatory biography of Ko Tha Byu. But when he focused on educational issues, Mason tended to portray the Karen as people who needed supervision from those who had been reared in an advanced civilization. Explaining that early in his career he had been intent on ordaining assistants, Mason found that "further acquaintance with the native character has raised insuperable obstacles in my mind." Mason encouraged groups of Karen Christians to abandon their seminomadic lifestyle to join a settled Christian community, under missionary supervision. These communities, Mason hoped, would help the Karens hold to Christian piety, develop educational systems, forge democratic decision-making processes, abstain from alcohol, adopt patterns of cleanliness, and develop economically prosperous practices of trade and agriculture.[28]

Interpreting Karen Christianity in America

We might wonder what the typical Baptist supporter of missions was to make of the "native character" of the Karen people, as she periodically paused in her Connecticut sitting room to reflect upon Asia after reading the *American Baptist Magazine*. In April 1842, she would have read Francis Mason say that the term "full grown children" gave the Karen people too much credit. In July 1844, she would have read Elisha Abbott explain that the Karen evangelists were "competent to preach the gospel," qualified to "lead and instruct Christian congregations," and ought to administer the ordinances. In fact, she would have read a report in which the missionary board itself agonized aloud over this question of indigenous leadership. The "privileges of the church of Christ" should not be "unnecessarily withheld from any who are entitled to them," the board wrote in 1844. Yet it could not decide "how far it is *safe* to entrust to native teachers, in their present comparative ignorance, the powers of the Gospel ministry."[29]

American Baptists attempted to reconcile these conflicting portrayals of Karen Christianity within a framework of issues pertinent to *American* culture, not Asian culture. In fact, the dominant issues for missionary thinking would have been particular to Baptists in the northeastern United States in the 1840s, 1850s, and 1860s, who at this time formed the backbone of support for the American Baptist Missionary Union, (ABMU).[30] Even more specifically, the perception eventually formulated by our hypothetical Connecticut supporter most probably grew from the issues she saw most pertinent to her personal religious life.

Our missionary supporter could have drawn upon several different cultural forces to inform her thinking. On the one hand, the descriptions of the Karen evangelists given by Elisha Abbott resonated with the Baptist heritage of democratized Christianity. This heritage found virtue in the abilities of the common, unsophisticated segments of society. Refusing to view to the clergy as a separate order of people, many Baptist evangelists in the first decades of the nineteenth century accepted the spiritual experiences of ordinary people at face value, without subjecting them to the scrutiny and authority of learned theologians. Emphasizing literacy and the perspicuity of truth, these Baptists placed a great emphasis on getting the Bible into the hands of ordinary people so that they could plainly read the truths of Christianity for themselves.[31] New England Baptists also enjoyed a heritage of disestablishmentarianism. In the early days of the republic, these Baptists had pitted themselves against Congregationalists by strenuously fighting for the separation of church and state and championing the right of ordinary people to choose and financially support their own religious affiliation.[32]

This heritage of democratized Christianity and disestablishmentarianism gave Baptists an outsider status that could feed ambivalence about their own culture. Evangelical theology and spirituality explicitly declared that membership within a "Christian civilization" or even a Christian denomination did not guarantee Christian status.[33] Indeed, the earliest Baptist missionary societies did not specifically define "missionary" work as an effort to take the gospel to people of different cultures, though it might involve that.[34] Thus, the earliest generation of Baptist missionaries did not seamlessly identify Christianity with American society. This heritage made it possible for Baptists like Elisha Abbott to see how Karen evangelists could qualify as effective Christian pastors, even though they did not demonstrate all the characteristics of Western civilization.

By the 1840s, though, Baptists in the Northeast were busy redefining their relationship to American society. Many Baptists in this region of the country had climbed from the ranks of the "ordinary" into the upper reaches of the American establishment, enjoying higher levels of education, economic prosperity, and social respectability. Baptists counted an increasing number of wealthy businessmen, high-ranking politicians, and college-educated Americans among their ranks. More and more Baptist ministers and their congregations in the Northeast donned the accoutrements of American Victorian religious gentility: organs, gothic architecture, and refined manners.[35] At the same time, middle-class women of the Northeast, who outnumbered men in evangelical congregations, began to adopt new ideals of domesticity and female virtue as the basis for moral education. Through their influence, northern Baptist churches increasingly situated education as the cornerstone of Christian civilization.[36] Therefore, our Connecticut supporter may have been quite concerned by Francis Mason's anxieties over the lack of education among the Karen evangelists.

We cannot say for sure which direction our Connecticut supporter would have gone on these issues. Francis Wayland, an ordained Baptist minister, president of Brown University, author of the most widely used textbook on moral philosophy in the United States, and undoubtedly the most prominent intellectual among American Baptists, demonstrated that high education and status did not guarantee the rejection of democratized Christianity. After decades of service in numerous positions within the ABMU leadership, including years in the influential post of corresponding secretary, Wayland had become convinced that the principles of democratized Christianity explained the rapid growth of Christianity among the Karen people, and he actively campaigned to adjust missionary policy according to these principles.

The most explicit articulation of these ideas came in the form of a report that Wayland presented to the ABMU at the annual meeting of delegates in 1854. In the report, the president of Brown University argued that the educational policies of the missionaries hampered the growth of indigenous Christianity. "If we teach the natives to rely upon us," Wayland declared, "nothing like a permanent impression can ever be made upon their character." Missionaries should not "attempt to transform the Oriental into the European character by any process of instruction," he argued, but should "strive to improve and perfect the forms of character now existing, instead of making them into our own." Pointing out the limited knowledge held by Americans of "a nation so very dissimilar from ourselves," Wayland urged upon his fellow Baptists a careful effort in which missionaries carried out "our ideas as being ourselves learners."[37] Wayland's report also upheld the need to ground seminary education in the vernacular. "Nothing could be more disastrous than to confine knowledge to a few and teach men to despise their native language," Wayland wrote. "We must improve them by making the vernacular rich in valuable truth, not by making it the language merely of serfs and peasants." The same principles applied to tracts, which "should be written with adaptation to the wants of the people, simple, brief and pungent."[38]

More clearly than any other American Baptist of his era, Francis Wayland articulated a vision of Karen Christianity as a movement that had been translated into a non-Western culture. He identified the significance of indigenous leadership, the key role of the vernacular, the value of Karen cultural identity, and the importance of finding limits to missionary oversight. Wayland even encouraged humility by admonishing American supporters to consider themselves learners in the entire missionary process.

From our perspective today, though, an odd silence trailed in the wake of these points in Wayland's report. Few Baptists challenged or championed Wayland's idea that the Karen people should respect the vernacular. Nobody in the 1850s argued against Wayland's idea that Asian Christians should eschew "Western character," but neither did anybody develop his suggestion that missionaries should build on Asian culture. Through the rest of the century, Baptist missionary spokespeople praised the virtues of the "native ministry" without giving much attention to its cultural implications. In fact, despite his brief forays into questions of the vernacular, Wayland himself grounded issues of class, not culture, as the fulcrum upon which missionary policy rested.[39]

These specific issues provoked little reaction, positive or negative, because American Baptists tended to believe that the most important issues facing Karen Christians and missionaries in Burma were the same sort of issues that Baptists faced in their churches in northeastern America. It is here where we find a rebound effect of Andrew Walls's indigenizing principle. Walls argues that because theology "springs out of practical situations, it is therefore *occasional* and *local* in character."[40] So it goes for missionary thinking. The extent to which nineteenth-century missionaries and missionary spokespeople recognized the process of indigenization in non-Western lands depended largely on the dynamics indigenous to Western culture.

In the 1850s, many northern Baptists believed the future vitality of their congregations depended on how they resolved issues of education and class in their religious life. That context explains the drama behind a speech that Francis Wayland gave at Rochester, New York, in July 1853 to mark the founding of a new Baptist seminary and college. Although commemorative speeches on theological education are not the sort of thing one usually associates with high drama, let alone popular interest, this one attracted about a thousand listeners, spawned numerous newspaper articles, and generated two publications.[41]

Francis Wayland's speech placed democratized evangelism and primitive Christianity at the center of healthy church life. Arguing for the strength of lay evangelism and initiative, Wayland warned against developing a "ministerial caste set apart by specialized education." In what must have been a hard sell to the founders of a theological seminary, Wayland declared that seminary education ought to be viewed as just one of several possible ways to educate ministers.[42]

Wayland then compared the vitality of American Baptist churches to the growth of Karen Christianity. Wayland believed that the explosive growth of the Baptists in America and the spread of Christianity among the Karen people came from similar populist sources. He told the Rochester audience that success among the Karen people in Burma came from "rude" and unlettered men, "hardly elevated at all above their brethren," who worked with only a few books, some tracts and the New Testament translated into their language. Christianity had spread in Burma, Wayland proclaimed, not because highly educated pastors had instructed congregations in Christian truths but because common people told their neighbors about Christ and then established churches where ministerial gifts manifested themselves. Similarly, the prosperity of Baptist schools, Baptist churches in western New York, and even the society he addressed grew from the efforts of earlier generations of "plain men, generally of ordinary education."[43]

When Wayland concluded his three-hour speech, another Baptist minister and intellectual, Barnas Sears, jumped to his feet to request that *he* be allowed to speak. After gaining consent, Sears embarked on a half-hour speech in which he disputed a number of Wayland's points. Sears feared that Wayland's plan would derail the progress Baptists had made toward effective theological education. Arguing that history had demonstrated that Christianity had thrived when pastors served as Christian teachers, Sears warned that no denomination could maintain its position in society without educated ministers to open channels of thought. "Rhapsodical and ranting preaching may produce high excitement with an ignorant people," Sears declared, referring to Baptists in western states who seem to have been an embarrassment to him, "but it will not elevate them, nor fit them for well-directed activity and influence." In his competing portrayal of evangelicalism, Sears argued that Baptists and Methodists owed their prosperity to the increased intelligence and influence of their ministry.[44]

In a portrayal of Karen Christianity that owed more to Francis Mason than to Elisha Abbott, Sears argued that these same principles explained Christian growth in Burma. Thirty or 40 years ago, Sears argued, hardly a person could be found in Burma who believed in the existence of an eternal God. But now, he claimed, two-thirds to three-fourths of the people believed in one, thanks to missionaries who had elevated the people "not so much by oral preaching, as by books and schools."[45]

In the long run, Sears carried the day, even though Francis Wayland probably perceived Karen Christianity more accurately than anyone in America.[46] Wayland had forged his understanding with tools that would be used less and less by Baptists of northeastern America. As northern Baptists joined the ranks of the mediating elites in America, issues of democratization and disestablishmentarianism dropped from sight. Like Barnas Sears, many middle-class American Baptists tied the health of their churches to higher education. Furthermore, shifts in gender roles enabled many women to find opportunities to minister through education, both in America and as missionaries. Female Baptist missionaries, who outnumbered males in the late nineteenth century, often perceived education as the force that built up Asian Christianity.[47]

As a result, American Baptist missionaries in the 1860s and 1870s embarked on extensive efforts to develop highly educated leaders among the Karen. They built seminaries, established normal schools, and founded a liberal arts college, Rangoon Baptist College. The thrust of this educational program, however, placed missionaries into custodial roles that conflicted with the ideals of Karen independence that had been established during Wayland's era. An 1866 convention of missionaries and Asian Christian leaders declared that though they worked for independence from "the guidance of foreign missionaries," it could not be achieved until the Asian leaders received "an education which shall approach in breadth and thoroughness that of their present foreign teachers."[48] That process would take some time. In 1873, ABMU leaders figured that effective education would enable missionaries to withdraw after another 20 years.[49] Two decades later, though, the missionaries remained, as they did well into the twentieth century.

American Baptist relations with Karen Christians, however, do not necessarily fit into a tidy colonial narrative of indigenous peoples clamoring for missionaries to go home. Although further research is needed to uncover all the dynamics involved, periodic requests by Karen Christian leaders for missionary teachers certainly encouraged an ongoing missionary presence. Education, of course, had been important to Karen Christians from the time of the first conversions. Missionaries remained their sole source of educational resources, a source that these financially strapped people did not want to lose. If, as the evidence hints, the dynamics between Karen Christians and Baptist missionaries were similar to those between Zimbabwean Christians and Baptist missionaries that Isaac Mwase describes elsewhere in this volume, then

Karen Christians may have had good reason to desire some sort of missionary presence, especially in areas where their resources were limited. A resolution by a committee of Karen pastors in 1854 declared their commitment to build financial independence of congregations from the missionaries, "but for books and schools we greatly need help, and we request that our dear brethren in America will continue to aid us in these things."[50]

Whatever the exact nature of the relationship between Karens and missionaries, Baptists in America interpreted Karen requests for education as evidence that Asians needed highly civilized custodians. Of course, a denomination that claimed an egalitarian heritage and defined itself in opposition to episcopal ecclesiastical systems needed to employ a few verbal gymnastics to justify the custodial role assumed by missionaries. While conceding that each Baptist missionary supervised 12 to 60 churches each, C. H. Carpenter reassured supporters in 1873 that the missionaries "have never received or assumed any official authority as bishops over the native pastors and churches." Carpenter explained that even though "the differences growing out of birth and education cannot be removed or overborne for generations to come, probably," missionaries worked hard to free Asian pastors from missionary dependency. "The missionary will long stand first among his native brethren," Carpenter's rather tortured reasoning ran, "but if a Baptist, he will be first among equals."[51]

This de facto, if not de jure, custodial role that Baptist missionaries assumed gives some indication as to how far American Baptists had gone toward reasserting mediating elites into their missionary vision. In the process, Baptists also reinterpreted the history of the growth of Karen Christianity, losing sight of the reality that Karen evangelists played the primary role in spreading Christianity among the Karen. L. P. Brockett's 1891 history of the Karen mission, marching in step with most late-nineteenth-century missionary literature, portrayed four male missionaries as the primary agents of conversion. Upholding the Karen mission "as an object lesson in missionary policy," the introduction lauded these American men for two major accomplishments: establishing a variety of educational institutions and "signally and courageously" insisting that the Karen pastors develop patterns of responsibility, independence, and self-government.[52]

By casting missionaries as the star actors and non-Western Christians in supporting roles, late-nineteenth-century missionary narratives also found a way to remold perceptions of non-Western Christianity into the dominant framework of civilization. Brockett's title gave the standard formula: *The Story of the Karen Mission in Bassein, 1838–1890: or, the Progress and Education of a People from a Degraded Heathenism to a Refined Christian Civilization*. This civilizing mission narrative not only lost sight of the agency of non-Western Christians but also tied Christianity to the progress of Western civilization.

These civilizing narratives cast a long shadow. Most obviously, they shaped the perceptions of succeeding generations of new missionaries, who often ar-

rived in non-Western lands with paternalistic notions of their expected relationships with non-Western peoples. For supporters in the United States, they
often reinforced the tidy notion that Christianity and Western civilization must
march side by side. They also obscured the reality that, on the ground, indigenous Christians were busy translating Christianity into a variety of forms that
did not fit the civilizing narrative. Many historians today, taking their cues from
civilizing narratives rather than from non-Western Christians, have yet to examine their own assumptions that conflate Christianity with Western culture.[53]

On the other hand, civilizing narratives by missionaries contained dynamics that swam against the current of American conceptions of race and civilization in the 1890s. By that decade, most concepts of civilization portrayed the
differences between Anglo-Saxons and non-whites either as an evolutionary
gulf that would take centuries to bridge or in even more pernicious racial terms
that posited inherited differences of superiority and inferiority. In American
universities, strands of social Darwinism and an ascendant scientific racism
imbued disciplines of anthropology, psychology, and biology with notions that
non-whites possessed inferior intelligence and fewer capabilities than whites.
Popular literature, travel writings, and public exhibitions like the 1894 Columbian Exposition painted distant "barbarian" peoples in oppositional relationships to those who had constructed "high civilization." In politics, new Jim
Crow legislation and a rising tide of lynchings enforced white supremacy in
the South, while most northern white reformers had long abandoned efforts
at establishing black equality. The first major law of immigration restriction
had used the argument of the racial incompatibility of the Chinese as the basis
to exclude them from America.[54]

Karen Christianity, however, kept racialized thinking by Baptist missionaries on a short leash.[55] By compelling American Baptists to ground their evangelistic hopes on the "native ministry," Karen Christianity not only helped
preserve missionary notions in the capabilities of non-Westerners but also
placed missionaries in roles designed to promote Asian agency and achievement, despite the paternalism of their rhetoric. In their efforts to build on the
evangelistic success of the Karen preachers, American Baptist missionaries
continued to ordain non-Western pastors, a number that had reached 280 by
1899. The ABMU also operated two liberal arts colleges in Asia, 7 seminaries,
38 high schools, and 1,330 primary schools, staffed primarily by national teachers.[56]

Asian Christianity also provided northern white Baptists with a model to
help establish colleges and seminaries for African Americans. As the Civil War
came to a close, the American Baptist Home Missionary Society (ABHMS),
which was deeply tied to and influenced by the foreign missionary movement,
turned its attention to the newly freed Blacks of the South. Comparing African
American skills in evangelism with those of the Karen evangelists, leaders of
the ABHMS decided to help train African American leaders by establishing

institutions of higher education.[57] Thus, a missionary in Burma found it perfectly sensible to uphold the success of Ko Thah Byu as proof that the theological training of barely literate people would produce the same results among
freed people of the American South.[58] Long after Reconstruction ended, White
northern Baptists continued to develop African American colleges and seminaries in the South, just as they supported educational efforts by missionaries
in Asia. Unlike northern philanthropists, who by the 1890s funded industrial
education in order to keep African Americans in the role of efficient working-
class laborers, leaders of the ABHMS sought to train African Americans as
ministers, businessmen, lawyers, doctors, scientists, and politicians. It was
Henry Morehouse, the head of the ABHMS and a long-term official of the
Baptist foreign missionary board, who coined the term "Talented Tenth," which
W. E. B. DuBois appropriated for his civil rights efforts.[59]

Home missionaries and foreign missionaries mirrored each other in additional ways. Just as foreign missionaries saw themselves civilizing Asians,
Morehouse and his fellow home missionaries saw themselves "uplifting" the
black race. Even with its declarations of social equality and achievement, the
missionary model of civilization implicitly upheld Anglo culture, with its flaws,
as a pure model toward which non-whites should aspire. Highly civilized
whites, who saw themselves as custodians of this process, often failed to see
how they were shaped by the sins, as well as the blessings, of Anglo culture.
The twentieth century, of course, exposed the flaws of the civilizing model, at
home and abroad.

Even in the nineteenth century, though, many missionaries pointed out
the inadequacies of a system that did not attempt to translate Christianity into
other cultures. William Ashmore, a Baptist missionary who first arrived in
China in 1850, wrote a two-part article in 1887 on "Discarded Missionary Methods," in which he devoted the entire second section to the mistake of "En-
deavoring to Westernize Asiatics." Missionaries were beginning to recognize
that they cannot combine "Christianity and Western civilization" but must
"plant Christianity alone" and "then leave it to develop its own civilization, as
it naturally must and surely will." The editor of the *Baptist Missionary Magazine*
in 1895 cited the Karen Mission in Burma as evidence for his argument that
missionaries should give the blessings of Christianity without introducing "any
element which shall be detrimental to all that is best in their national life, and
without imposing on them obligations which shall weaken their character as
a nation."[60]

Missionaries in other denominations recognized similar dynamics of the
translation process. In 1886, the denominational newspaper of southern Methodists published an article by a missionary in Brazil who upheld the superior
evangelistic abilities of "the native ministry." He asked, "Do we not needlessly
envelop the gospel in the swaddling-bands of our Western civilization?"[61] William Taylor, a popular missionary in the northern Methodist church, believed

Christianity ought to draw resources from African religions, which he said acknowledged the eternality of the soul, Old Testament law, and circumcision. Taylor told his supporters that Africans knew of the same God as Western Christians but used their own African terms to refer to him.[62] The editor of the flagship newspaper for black Methodists, the *Christian Recorder*, argued in 1895 that "one of the reasons why the missionary effort has not had greater success is that Christianity often goes . . . representing a certain civilization, and the heathen is taught he must be transformed into the habits, manners and customs of the missionary.[63]

Of course, counterexamples of missionaries promoting Western civilization could also be given. The point is not that nineteenth-century missionaries understood the complexity of these cultural questions but that the missionary experience, especially the development of non-Western Christianity, challenged the nineteenth-century American tendency to conflate Christianity with Western civilization. Whenever evangelical missionaries tried to conflate Christianity with Westernization, they stumbled into the realities of indigenous leadership and translated Christianity. At the same time, though, we must recognize that the specific terms of those conflicts varied according to the issues believed most pertinent to a given place and time. American supporters of the missionary enterprise believed that their faith tied them to people all over the globe, but they viewed non-Western Christianity through the lens of the culture of their own time and place. The history of the missionary movement shows us, then, that even missiology and theologies of mission are expressions of contextualized Christianity.

NOTES

1. "Mr. Boardman's Journal," *American Baptist Magazine,* July 1829, 242–44. For variations on this account, see Edward Judson, *The Life of Adonirum Judson* (Philadelphia: American Baptist Publication Society, 1883), 377–81; Roger G. Torbet, *Venture of Faith: The Story of the American Baptist Foreign Mission Society and the Woman's American Baptist Foreign Mission Society, 1814–1954* (Philadelphia: Judson Press, 1955), 42–46.

2. "Mr. Boardman's Journal," *American Baptist Magazine,* May 1829, 170–11; July 1829, 242–44; Aug. 1829, 278, 281; Sept. 1829, 317; Nov. 1829, 386–88.

3. In addition to the 5,000 members in 1852, it was estimated that another 6,000 awaited baptism and that an additional 5,000 Christian Karens had died from disease, famine, and violence during the Second Anglo-Burmese War. L. P. Brockett, *The Story of the Karen Mission in Bassein, 1838–1890* (Philadelphia: American Baptist Publication Society, 1891), 149–50.

4. Andrew F. Walls, *The Missionary Movement in Christian History: Studies in the Transmission of Faith* (Maryknoll, N.Y.: Orbis Books, 1996); Lamin Sanneh, *Translating the Message: The Missionary Impact on Culture* (Maryknoll, N.Y.: Orbis Books, 1989).

5. The impact of Karen Christianity on American Baptist thinking in the nine-teenth century has yet to be fully explored, but it certainly loomed large. One can scarcely find an issue of the *Baptist Missionary Magazine* after 1835 where some as-pect of Christianity among the Karen is not discussed. American Baptists published more than a dozen books in the nineteenth century addressing Karen Christianity, either as histories of the mission or biographies of missionaries who worked with the Karen. This consciousness of Karen Christianity spread from the Baptists to other evangelical organizations. As late as 1900, when John Mott wanted to give proof to the delegates of the Ecumenical Missionary Conference in New York that the world could be evangelized in one generation, he upheld the Karen as one of several "recent missionary achievements of the Church." American Tract Society, *Report of the Ecu-menical Conference on Foreign Missions* (New York: American Tract Society, 1900), 1: 97. See also the bibliography in Torbet, *Venture of Faith*, 599–612.

6. Martin Smith, *Burma: Insurgency and the Politics of Ethnicity* (Dhaka, Bangla-desh: University Press, 1999), 44; John Frank Cady, *A History of Modern Burma* (Ith-aca, N.Y.: Cornell University Press, 1958), 73–80.

7. U Zan and Erville E. Sowards, "Baptist Work among the Karens," in *Burma Baptist Chronicle, Book II, The Burma Baptist Chronicle by Language Groups*, ed. Gene-vieve Sharp Sowards and Erville E. Sowards (Rangoon, Burma: University Press, 1963), 305.

8. Lamin Sanneh has described a similar process in Africa in *Translating the Message*. See esp. 157–90.

9. Saw Doh Say, "A Brief History and Development Factors of the Karen Baptist Church of Burma (Myanmar)" (master's thesis, Fuller Theological Seminary, 1990), 41–44.

10. Francis Mason, *The Karen Apostle, or Memoir of Ko Tha Byu, the First Karen Convert, with Notices concerning His Nation* (Bassein, Burma: Sgau Karen Press, 1884), 127–55; "Karen Traditions," *Baptist Missionary Magazine*, May 1999, 120–21.

11. Smith, *Burma*, 44; Zan and Soward, "Baptist Work," 312–13; Maung Shwe Wa, *Burma Baptist Chronicle, Book I, Introducing the Tree of Life on the Banks of the Irra-waddy* (Rangoon, Burma: University Press, 1963), 126; Torbet, *Venture of Faith*, 238.

12. "Mr. Boardman's Journal," *American Baptist Magazine*, July 1829, 242–44; Aug. 1829, 278.

13. Torbet, *Venture of Faith*, 68–69.

14. Saw Doh Say, "Brief History," 84; Dana Robert, "Evangelist or Homemaker? Mission Strategies of Early Nineteenth-Century Missionary Wives in Burma and Ha-waii," *International Bulletin of Missionary Research* 17, no. 1 (1993): 4–10; Torbet, *Ven-ture of Faith*, 47–49, 61–69; Shwe Wa, *Burma Baptist Chronicle*, 174; Brockett, *Story of the Karen Mission*, 149–50.

15. "Letter from Henry Van Meter," *Missionary Magazine*, Aug. 1852, 327–30. Karen beliefs in spirits and revelations by through dreams seem to have persisted through the nineteenth century. See, for example, the comments by a "Miss Batson" in *Helping Hand*, Aug. 1879, 59.

16. Adam Kuper, *Culture: The Anthropologists' Account* (Cambridge: Harvard Uni-versity Press, 1999), 29–36.

17. Francis Paul Prucha, *American Indian Treaties: The History of a Political*

Anomaly (Berkeley: University of California Press, 1994), 9–14, 118–19; Robert F. Berkhofer Jr., *The White Man's Indian: Images of the American Indian from Columbus to the Present* (New York: Alfred A. Knopf, 1978); George M. Frederickson, *The Black Image in the White Mind: The Debate on Afro-American Character and Destiny, 1817–1914* (New York: Harper & Row, 1971), 5–19; Ronald Takaki, *Iron Cages: Race and Culture in 19th-Century America* (New York: Oxford University Press, 1990); Reginald Horseman, *Race and Manifest Destiny: The Origins of American Racial Anglo-Saxonism* (Cambridge: Harvard University Press, 1981); George W. Stocking Jr., *Victorian Anthropology* (New York: Free Press, 1987); Wilson Jeremiah Moses, *The Golden Age of Black Nationalism, 1850–1925* (Hamden, Conn.: Archon Books, 1978); Robert T. Handy, *A Christian America: Protestant Hopes and Historical Realities* (London: Oxford University Press, 1971).

18. David Brainerd had been an eighteenth-century missionary to the American Indians. When George Boardman set off on his first tour of Karen villages, he carried a Bible and Brainerd's memoirs. He regularly turned to Brainerd's memoirs for inspiration. Alonzo King, *Memoir of George Dana Boardman, Late Missionary to Burmah* (Boston: Gould, Kendall & Lincoln, 1839), 210, 213, 268; Joseph Conforti, "Jonathan Edwards' Most Popular Work: 'The Life of David Brainerd' and Nineteenth-Century Evangelical Culture," *Church History* 54 (1985): 188–201; William Hutchison, *Errand to the World: American Protestant Thought and Foreign Mission* (Chicago: Chicago University Press, 1987), 63–64.

19. Brian Stanley, *The History of the Baptist Missionary Society, 1792–1992* (Edinburgh: T. & T. Clark, 1992), 47–52.

20. Roger G. Torbet, *A History of the Baptists*, 3rd ed. (Valley Forge, Pa.: Judson Press, 1963), 247–49; "Necessity of Christianity to India," *American Baptist Magazine and Missionary Intelligencer*, Jan. 1821, 36; "Report," *American Baptist Magazine*, June 1828, 167. See also "Extract of a Letter from Mrs. Judson, to Mrs. Kendall, of Boston, Rangoon, Mar. 5, 1821," *American Baptist Magazine and Missionary Intelligencer*, Jan. 1822, 254; "Letter from Mrs. Judson, to Dr. Baldwin, Dated Calcutta, Dec. 8, 1821," *American Baptist Magazine and Missionary Intelligencer*, May 1822, 346; "Letter on the Burman Mission, Addressed to the Corresponding Secretary by a Professor in One of the New England Colleges, Jan. 23, 1827," *The American Baptist Magazine*, Mar. 1827, 77; "Rev. Mr. Wade's Journal, Addressed to the Corresponding Secretary," *American Baptist Magazine*, Jan. 1828, 14.

21. "Sketches of India," *American Baptist Magazine*, Feb. 1826, 53–54; "Remarks on the Manners and Character of the Burmese," *American Baptist Magazine*, Apr. 1826, 109–11; May 1826, 143–47.

22. "Mr. Boardman's Journal," *American Baptist Magazine*, July 1829, 242–43; King, *Memoir of Boardman*, 165.

23. See, for example, "Report of the Committee on Asiatic Missions," *Baptist Missionary Magazine*, July 1845, 154.

24. C. H. Carpenter, *Self-Support, Illustrated in the History of the Bassein Karen Mission from 1840–1880* (Boston: Rand, Avery, 1883), 44.

25. "Journal of Mr. Abbott," *American Baptist Magazine*, Apr. 1842, 87–90; Carpenter, *Self-Support*, 75; Saw Doh Say, "Brief History," 84–85.

26. "Report of the Committee on Asiatic Missions," *American Baptist Magazine*, July 1844, 203.

27. "Report of the Committee on Asiatic Missions," *American Baptist Magazine*, June 1843, 154–55.

28. Mason, *The Karen Apostle*; "Letter from Francis Mason," *American Baptist Magazine*, Apr. 1842, 84–85. Torbet, *Venture of Faith*, 64–65.

29. "Report of the Committee on Asiatic Missions," *American Baptist Magazine*, July 1844, 203; Carpenter, *Self-Support*, 73.

30. After the Baptists split into northern and southern regions in 1845, the missionary agency for northern Baptists, the American Baptist Missionary Union, conducted the Baptist missionary work in Burma. Although the Baptist missionary organization divided into northern and southern systems in 1845, all but four of the 69 missionaries appointed to Burma from 1814 to 1846 had been born in New England or the Mid-Atlantic states. Of those who were not, two had been born in Great Britain and immigrated to America (Francis Mason and Thomas Simons), one was a British woman born in India who married a American Baptist (Barbara McBain Kincaid), and one was born in Georgia. "Missionaries and Assistant Missionaries of the General Convention," *American Baptist Magazine*, July 1846, 236–37.

31. Henry May, *The Enlightenment in America* (New York: Oxford University Press, 1976). Also, see articles by George Marsden, "Everyone One's Own Interpreter? The Bible, Science, and Authority in Mid-Nineteenth-Century America," and Nathan O. Hatch, "Sola Scriptura and Novus Ordo Seclorum," in *The Bible in America: Essays in Cultural History*, eds. Nathan O. Hatch and Mark A. Noll (New York: Oxford University Press, 1982), 80–95, 60–78.

32. Nathan Hatch, *The Democratization of American Christianity* (New Haven: Yale University Press, 1989); Rhys Isaac, *The Transformation of Virginia, 1740–1790* (Chapel Hill: University of North Carolina Press, 1982); William G. McLoughlin, *Isaac Backus and the American Pietistic Tradition* (Boston: Little, Brown, 1967).

33. As Andrew Walls has stated, "Historic evangelicalism is a religion of protest against a Christian society that is not Christian enough." Andrew Walls, "The Evangelical Revival, The Missionary Movement, and Africa," in *Evangelicalism: Comparative Studies of Popular Protestantism in North America, the British Isles, and Beyond, 1700–1900*, eds. Mark A. Noll, David W. Bebbington, and George A. Rawlyk (New York: Oxford University Press, 1994), 311.

34. Baptists had formed the Philadelphia Association in 1771 to organize evangelistic forays into the South, the Shaftesbury Association in 1780 to carry on domestic missionary work in Vermont, and the Massachusetts Domestic Missionary Society in 1802 to evangelize both Whites and Native Americans in the western regions of America. Torbet, *History of the Baptists*, 245–46.

35. Richard Bushman, *The Refinement of America: Persons, Houses, Cities* (New York: Alfred A. Knopf, 1992), 313–53.

36. Susan Hill Lindley, *"You Have Stept Out of Your Place": A History of Women and Religion in America* (Louisville, K.Y.: John Knox Press, 1996), 90–106; Colleen McDannell, *The Christian Home in Victorian America, 1840–1900* (Bloomington: Indiana University Press, 1986); Dana Robert, *American Women in Mission: A Social History of Their Thought and Practice* (Macon, GA.: Mercer University Press, 1996), 81–124; Kathryn Kish Sklar, *Catherine Beecher: A Study in American Domesticity* (New Haven: Yale University Press, 1973).

37. "Report," *Baptist Missionary Magazine*, July 1854. Wayland's full report is found on pages 218–26.

38. "Report," *Baptist Missionary Magazine*, July 1854, 218–26.

39. This populist thinking mirrored Wayland's attempts to implement anti-elitist curriculum reforms at Brown University. Theodore R. Crane, *Francis Wayland: Political Economist as Educator* (Providence, R.I.: Brown University Press, 1962).

40. Italics in original. Walls, *Missionary Movement in Christian History*, 10.

41. Kenneth R. M. Short, "Baptist Training for the Ministry: The Francis Wayland–Barnas Sears Debate of 1853," *Foundations* 11 (1968): 227–34; Glenn T. Miller, *Piety and Intellect: The Aims and Purposes of Ante-Bellum Theological Education* (Atlanta: Scholars Press, 1990), 327–30.

42. Francis Wayland, *The Apostolic Ministry: A Discourse Delivered in Rochester, N.Y, before the New York Baptist Union for Ministerial Education, July 12, 1853* (Rochester: Sage & Brother, 1853).

43. Wayland, *Apostolic Ministry*, 18–19, 51.

44. Barnas Sears, *An Educated Ministry: An Address Delivered Before the N.Y. Baptist Union for Ministerial Education, at Its Anniversary, Held in Rochester, July 12, 1853* (New York: Lewis Colby, 1853), 11.

45. Sears, *An Educated Ministry*, 9, 12.

46. Sears not only managed, ultimately, to prevail in missionary policy but also assumed the presidency of Brown when Wayland retired and reversed Wayland's academic reforms. Crane, *Francis Wayland*.

47. See, for example, *The Helping Hand*, Feb. 1878, 10; June 1878, 42; Dec. 1878, 98. Patricia R. Hill, *The World Their Household: The American Woman's Foreign Mission Movement and Cultural Transformation, 1870–1920* (Ann Arbor: University of Michigan Press, 1985); Robert, *American Women in Mission*.

48. "Resolution on Education," *Baptist Missionary Magazine*, July 1866, 225.

49. "General View of the Work," *Baptist Missionary Magazine*, July 1873, 223–24.

50. Quoted from Saw Doh Say, A "Brief History," 92.

51. "Chief among Equals," *Baptist Missionary Magazine*, Apr. 1873, 97.

52. Brockett did write that "many of the native pastors also have done their part" and "devout women . . . have helped forward the good work," but the overall thrust of his work credits the male missionaries with bringing about the growth of Karen Christianity. Brockett, *Story of the Karen Mission*, 131.

53. A wide range of historians asking quite different questions about missionaries have made these assumptions. For representative examples, see Patricia Grimshaw, "'Christian Woman, Pious Wife, Faithful Mother, Devoted Missionary': Conflicts in Roles of American Missionary Women in Nineteenth Century Hawaii," *Feminist Studies* 9 (1983): 489–521; Edward H. Berman, *African Reactions to Missionary Education* (New York: Teachers College Press, 1975), 6; George Tinker, *Missionary Conquest: The Gospel and Native American Cultural Genocide* (Minneapolis: Fortress Press, 1993); Sylvia Jacobs, "The Historical Role of Afro-Americans in American Missionary Efforts in Africa," in *Black Americans and the Missionary Movement in Africa*, ed. Sylvia Jacobs (Westport, Conn.: Greenwood Press, 1982), 6.

54. Matthew Fry Jacobson, *Barbarian Virtues: The United States Encounters Foreign Peoples at Home and Abroad, 1876–1917* (New York: Hill and Wang, 2000); Stock-

ing, *Victorian Anthropology*; Gail Bederman, *Manliness and Civilization: A Cultural History of Gender and Race in the United States, 1880–1917* (Chicago: University of Chicago Press, 1995); Robert C. Morris, *Reading, 'Riting, and Reconstruction: The Education of the Freedmen in the South, 1861–1870* (Chicago: University of Chicago Press, 1981); Eric Foner, *Reconstruction: America's Unfinished Revolution, 1863–1877* (New York: Harper & Row, Publishers 1988).

55. World Christianity, as interpreted by American missionaries, seems to have produced a different strain of thinking for those with ties to religious denominations. In his history of the discipline of anthropology, George Stocking notes that as the nineteenth century wore on, the growing belief in the incapabilities of "savages" was especially pronounced among scientists who had lost their religious faith. Stocking, *Victorian Anthropology*, 92.

56. "Table of Statistics," *Baptist Missionary Magazine*, July 1899, 401–2; Torbet, *Venture of Faith*, 167.

57. See, for example, *The Macedonian and Record*, July 1868, 25; July 1868, 27; Feb. 1872, 7; *Home Mission Monthly*, Jan. 1879, 100; June 1879, 190; Aug. 1880, 149; Aug. 1881, 170; Dec. 1881, 254; *Home Evangelist*, July 1863, 26; Mar. 1866, 9.

58. "Letter from J. L. Douglass," *Missionary Magazine*, Feb. 1867, 39–40.

59. See Jay Riley Case, "From the Native Ministry to the Talented Tenth: The Foreign Missionary Origins of White Support for Black Colleges," in *The Foreign Missionary Enterprise at Home: Explorations in North American Cultural History*, ed. Daniel H. Bays and Grant Wacker (Tuscaloosa: University of Alabama Press, 2003), 60–74. For the "Talented Tenth" speech by Henry Morehouse, see *The Home Mission Monthly*, Aug. 1896, 277.

60. "Discarded Missionary Methods," *Baptist Missionary Magazine*, Dec. 1887, 453–56; "Discarded Missionary Methods–II," *Baptist Missionary Magazine*, Jan. 1888, 11–15; "Civilization or Christianity?" *Baptist Missionary Magazine*, Nov. 1895, 554–55.

61. "Letter from J. Ransom," *Christian Advocate* (Nashville), 23 Jan. 1886, 14.

62. William Taylor, *Christian Adventures in South Africa* (New York: Phillips & Hunt, 1880), 390–423; William Taylor, *Story of My Life: An Account of What I Have Thought and Said and Done in My Ministry of More Than Fifty-Three Years in Christian Lands and among the Heathen*, ed. John Clark Ridpath (New York: Eaton & Mains, 1895), 455–70.

63. "Civilization," *Christian Recorder*, 17 Oct. 1895, 2.

8

Missionary Thinking about Religious Plurality at Tambaram 1938: Hendrik Kraemer and His Critics

Richard J. Plantinga

In a letter dated 17 July 1845, Ralph Waldo Emerson related a novelty in his community. In his words: "The only other event is the arrival in Concord of the 'Bhagavat-Geeta,' the much renowned book of Buddhism."[1] Given the time in which it was written, Emerson's glaring error is understandable and forgivable. But his blunder is also instructive. It seems highly unlikely that a well-educated and well-read person living in 1945 or 1995 would make such a gaffe, for Westerners have become increasingly knowledgeable about the world's great religious traditions during the course of the last century—a reality evidenced by an ever-growing educational industry that seeks to raise awareness about humanity's long and many-sided religious quest.[2] In turn, recognition of religious plurality in the last century has led many devout Christian believers into both theological turmoil (at least some non-Christian religions do not seem to exist in utter darkness) and existential *angst* (many non-Christian persons are indeed wonderfully warm and moral). Accordingly, academic theological scholarship in the West, particularly in the second half of the twentieth century,[3] has taken as one of its agenda items the project of thinking Christianity's relationship to the religions of the world.

Before academic theological scholarship had suited up for the new challenge, however, missionary theological scholarship had been centrally engaged in thinking about Christianity's encounter with religious plurality. This chapter seeks to mine some of the wisdom offered by Protestant missionary scholarship on the subject of Christianity's theological relationship to the religious traditions of the world. More specifically, it seeks to investigate the thinking offered in connection with the third international missionary conference of the International Missionary Council, Tambaram 1938, held at Madras Christian College in India (figure 8.1).

The dominant voice in the discussion at Tambaram in 1938 was that of the Dutch scholar and missionary Hendrik Kraemer (1888–1965), whose approach "dominated nearly a generation of Protestant missionary thinking."[4] Kraemer's influence came at a critical juncture in the history of Christianity,

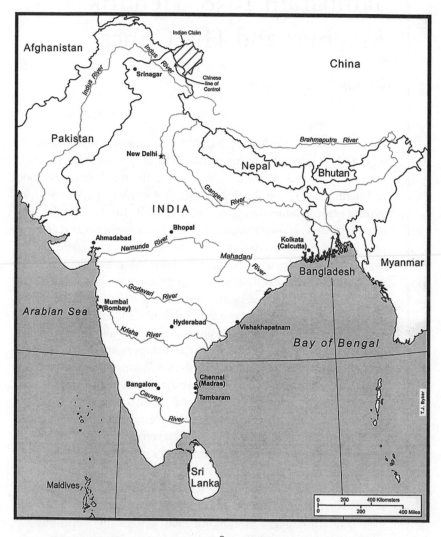

FIGURE 8.1. India

that is, at the very time when world Christianity was in the early stages of formation.[5] The position that he argued in his *The Christian Message in a Non-Christian World*[6] met with mixed reviews, more critical than not, both at the conference and in postconference developments. This chapter seeks to contextualize and delineate Kraemer's position, weigh the responses to it both at Tambaram and in the published post-Tambaram discussions, and estimate reactions to the conference and to Kraemer's position offered by scholarship in the second half of the century, with particular attention to publications produced in 1988 in connection with the fiftieth anniversary of Tambaram 1938. In his theological estimation of the status of non-Christian religious traditions, Kraemer defended a position consistent in important respects with the dictates of Christian scripture and tradition but attended by an excessively narrow and insufficiently clarified conception of revelation derived from his Dutch Reformed milieu and bolstered by Swiss dialectical theology, a conception, moreover, that prevented him from articulating a nuanced and more desirable position with respect to central theological issues in thinking about religious plurality.

International Missionary Developments Prior to Tambaram 1938

The rich and varied developments in international Protestant missionary discussions in the first decades of the twentieth century cannot be given justice in the space of a few paragraphs. However, a few words about the line from Edinburgh 1910, the first international missionary conference, through Jerusalem 1928, the second, to Tambaram 1938, the third, are essential for understanding Kraemer's theological view of non-Christian religions.

 The international missionary conference held in Edinburgh during June 1910 was a milestone in the development of both Protestant missions and ecumenicity.[7] Reflecting "the high tide of Western European optimism and imperialism"[8] at the end of the nineteenth century, Edinburgh 1910 sought to inaugurate the process that would end in the Christianization of the globe. This lofty goal, which would require a deliberate and ecumenical strategy, as well as the inspiration and conscription of the next generation of enthusiastic missionaries—among whom was the young Hendrik Kraemer[9]—was expressed through a watchword borrowed from the Student Volunteer Movement: "The evangelization of the world in this generation."[10] The fervent wish at the heart of this watchword was expressed every day at the conference, when a half hour of prayer was observed at noon for the cause of world mission, which, it was believed, had reached a "decisive hour."[11] With its emphasis on imminent Christianization, the focus of Edinburgh's conversion strategy fell on the non-Christian world, the religions of which it tended to understand

along empathetic and inclusivistic lines typical of liberal Protestantism. Edinburgh 1910 assumed that the non-Western, non-Christian world was ready to
be toppled and that the Western, Christian world was up to the task of bringing
about its downfall. Not surprisingly, the conference was dominated by Western
Christians. Of the 1,200 participants, only 17 were non-Western; its chair was
an American (John Mott) and its secretary a Brit (J. H. Oldham). Among Edinburgh 1910's many accomplishments was the creation of a "continuation
committee." One of the committee's fruits was the foundation in 1921 of the
International Missionary Council; another, it could be argued, was the formation of the World Council of Churches in 1948.

After the assumptions and heady optimism expressed at Edinburgh 1910
were dashed by the harsh realities of World War I and its existential and political aftermath, Protestant missions began the work of rethinking its global
strategy. Some of this rethinking came to expression at the second international
missionary conference, held at the Mount of Olives in Jerusalem during Easter
of 1928.[12] In a real sense, Jerusalem took place in a different century than did
Edinburgh; that is, Edinburgh was very much nineteenth century in its outlook
and Jerusalem decidedly twentieth century in its approach. Accordingly, a
rather different ethos pervaded Jerusalem 1928 than the one that dominated
Edinburgh 1910: "subdued tones" replaced assured ones, and the "earlier confident belief that 'non-Christian' religions would soon die out had now turned
into fear"; some delegates at Jerusalem held to "the view that religions were
doomed to disappear with the rise of a scientific, secular way of thinking"[13]—
and that, accordingly, secularism in its many ideational and political guises
ought to be specified as the common enemy of all religions and the consequent
focus of missions. Other delegates, however, under the influence of Karl
Barth's theological revolt in Europe, opposed this line of thinking and focus.
Particularly important at Jerusalem was its deliberation on the theme of the
Christian life and message in relation to non-Christian systems of life and
thought. Apropos of this theme, there was conflict at Jerusalem, and thereafter,
between the Barthians and the Anglo-American proponents of transreligious
commonality. Anglo-American missionary thinking favored a more experience-
based approach to other faiths, whereas Continental missionary thinking, in
part inspired by dialectical theology, called for a strict theological approach to
non-Christian religions. In the emerging debate, the Anglo-American camp
assumed a relationship of continuity between Christianity and the religions of
the world, and the Continental camp assumed discontinuity in the same relationship. In the post-Jerusalem discussions and in light of the geopolitical
situation, those who favored the continuity approach specified secularism as
one of the major issues—if not the major issue—facing Christianity and Christian missions. The argument that secularism represents the chief challenge
for missions, and that all religions ought to join together in the fight against
it, came to influential and controversial expression in the 1932 report headed

by the American philosopher W. E. Hocking, *Rethinking Missions: A Laymen's Inquiry after One Hundred Years*.[14] The assumption that this much-disputed report had at its core—that a relationship of continuity exists between Christianity and the religions of the world—is what Kraemer would challenge head-on in the years to come.[15]

From the early 1920s through the mid-1930s, Kraemer served as a missionary in Indonesia, where opposition to Dutch colonialism and a resurgent Islam had begun to manifest themselves. This situation presented particular challenges for missionaries stationed there and required of them not just sensitivity but special expertise. Kraemer came well equipped, with a pronounced knowledge of Islam and a deep understanding of Christian theology—both of which he had acquired through his doctoral studies at the University of Leiden. In the mid-1930s, Kraemer became involved with the preparatory work for Tambaram 1938. Specifically, he was asked by the International Missionary Council (IMC) in preparation for the conference to write "a book on evangelism in the modern world, with especial reference to the non-Christian religions."[16] In a real sense, Kraemer's volume was intended by the IMC and by Kraemer himself as a countermeasure to the *Laymen's Inquiry*.[17] As part of his preparation for writing *The Christian Message in a Non-Christian World*, Kraemer corresponded with missionaries in various countries in an attempt to survey the world's current missionary situation. He also spent time working on theological issues that the book would raise. In the fall of 1937, Kraemer composed the bulk of his book in a seven-week period. The final manuscript was finished in December, 1937.[18] The author felt intellectually cramped and constrained by his audience, as he confided in a letter to William Paton dated 18 December 1937:

> All the time I have been writing my book I have been very uneasy about it. In the first place the subject of the book is big and complicated. In the second place I had constantly to suppress many thoughts that I wanted to express because I had to keep in mind that this book may not be too long. It has perhaps cost me more time to think about what had to be left out than the writing itself has cost me. In the third place my difficulty was that I had to write for all the world, for Englishmen, who like practical and not too heavy stuff, for Americans who are easily deterred by a systematic dissertation, for Continentals, who certainly will be amazed to hear that Anglo-Saxons speak of the massiveness of the book, for Orientals, who have a very different background and who have the peculiarity of being vehemently interested in their own problems and of being prone to find problems unknown to them rather dull and difficult. If I had written the book to my own satisfaction I would have written it in a far more massive way than it has been done but I felt

> I could not treat the subject for Anglo-Americans in a way that is, perhaps, only congenial to Continentals.[19]

Even so, the task was done, the audience would indeed be wide, and Kraemer's position for the ensuing debate was established.

Kraemer's Tambaram Position

The three international missionary conferences in the first half of the twentieth century moved ever eastward, from Scotland in 1910, to Palestine in 1928, and to India in December 1938 for the third international missionary conference. The redoubts of Western Christendom were half a world away, and the Indian setting doubtless gave point and relevance to the issues the conference examined. Kraemer's trip from Europe represented a significant investment of time, but it turned out to be important preparation. In his reflections on traveling to Tambaram, he reported that there was an informal "pre-conference" on the ship. Kraemer learned that his new book made many people uneasy. At the conference itself, Kraemer participated in Section One ("The Faith by Which the Church Lives") of 16 sections in total. Although he is widely assumed to have dominated the conference proceedings in general, he did not address the delegates at Tambaram—half of whom were non-Western—as a whole. His influence was made manifest more by means of the written word than by the spoken word.[20]

The heart of Kraemer's position at Tambaram is expressed in both his book, *The Christian Message in a Non-Christian World* (particularly its fourth chapter, "The Attitude towards the Non-Christian Religions"), and in an essay published after the conference, "Continuity or Discontinuity."[21] Prior to presenting his theological position in the pivotal fourth chapter of *The Christian Message*, Kraemer attempts a "realistic" sketch of the world situation in the West and in the East.[22] In the West, he discerns the problem of religious uncertainty and the corresponding specter of relativism. In the East, the problem concerns the Western invasion of the East and the East's reaction to it—an observation no doubt bolstered by his experience as a missionary in Indonesia.[23] In such a world, Kraemer says, the church must witness to the truth of the Christian gospel. In so doing, the church must realize that the call "to missionary expression in the non-Christian world is more urgent than ever."[24] Such a realization calls for "realism," and not just of the human kind: what is needed is "divine realism," which takes

> man and God radically and seriously: man in his high origin and destiny as well as in his utter corruption and frustration; God in His radical rejection and condemnation of man, and in His never-weakening faith in and saving grace for man. Here we can learn the

right and saving kind of realism that looks realities honestly in the face and exposes them to the light of the divine judgment. We learn from the Gospel that God is not to be treated as an appendix—usually a rather disconnected one—to our human reasonings and analyses, but as the all-pervading centre in total reality.[25]

Such divine realism requires careful listening to the radically religious and theocentric record of divine revelation, namely, the Bible.[26]

"Biblical realism," one of the central concepts in *The Christian Message* (but largely abandoned in Kraemer's writings in the 1950s and 1960s), focuses on the idea that "the essential message and content of the Bible is always the Living, eternally-active God, the indubitable Reality, from whom, by whom and to whom all things are."[27] Biblical realism takes seriously the "radically religious character of the Bible and of the Christian faith."[28] Taking "Biblical realism as the fundamental starting-point and criterion of all Christian and theological thinking exposes all problems to an unexpected and revealing light."[29] Roughly synonymous with the record of divine revelation in scripture—or so at least it seems, for Kraemer is infamously unclear on this matter—to know and testify to the truth of the Christian faith involves continually confronting Biblical realism cum divine revelation. With regard to his somewhat murky but pivotal conception of revelation, Kraemer notes the following: "Revelation in its proper sense is what is by its nature inaccessible and *remains so, even when it is revealed.* The necessary correlate to the concept of revelation is therefore faith" [emphasis added].[30] As the witness to and record of revelation, the Bible testifies to the fact that God was simultaneously revealed and hidden in Jesus Christ. Revelation is, therefore, not accessible to humanity by nature. In fact, the "essential, absolutely unique feature in the revelation of God in Christ is that, contrary to all human conceptions, God's revelation is an offence to man."[31] "This," Kraemer says, "is the stern teaching of Biblical realism."[32]

With the foundational analysis of his conception of biblical realism complete, Kraemer turns to the matter of other faiths in the fourth chapter of *The Christian Message*. The revelation of God in Christ, he reminds the reader, revolves around two poles: (1) a special kind of knowledge of God that upsets all other kinds of knowledge of God and (2) a special kind of knowledge of humanity that reveals humanity's dual condition of greatness and misery.[33] How does this conception of revelation enlighten Christianity's relationship to non-Christian religions? According to Kraemer, there are really two fundamental positions on this question: continuity and discontinuity. The former was classically articulated by Clement of Alexandria and expresses itself with the terms *fulfillment, general revelation,* and *natural theology.* The latter has been best articulated by Karl Barth and rejects the ideas of fulfillment, general revelation, and natural theology. These two diametrically opposed positions, Kraemer argues, necessitate a choice: either one starts from a general idea of the essence of religion and makes that one's standard of reference, or one derives one's idea and evaluation of religion from the revelation in Christ and makes that one's standard of reference. Kraemer, it should be clear by this point, favored the second, Christocentric option, for which he was prepared by his Dutch milieu and to which his encounter with Swiss dialectical theology further inclined him.[34]

Advocating a position of discontinuity, then, Kraemer seeks to examine non-Christian religions from the viewpoint of Christian revelation. In doing so, he argues, the matter of Christianity's dialectical attitude to the world and to religion needs to be addressed, as do the issues of general revelation and natural theology. With regard to the former, Christianity must say yes and no to the world, reflecting divine ambivalence—that is, both judgment of and love for the fallen creation.[35] With regard to the latter, Kraemer reflects the common terminology used to express the problem of Christianity's relationship to other religions, although he was uncomfortable with the terminology.[36] What is the relationship of Christian revelation to nature, history, and reason? Is there truth outside Christianity? The only basis for certitude and the only firm foundation for Christian witness in the world, Kraemer says, is the "faith that God has revealed *the* Way and *the* Life and *the* Truth in Jesus Christ and wills this to be known through all the world."[37] Alternately put, "Christ, as the ultimate standard of reference, is the crisis of all religions, of the non-Christian religions and of empirical Christianity too. This implies that the most fruitful and legitimate way to analyze and evaluate all religions is to investigate them in the light of the revelation of Christ."[38]

With Christic revelation as the standard for evaluating of religion and religions, what then of extra-Christian revelation? Or, as Kraemer poses the question: From the point of view of Christian revelation, does "God—and if so, how and where does God—reveal Himself in the religious life as present in the non-Christian religions?"[39] Again, on this question, one looks in vain in Kraemer's writing for a clear and unambiguous answer. On the one hand, he argues that the idea of the *sensus divinitatis*, as given expression by Calvin, is one of the Bible's key teachings.[40] On the other hand, he says that general revelation is a contradiction in terms, "for what lies on the street has no need to be revealed."[41] In other words, by its nature, revelation must be special because revelation is a divine act of condescension—and not a human act of ascension. Accordingly, revelation is not and cannot be *possessed* by any religious group. Therefore, Christians must point "gratefully and humbly to Christ: 'It has pleased God to reveal Himself fully and decisively in Christ; repent, believe and adore.'"[42]

On the related subject of natural theology, Kraemer clearly appreciates Barth's criticism of the notion, but he is also critical of Barth's rigid doctrinalism. Not entirely surprisingly, then, in the Barth-Brunner debate of 1934,

Kraemer tended to side with Brunner.[43] Therefore, despite reservations, he holds that there is some qualified, conditional legitimacy to the idea of natural theology; it is necessary to "try to speak in the light of the Christian revelation in Christ about the religious reality of man outside the sphere of 'special revelation.'"[44] But one must always be reminded that, however necessary such speaking may be, the endeavor will always be subject to error:

> The terms "general revelation" and "natural theology" cannot forthwith be used in the customary loose way. It will no more be permitted to call, as so often is done undiscerningly, sublime religious and moral achievements the pure and unmistakable evidences of divine revelation of the same sort and quality as the revelation in Jesus Christ.[45]

Kraemer's guarded position, it should be observed, does not ultimately concern the *reality* of extra-Christian revelation but its putative *transitional efficacy*. That is, he cannot finally bring himself to deny flatly that extra-Christian revelation exists—although he emphasizes that it is incomparable with Christian revelation (i.e., in Christ). But—and this is the key point for Kraemer—it can never function as a *praeparatio evangelica* or as a preamble to "the realm of grace and truth as manifest in Jesus Christ," for general revelation is not self-illuminating; it becomes visible only in the light of Christ.[46] Accordingly, one should rejoice "over every evidence of divine working and revelation that may be found in the non-Christian world. No man, and certainly no Christian, can claim the power or the right to limit God's revelatory working."[47] But one should never regard such glimpses of revelation as preparations for the gospel; conversely, one should never regard Christian revelation as the fulfillment of humanity's religious striving. The concepts of preparation and fulfillment presuppose a relationship of continuity between Christianity and non-Christian religions. And in Kraemer's view, the road from Banaras or Beijing does not lead naturally to the cross, for the cross "is antagonistic to all human religious aspirations and ends."[48] Conversion and regeneration are required for those who would come to Christ. Bearing in mind the dialectical attitude of biblical realism, then, "the attitude towards the non-Christian religions is a remarkable combination of down-right intrepidity and of radical humility."[49]

The vast majority of the remaining presentation in *The Christian Message* falls outside the purview of the present discussion. What is relevant, however, is Kraemer's theological approach to non-Christian religions (chapter 4) as it informs his missionary approach (chapters 8 and 9). According to Kraemer, mission has one motive and purpose: "to call men and peoples to confront themselves with God's acts of revelation and salvation for man and the world as presented in Biblical realism."[50] Such an approach has no place for attitudes of superiority or pride. Rather, the apostolic attitude calls for humble witness, for all human beings are sinners before the face of God and lost apart from God. Therefore, evangelization and conversion must be the heart of the missionary enterprise.[51]

At this point in his presentation, Kraemer turns his attention to what he calls "adaptation." Opposing both the overly aggressive and overly sympathetic approaches of past missionary efforts, Kraemer advocates a mediating "evangelistic" approach, which emphasizes humble witness and the offer of a divine gift.[52] Such an approach involves adaptation, which is largely similar to what some recent theorists have called "translation."[53] Adaptation requires that the Christian message be made understandable to a given culture, that is, in terms that are meaningful to it, but in so doing, it must also highlight how the culture in question is inadequate and even in conflict with the Christian message. In Kraemer's view, this was the approach of St. John and St. Paul in the New Testament. In other words, the strategy in adaptation is to reveal both bridges and gulfs. And because the Christian message admits of many embodiments, no one embodiment can claim absoluteness or finality. Western cultural imperialism, therefore, is unjustified and unjustifiable.[54] The challenge is to "help in paving the way for the expression of the religion of revelation in indigenous forms so as to be a true and vigorous expression of its real character."[55]

In concluding his substantial volume, which he thought was incomplete because of its focus on the mere fundamentals, Kraemer reiterates what is in some sense his chief claim in the book, namely, that the "core of the Christian revelation is that Jesus Christ is the sole legitimate Lord of all human lives and that the failure to recognize this is the deepest religious error of mankind. . . . Seen in this light, not to recognize Him as the sole legitimate Lord is to serve false Gods."[56]

Immediate Post-Tambaram Reactions to Kraemer's Position

Kraemer himself admitted that *The Christian Message* caused "a storm of criticism" and controversy.[57] The written reactions to his position at Tambaram are contained in the first volume of the Tambaram Madras Series edited by William Paton, called *The Authority of the Faith*.[58] In his essay in this volume, Kraemer notes some problems with his position as stated in *The Christian Message*, including his own admission of a partial and imperfect grasp of the standard for evaluating religion and religions, namely, "the Christian revelation."[59] It is precisely on his central conception of revelation that, instructively, several of Kraemer's critics focus.

In T. C. Chao's chapter "Revelation," the author points out that Kraemer demands careful study and interpretation of the Bible, but he does not tell the reader of his book how to do so.[60] On the premise that God has given himself to the world, Chao also has difficulty accepting the seeming Kraemerian proposition that in light of the personal and unique revelation of God in Christ, there can be no revelation in creation and history: "All the nations, with their various religions, have seen God more or less clearly, although the forms in which their visions have been clothed are incomplete, insufficient and unsatisfactory."[61]

In "The Christian Attitude to Non-Christian Faith," A. G. Hogg, whom Kraemer regarded as his most perceptive critic, investigates the human correlate to the divine act of revelation, as the chapter's title indicates.[62] In his treatment of non-Christian faith, with an emphasis on the singular and not the plural faiths, Hogg's first order of business is to argue that such must exist. That is, non-Christian religions represent not mere endless searches but actual divine-human exchanges—something in Hogg's judgment about which Kraemer seems ambivalent and which he therefore seems hesitant to grant. Hogg asks if Kraemer perhaps speaks with two voices, "one more Barthian than the other."[63] At the heart of Hogg's criticism of Kraemer is his concern that the Dutch scholar puts the Christian religion and non-Christian religions in different camps, in which the former is seen as arising from revelation while the latter are regarded as mere human articulations. Do not, Hogg wonders, other religions also arise from an encounter with revelation? Have non-Christians not seen something to which they testify? He answers unambiguously: "Whether to Christian faith or to non-Christian, God reveals *Himself*."[64] One cannot easily specify where revelation (God) ends and religion (humanity) begins. How does one know that non-Christian faith exists? Hogg offers as evidence his own testimony: he claims to have seen non-Christian faith, and he therefore concludes that Kraemer's discontinuity position is problematic. With appreciation for Kraemer's contributions, Hogg simply disagrees with Kraemer's central argument that "Christianity is unique because it is created by the *occurrence* of revelation. . . . Without the revealing initiative of God there would be *no* religions" [emphasis in original][65] For Hogg, Christianity's uniqueness lies not in the fact of its origin in revelation but in the content of its revelation.

Walter Marshall Horton and H. H. Farmer should be placed in a somewhat different camp in the post-Tambaram discussions than T. C. Chao and A. G. Hogg. Unlike Chao and Hogg's dominant critical focus on Kraemer's conception of revelation, Horton and Farmer, while nonetheless critical of Kraemer, seek to clarify the debate at Tambaram and in so doing to occupy something of a mediating position. The title of Horton's chapter gives an indication of his desire to mediate and even of his indecision: "Between Hocking and Kraemer." Favorably disposed toward the general approach counseled by Jerusalem 1928 and the *Laymen's Inquiry*, Horton reports that he nonetheless found himself appreciative of some of Kraemer's views. After listening to the discussions at Tambaram and on further reflection, he argues that Hocking and Kraemer are not in complete disagreement. In particular, Horton salutes Kraemer's call for a warm, human, humble approach to non-Christians. Kraemer, he points out in a comment indicative of approval, offers non-Christians "no ready-made system of thought, no imposing—and invading—body of full-fashioned cultural patterns, but simply a piece of news of transcendent importance for all the world."[66] However, like Hogg, Horton balks at Kraemer's characterization of non-Christian religions. Given that one can observe humility and awe in the postures of non-Christians, must one not conclude that non-Christian religions are rooted in revelation? Kraemer, Horton points out, is hesitant to grant this point, qualifying his recognition of revelation outside of Christianity: only "here and there," only "now and then."[67] Horton diagnoses a conflict between Hocking and Kraemer in their appropriations of conceptions of revelation drawn from, respectively, Protestant liberalism and neo-orthodoxy. In other words, the difference concerns a notion focused on "tokens" of progressive revelation, on the one hand, and a notion focused on "those few supremely significant mighty acts of God, culminating in the Incarnation,"[68] on the other. As appreciative as he is of Kraemer's and Barth's position(s), Horton favors the tradition rooted in Justin Martyr, Clement of Alexandria, and Protestant liberalism.

Farmer's chapter, "The Authority of the Faith," seeks to clarify the two chief points of view expressed in the debate at Tambaram. In Farmer's judgment, the key term in the Tambaram debate was *fulfillment*, which was used ambiguously at the conference, also by Kraemer. In one sense, the term has to do with the necessary correction or development of insights found in the world's religions. In this sense, Farmer avers, the term is problematic, for what could lead up or prepare for the incarnation? In another sense, the term has to do with religious yearning finding its completion in Christ. In this sense, Farmer argues, the term is not problematic, as even Kraemer hesitatingly admits, despite his commitment to the idea that Christ negates and cancels human religious striving.[69] Behind this ambivalence on Kraemer's part, Farmer suspects, is his view of non-Christian religions as human achievements, that is, as not real responses to revelation, owing to his apparent view that revelation is exclusively Christic. This view of religions, in turn, reflects Kraemer's general theological commitments and his view of God in particular. Rather than conceiving God as loving and fatherly, Kraemer seems to understand God as a demanding and sovereign. The divine-human relation is therefore not one of loving reciprocity but of rebellious over-againstness.[70]

Kraemer's Tambaram critics sent him back to his study—not, it should be noted, to construct a new position but to clarify and refine the position he had defended at Tambaram. He would have to wait, however. Less than a year after the end of the conference, Europe was once again engulfed by war. For most of the 1940s, Kraemer's energies were focused on his home country, his home church, his university position at the University of Leiden, and his new position as director of the Ecumenical Institute at the newly formed World Council of Churches. He would pick up his pen again and return to the issues raised at Tambaram in the 1950s and 1960s.[71]

Kraemer's Key Publications in the 1950s and 1960s

As director of the Ecumenical Institute of the World Council of Churches, based in Switzerland, Kraemer delivered a series of lectures at the University of Geneva in 1953–54. These became the basis for another of his major works, *Religion and the Christian Faith*. Perhaps still wary from the backlash that greeted *The Christian Message*, which *Religion and the Christian Faith* was intended to clarify and on which it was to improve, Kraemer notes that the frank tone of the book was likely to evoke criticism. In linking *Religion and the Christian Faith* with his Tambaram volume, Kraemer emphasizes that he has not substantially changed his mind on any key matter. But in attempting to specify *how* God works outside the realm of Christian revelation, he seeks in the later book "to point out the religious consciousness as the place of dialectic encounter with God."[72]

The heart of *Religion and the Christian Faith* is the investigation of "the great human fact: Religion, in the light of Biblical revelation, particularly in the light of Jesus Christ, the Way, the Truth and the Life."[73] Such investigation of religion necessitates asking the question of the status of non-Christian religions as well as the question of truth.[74] And such investigation of "the whole problem of religion and religions . . . calls for a theological treatment."[75] After some comments about the justification of a theological evaluation of religion, Kraemer offers a historical overview of Christian theological assessments of religions. Several things about this overview stand out as instructive. First is Kraemer's criticism of the Justin-Clement-Aquinas line of thinking, focused on the conception of continuity. Second is his praise of Calvin's doctrine of the *sensus divinitatis*, which Kraemer takes to be a concept equivalent to what he calls "human religious consciousness" in *Religion and the Christian Faith*. Third is his careful assessment of the contributions of Barth and Brunner, who represent the antithesis of the Justin-Clement-Aquinas tradition, and his overall preference for the views of Brunner over those of Barth.[76]

With this survey complete, Kraemer turns to a lengthy examination of the Bible's verdict about religion and religions, which was largely absent from his Tambaram book. In setting out on this journey, Kraemer reiterates his basic assumptions: (1) "that Jesus Christ is *the* Way, *the* Truth and *the* Life, by whom alone man comes to the Father, and by whose light alone all problems can be seen in their proper perspective" and (2) that Christians have access to God's revelation in Jesus Christ through the Bible, "the record of the peculiar mode of God's self-disclosing activity."[77] In his treatment of texts and themes in the Old and New Testaments, Kraemer finds the justification for his anthropological dictum regarding human religious consciousness: "*related to God—separated from Him: sought by God . . . and haunted by Him—rebelling against Him and yet groping towards Him*. This dialectical condition is the constitutive element of man's religious consciousness" [emphasis added][78] Humanity's dialectical condition, along with the dialectical situation of God's judgment and mercy, "are the crucial points of orientation for our problem of the meaning of religion and religions."[79] Humanity can know God but does not know God; God is in dialogue with humanity but humanity misunderstands.[80] "Even in its most degraded form religion is evidence that man is haunted by God. He cannot get rid of Him."[81] The ineradicability of human wrestling with the divine is a function of human religious consciousness. The world of religion, then, "does not stand outside the sphere of God's self-revealing activity."[82] Recognition of this truth, however, does not minimize the "indispensability of God's decisive act in Christ."[83] Jesus Christ, moreover, "turns all standards and conditions of ability of knowing God . . . upside down."[84]

Kraemer's biblically based, dialectical approach to religion and religions indicates that God is at work in human religious consciousness. Yet, Kraemer warns, it is "illegitimate to speak of a rectilinear transition from the world of religion . . . to the world of revelation."[85] Adopting an identity as a follower of Christ requires one to make a fundamental break with one's past because Christ is the crisis of all religions. Accordingly, there can never be assumptions of continuity or notions of "gradual transition." Using a phrase from *The Christian Message*, Kraemer states that those who testify to Christ must therefore approach non-Christians "with downright intrepidity and radical humility."[86]

Kraemer's dialectical approach in *Religion and the Christian Faith* sometimes gives the impression of organizational infelicity that more than once leaves the reader unsure of his final position. Returning once again to the critical issue of general revelation, he dialectically observes: "God reveals, discloses constantly, uninterruptedly, His eternal power and divinity, so that man can and ought to know Him; but in fact man does not know God because his heart refuses it (he wills not), and, therefore, is inexcusably guilty."[87] Is there general revelation or not? Kraemer's failure to provide an unambiguous answer is rooted in his conception of revelation as a divine act of self-disclosure; all revelation is therefore special. In other words, the designation *general revelation* is self-contradictory and the term *special revelation* is pleonastic. The general-special distinction, Kraemer concludes, ought to be abandoned at a maximum or very carefully qualified at a minimum. The term *revelation* must therefore be used with great circumspection:

> Revelation in the Bible is objective divine action, decisively in the
> person and work of Jesus Christ, the "Word made flesh." Strictly
> speaking, the word should be confined to this basic divine history. It
> is, however, the custom, which is to a certain extent acceptable, to
> speak about the transmission of the *kerygma* regarding this history
> by means of persons and writings also as "revelation." This is "reve-

lation" in a subjective, secondary sense. Into this category falls the
Bible, when we speak about this book as "God's revelation."[88]

With this sui generis conception of revelation in mind, one can see that the
other modes "of revelation . . . are that of God's eternal power and divinity, that
of God's wrath, that of God's revelation in the conscience of man. These modes
of revelation . . . teach clearly that God, according to the Bible, discloses Himself in Christ, in nature, . . . in historical human life and activity, and human
consciousness."[89]

Clearly—or at least dialectically—there is "revelation in nature and history,
it is an undeniable fact that the Bible says so."[90] But this revelation "can only
be legitimately expressed in the light of the revelation in Christ."[91] Again, great
care and qualification must be applied in the use of the notion of "revelation
in nature and history." And hierarchical arrangements of the modes of revelation are illegitimate: "the central or focal revelation is the revelation of the
righteousness of God in Christ . . . the other modes are all of them revelations
of God's righteousness in their own specific way [and] are all related to the
central one, and yield their true significance through it, because they all happen
through Christ and to Christ."[92]

Kraemer's conception of revelation—that is, Christic revelation—is the key
to his view of Christianity's "intolerant exclusivism" regarding "ultimate
truth."[93] Christianity's "offensive exclusivism is a fact, and should remain so.
It belongs to the heart of the Biblical message. The least surrender on this
point means in principle the total surrender of the Biblical truth. God is God
or He is not God at all. Jesus Christ is *the* Truth, or there is no truth in Him
at all."[94] Christians therefore claim exclusiveness not because they have the
truth but because the truth (Jesus Christ) has them.

The Christian Message in a Non-Christian World and *Religion and the Christian Faith* are Kraemer's two major statements on these themes, but late in his
life he published a short summative work, *Why Christianity of All Religions?*[95]
Always the presuppositionalist, Kraemer declares his point of departure and
standard for judgment to be the person of Jesus Christ, *the* revelation of God
and *the* Truth, to whom the Bible bears witness and who confronts human
beings with a choice. Kraemer's Christocentric answer to the question posed
in the book's title presupposes a rigorous distinction between revelation and
religion, as in his earlier writings.[96] Reiterating his view that all religions are
"a mixture of sublimity and perversion, of evil, falsehood and sheer absurdity
. . . reflect[ing] the equivocal and inwardly divided state of human nature,"
Kraemer urges that a committed Christian approach must "search out . . . the
evidences for revelatory activity on the part of that same God in all religions—
but tracking down also the demonic and devilish forces in them [including
historical Christianity]."[97] In light of the dialectical character of all religions and

based on the criterion of Jesus Christ, it must be recognized that non-Christian religions "in regard to their deepest, most essential purport . . . are all in error. . . . They are all noble, but misguided and abortive, attempts to take the fundamental religious questions . . . and to answer them in their own terms."[98] Surrender to Jesus Christ requires one to make a break with one's religious past. In other words, conversion is required.[99] Summarizing his position in *Why Christianity?*—and, indeed, his position in general—Kraemer writes: "A fundamental being in error; a field in which we can trace God's own footmarks; noble aspiration and a tremendous capacity for creative action; and, in the light of Jesus Christ, humiliating aberration: these form the main outline of what I have be trying to say."[100] What makes Christianity the religion different? Only this: "although it enjoys its full share of human frailty, Christianity does arise out of the Revelation of God in the Person of Jesus Christ."[101] Christianity as a religion is not absolute, therefore; but the revelation of God in Christ is.[102] Kraemer ends where he began.

The 1988 Assessment: Tambaram and Kraemer in Retrospect

In 1988, a group of scholars met on the same premises in Tambaram that the delegates to the third international missionary conference had 50 years earlier. An account of their discussion and the conference's written contributions were published in the *International Review of Mission*.[103] This discussion had, it seems, two issues in focus: (1) the historical significance of Tambaram 1938 and the status of Christian missions and (2) Kraemer's theological evaluation of non-Christian religions.

On the first issue, Carl Hallencreutz offers the historical judgment that Tambaram 1938's significance lay in its transformative role. Especially at this third international missionary conference, he holds, Christianity shed its identity as the religion of the West and *again* came to understand itself as a world religion.[104] In other words, Tambaram is an important milestone on the road to world Christianity, and Kraemer can be regarded as a pioneer of Christianity's new global status.[105]

In another historical judgment, Stanley Samartha contends that the

> significance of Tambaram is that at such a time of confusion and
> danger a representative group of Christians met together to affirm
> the fundamentals of the Christian faith. Tambaram was an attempt
> to recover the spiritual vision, theological strength, moral power and
> missionary enthusiasm of the church in the world.[106]

But making a stronger philosophical and theological claim, Samartha calls for a "drastic revision of the conceptual framework" of Tambaram 1938. Key for Samartha in such a postcolonial, postexclusivistic, and post-Kraemerian revision is the relation between missions and dialogue, in which much greater emphasis must fall on the latter.[107]

On the second issue, Wilfred Cantwell Smith observes that the Christian Church has often made errors of judgment in the past. He views Kraemer's *The Christian Message in a Non-Christian World* as another such instance of error. The era of traditional missions is over, Smith insists; dialogue is God's will for us in our world. Smith argues that at some level Kraemer recognized these realities. Accordingly, he diagnoses a division in Kraemer between what he felt and knew experientially and what he had been taught to believe theologically. This tension, Smith contends, accounts for Kraemer's tendency to write in such a way that each successive book is a partial clarification of the position articulated in its predecessor. At bottom, Smith concludes—and, in so doing, he speaks for many of Kraemer's critics—Kraemer's theories do not do justice to "modern awareness."[108]

In a Smithian spirit, Diana Eck censures Kraemer for his approach to the question of revelation outside Christianity. On the assumption that the era of missions is over and the era of dialogue has dawned, she points out that Kraemer does not engage in dialogue with non-Christians in order to inquire about the possibility and reality of revelation in their religious traditions. Rather, she argues, he concludes in an a priori theological fashion that no such revelation can exist outside Christian revelation. This approach is puzzling to non-Christians, and "this exclusive understanding of revelation . . . is also folly to many Christians."[109]

Aside from scattered minor notes of appreciation at Tambaram 1988 for Kraemer's contributions, the one thinker who offers a positive assessment of Kraemer's position is Lesslie Newbigin. Newbigin judges Kraemer's importance to be his overturning of the *Laymen's Inquiry* and its attempt to "domesticate the gospel" within the West's plausibility structure.[110] Siding with Kraemer over against Hogg in their famous exchange, Newbigin writes:

> If we are speaking about religious ideas, or about religious experiences, then certainly to claim uniqueness and finality for one's own is intolerable arrogance. Kraemer's whole point is that we are not; we are talking about facts of history. If, in fact, it is true that almighty God, creator and sustainer of all that exists in heaven and on earth, has—at a known time and place in human history—so humbled himself as to become a part of our sinful humanity and to suffer and die a shameful death to take away our sin and rise from the dead as the first-fruit of a new creation; if this is a fact, then to affirm it is not arrogance. To remain quiet about it is treason to our fellow human beings.[111]

The reflections at Tambaram 1988 as recorded in the *International Review of Mission* were not the only marker of the fiftieth anniversary of Tambaram

1938. Significant space in the *Ecumenical Review* was devoted to the results of a symposium on the relevance for our times of Kraemer's Tambaram theology of religions. In the published papers, Philip A. Potter and D. C. Mulder are broadly appreciative of Kraemer's contributions, although not without reservation,[112] while S. Wesley Ariarajah and Bert Hoedemaker present rather critical assessments. Ariarajah argues that a certain perceived fear of other cultures is grounded in a Christian theological position, rooted in a rigorous distinction between revelation and religion, which runs through the Protestant Reformers, Barth, and Kraemer. Kraemer's discontinuity verdict, Ariarajah avers, was influential in Asian missions and churches and made dialogue and relations with non-Christians strenuous. Accordingly, he argues that a broader conception of revelation and a more positive approach to non-Christian religions are required.[113]

In his assessment, Hoedemaker notes that "it is virtually impossible to ignore the traces of Kraemer's influence in present-day discussions on pluralism, mission and dialogue," insofar as Kraemer "helped formulate the basic alternatives of any theology of religions" in the middle third of the twentieth century.[114] Hoedemaker regards Kraemer as a necessary corrective to figures such as Troeltsch and Hocking, but he argues that the time has come to get beyond Kraemer's position by emphasizing "God's active presence in the whole of creation."[115] The root of this problem, says Hoedemaker, lies in Kraemer's theological position on revelation. It is time to subject that position to a concluding critical assessment.

Conclusion: A Dialectical Theological Assessment

Kraemer's evaluation of non-Christian religions turns on his conception of revelation, as many of his critics have noted.[116] This conception of revelation, as the foregoing discussion has indicated, is Christocentric. I am tempted to say Christomonistic, but so saying would be to risk too strong a statement.[117] Kraemer's conception of revelation, moreover, must be seen as rooted in his doctrine of God, but Kraemer never carefully and systematically discussed his doctrine of God and the closely connected doctrines of Christ and creation.[118] In the absence of clear articulations, Kraemer forces his interpreter to speculate.

Kraemer's Christocentric conception of revelation seems to be rooted in a somewhat mysterious and rather untrinitarian, unipersonal conception of God.[119] Accordingly, Kraemer's theology of religion does not pay sufficient attention to the persons of the Father and the Spirit and their work in creation and redemption. As a result, Kraemer could not bring himself unambiguously to grant the existence of extra-Christian revelation. If the person of God, in the end, *is* the person of Jesus Christ, then God's self-revelation *is* Jesus Christ.

Admitting the existence of revelation outside Christ cannot be permitted without qualification. Even so, as the preceding presentation has shown, Kraemer recognizes that St. Paul, Calvin, Brunner, and others point to *something* in humanity ultimately rooted in *theos* that cries out for *logos*.[120] But whatever the something may turn out to be, Kraemer never tired of pointing out, it can never lead in a natural or continuous way to *the* revelation of God in Christ. Kraemer derived this view of revelation, his central theological axiom, from his Dutch milieu and training. As an ethical theologian, he was led to embrace a strong incarnational (i.e., Christocentric) conception of revelation, and this conception was bolstered by his encounter with Swiss dialectical theology in the 1930s and beyond.[121] But in the end, Kraemer left too much unsaid with respect to the context, content, and implications of his own starting point and criterion: Jesus Christ.

A balanced and properly dialectical Christian view of non-Christian religions, rooted in a full-orbed trinitarian understanding of God, demands—pace Kraemer—greater recognition of continuity and a broader conception of revelation.[122] First, the idea of natural or general revelation is warranted by Christian scripture and tradition.[123] The Christian God who is agapic love—Father, Son, and Holy Spirit—has never left himself without a witness. Second, recognition that human beings outside Christianity respond to something real (i.e., revelational) in creation makes sense of the various human quests for transcendence. In other words, instead of seeing the religions of the world either as areas of complete darkness (in theological fashion à la Barth or in psychological fashion la Marx or Freud) or as equally efficacious paths to the divine (à la Hick), one could see such as legitimate products of revelation with a proper (that is to say, divinely granted) point of departure but in need of further divine light to come to their proper end.

So saying brings up the usual typology employed in Christian theological discussions of non-Christian religions in current scholarship: exclusivism, inclusivism, pluralism.[124] This typology is flawed, it seems to me, for at least two reasons. First, the focus is too narrowly trained on salvation, generally construed in an ultimate, other-worldly sense. Second, more distinctions are needed to discuss the complex of theological matters involved in thinking about religions. In particular, the following issues need to be addressed: revelation, knowledge of God, truth, salvation, and the study of religion. In what sense, then, should one be exclusivist, inclusivist, or pluralist?[125]

On the matter of revelation, one should be inclusivist and possibly even pluralist, in recognition that some kind of divine disclosure—evidenced externally in creation and internally in the *sensus divinitatis*—is available universally. On this front, Kraemer's position is inadequate. At best, he was willing to admit that something was there to be talked about but he was hesitant or unwilling to go further. On the closely related matter of knowledge of God, one should also be inclusivist or perhaps even pluralist, but in recognition of different levels of knowing: one might argue that non-Christians know *that* God exists, perhaps as creator, but do not know God tripersonally as creator, redeemer, and sanctifier—as Father, Son, and Holy Spirit. Kraemer, as the preceding discussion has attempted to demonstrate, was insufficiently nuanced on this point. On the matter of truth, one should also be inclusivist and possibly even pluralist, but in recognition of different levels of truth: non-Christians can surely reach many true conclusions about the world and its workings (i.e., on either a correspondence or a coherence conception of truth) but cannot finally recognize the truth of the mystery of human existence vis-à-vis the divine apart from special revelation, that is, as exemplarily disclosed in the incarnation. Again, in reflection of his conception of revelation and knowledge, Kraemer did not articulate requisite distinctions in this regard. On the matter of salvation, an orthodox Christian would want to be rigorously exclusivist—and here Kraemer was right in his defense of Christianity's theocentrism[126] and offensive, evangelistic claim. If the sovereign God and the dependent world are indeed distinct in being, there can be no power or thing in creation that can save creation. God alone, in Jesus Christ, is the savior of the world. And although Christ is the sole *means* of salvation, this truth does not necessarily entail that the *scope* of salvation must be exceedingly narrow; in fact, Christians have grounds for hoping that the scope of salvation will be lovingly and gracefully expansive. On the matter of the study of other religions, finally, one would want to proceed in an empathetic fashion, recognizing in the religions of the world some intuitive integrity yet misdirection in their quest for fulfillment. In other words, Kraemer was right in his dialectical estimate of religions and his phenomenological and theological approach to them.[127]

To sum up: rather than declaring oneself to be exclusivist, inclusivist, or pluralist in a straightforward manner, I would argue that a Christian theologian committed to both orthodoxy (i.e., fidelity to scripture and tradition) and coherence (i.e., fidelity to reason and experience) ought to be a qualified inclusivist (or perhaps even pluralist) about matters of revelation, knowledge of the divine, and truth in other religions, but an exclusivist in matters pertaining to salvation, and an empathetic phenomenologist in the study of religion. Of these five areas, Kraemer was on the mark in the last two, but his position is flawed on the first three. And these three are, in some sense, one: with a strong emphasis on particularity, missing in Kraemer's theology is adequate attention to the dimension of universality in Christianity.[128] The triune God was revealed particularly and decisively in Jesus Christ, but the triune God is the God— creator, redeemer, and sanctifier—of the *whole world*. How was and is the triune God active outside the sphere of Christian revelation? Is there hope of ultimate redemption for non-Christians? Kraemer does not say.

To understand and criticize Kraemer the dialectician, we need a dialectical assessment. That was the approach of this essay. Unjustifiably one-sided in several important theological respects, Kraemer was precisely and correctly centered in some others. In the face of Western theologians' growing recognition of the profundity of other faiths and their guilt over their own imperialism, Kraemer held the line on some crucial theological matters when it was not easy or popular to do so. As a Christian theologian, an expert in Islam, a missionary, and an ecumenist, Kraemer was superbly qualified to make the judgments that he did. For these reasons, he deserves the respect and thanks of mission-minded Christians who came after him, and his corpus merits careful study by Christian scholars. The *prima vox* of Tambaram 1938 and pioneer of world Christianity therefore "remains an invaluable resource"[129] for contemporary theology and missiology in a religiously pluralistic age, an age that is slowly coming to terms with the realities and challenges of a truly global Christianity.

NOTES

1. Cited in Eric J. Sharpe, *The Universal Gītā: Western Images of the* Bhagavadgītā (London: Gerald Duckworth, 1985), 22.

2. On some of the factors that have contributed to heightened Western awareness of religious plurality, see Richard J. Plantinga, ed., *Christianity and Plurality: Classic and Contemporary Readings* (Oxford: Blackwell, 1999), 1–3. On the development of education about religious plurality, consider the following two large and influential undertakings. First, there is the film series *The Long Search*, 13 vols. (New York: Ambrose Video Publishing, 1977), which has appeared on BBC in the United Kingdom and on PBS in the United States and found its way into numerous curricula. Second, there is "The Pluralism Project" headed up by Harvard's Diana Eck (an outspoken critic of Hendrik Kraemer's theological position regarding non-Christian religious traditions, as the following discussion will reveal). The Pluralism Project has produced a number of publications dealing with the increasing presence of the world's religious traditions in the United States, including Diana L. Eck and Elinor J. Pierce, *World Religions in Boston* (Cambridge, Mass.: The Pluralism Project. Harvard University, 1998) and Diana L. Eck, *On Common Ground: World Religions in America* (New York: Columbia University Press, 1997). For further information, see its Web site at http://www.pluralism.org/.

3. See John Hick and Brian Hebblethwaite, eds., *Christianity and Other Religions* (Philadelphia: Fortress Press, 1980). Their selection focuses on developments in the second half of the twentieth century.

4. Gerald H. Anderson, "Religion as a Problem for the Christian Mission," in *Christian Faith in a Religiously Plural World*, ed. Donald G. Dawe and John B. Carman (Maryknoll, N.Y.: Orbis Books, 1978), 106. Eric J. Sharpe refers to Kraemer as a "massive figure" (*Faith Meets Faith: Some Christian Attitudes to Hinduism in the Nineteenth and Twentieth Centuries* (London: SCM Press, 1977), 43). A. C. Bouquet calls Kraemer "the ablest and most learned opponent of the more liberal attitude towards non-Christian religions" (*The Christian Faith and Non-Christian Religions* (New York: Harper, 1958), 397–98). Antonio Gualtieri points out that Kraemer has been influential either by way of "endorsement or . . . repudiation" ("The Failure of Dialectic in Hen-

drik Kraemer's Evaluation of Non-Christian Faith," *Journal of Ecumenical Studies* 15/2 (Spring 1978), 275). Origen Vasantha Jathanna argues the necessity of getting beyond the point of seeing Kraemer "as a figure of the distant past, often hidden behind a smoke-screen of undiscriminating criticism in terms of over-simplified position-defining catch-words" (*The Decisiveness of the Christ Event and the Universality of Christianity in a World of Religious Plurality: With Special Reference to Hendrik Kraemer and Alfred George Hogg as Well as to William Ernest Hocking and Pandipeddi Chenchiah*, Studies in the Intercultural History of Christianity 29 (Berne: Peter Lang Publishers, 1981), 47). Further on the reception of Kraemer's thought (i.e., ignorance, misunderstanding, or caricature), see T. S. Perry, "The Significance of Hendrik Kraemer for Evangelical Theology of Religions," *Didaskalia* 9 (Spring 1998), 38 (especially n. 6), 59. For biographical data on Kraemer, see Willem A. Bijlefeld, "Kraemer, Hendrik," *The Encyclopedia of Religion*, ed. Mircea Eliade, volume 8 (New York: Macmillan, 1987), 380–81; Libertus Hoedemaker, "The Legacy of Hendrik Kraemer," *Occasional Bulletin of Missionary Research* 4/2 (Apr. 1980), 60–64; Jathanna, *Decisiveness*, 62–69; E. Jansen Schoonhoven, "Kraemer, Hendrik," *Biografisch Lexicon voor de Geschiedenis van het Nederlandse Protestantisme*, ed. D. Nauta, vol. 1 (Kampen: J. H. Kok, 1978), 104–11; A. T. Van Leeuwen, *Hendrik Kraemer. Dienaar der wereldkerk* (Amsterdam: Uitgeverij W. Ten Have N.V., 1959).

5. Kraemer could well be considered a pioneer of world Christianity. This status is signaled by A. T. Van Leeuwen in the title of his biography: *Hendrik Kraemer. Dienaar der wereldkerk* (*Hendrik Kraemer: Servant of the World Church*). Kraemer's lifelong concern with missions and a truly global Christianity comes to various expression in his corpus, including his autumnal and forward-looking *World Cultures and World Religions: The Coming Dialogue* (Philadelphia: Westminster Press, 1960).

6. See Hendrik Kraemer, *The Christian Message in a Non-Christian World*, 3rd ed. (Grand Rapids, Mich.: Kregel, 1956). In what follows, this will work be referred to as *CMNCW*.

7. On the following summary of Edinburgh 1910, see Carl Hallencreutz, "Tambaram Revisited," *International Review of Mission* LXXVIII (July 1988), 348–50; W. Richey Hogg, "Edinburgh 1910–Perspective 1980," *Occasional Bulletin of Missionary Research* 4/4 (Oct. 1980), 146–53; William Hutchison, *Errand to the World: American Protestant Thought and Foreign Missions* (Chicago: University of Chicago Press, 1987), 125–38; Harry Sawyerr, "The First World Missionary Conference: Edinburgh 1910," *International Review of Mission* 67/267 (July 1978), 255–72; J. J. E. Van Lin, *Protestantse theologie der godsdiensten. Van Edinburgh naar Tambaram (1910–1938)* (Assen: Van Gorcum, & Comp. B. V., 1974), 1–35; T. E. Yates, "Edinburgh Revisited: Edinburgh 1910 to Melbourne 1980," *Churchman* 94/2 (1980), 145–55.

8. Hogg, "Edinburgh 1910–Perspective 1980," 146.

9. See: Carl F. Hallencreutz, *Kraemer Towards Tambaram: A Study in Hendrik Kraemer's Missionary Approach*, Studia Missionalia Upsaliensia, 7 (Lund, Sweden: C. W. K. Gleerup, 1966), 21; Carl F. Hallencreutz, *New Approaches to Men of Other Faiths: 1938–1968: A Theological Discussion*, Research Pamphlet 18 (Geneva: World Council of Churches, 1970), 21.

10. Yates, "Edinburgh Revisited: Edinburgh 1910 to Melbourne 1980," 145.

11. Hallencreutz, "Tambaram Revisited," 349.

12. On the following summary of Jerusalem 1928, see David Bosch, "The Church in Dialogue: From Self-Delusion to Vulnerability," *Missiology* 16/2 (Apr. 1988), 132–34; J. R. Chandran, "Christianity and World Religions: The Ecumenical Discussion," *Indian Journal of Theology* 30/1 (Jan.–Mar. 1981), 187–89; Hallencreutz, "Tambaram Revisited," 350–52; Hallencreutz, *Kraemer Towards Tambaram*, 167–98; Gérard Vallée, *Mouvement Oecuménique et Religions Non Chrétiennes: Un débat oecuménique sur la rencontre interreligieuse De Tambaram à Uppsala (1938–1968)*, Recherches 14 (Montréal: Bellarmin, 1975), 19–31; Van Lin, *Protestantse theologie der godsdiensten*, 110–73.

13. Bosch, "Church in Dialogue," 133.

14. See W. E. Hocking et al., *Re-Thinking Missions: A Laymen's Inquiry after One Hundred Years* (New York: Harper, 1932). The project that resulted in the publication of this volume was undertaken by a group of laymen, as its title suggests, and not by the International Missionary Council. On Hocking and the debate about *Re-Thinking Missions*, see Hutchison, *Errand to the World*, 158–75.

15. Kraemer was an active participant at Jerusalem 1928, seeking to mediate between members of the International Missionary Council and the dialectical theologians from Europe. It is clear that he did not favor the Anglo-American approach to the question of the focus of missions or the classical liberal estimation of non-Christian religions that prevailed at Jerusalem. In a discussion of the much-emphasized theme of "values" in non-Christian religions, he publicly questioned the theological value of such values. See Van Leeuwen, *Hendrik Kraemer*, 48, 97; Hallencreutz, *New Approaches to Men of Other Faiths*, 22.

16. IMC Minutes, cited in Hallencreutz, *Kraemer Towards Tambaram*, 253. Significant in this quotation is the expressed (re)focus of evangelism: not secularism but non-Christian religions.

17. Even as Karl Barth had replied strongly to Emil Brunner in their famous 1934 exchange ("Nein!"), in parallel fashion, it seems, so did Kraemer in his debate with Hocking. See Emil Brunner and Karl Barth, *Natural Theology: Comprising "Nature and Grace" by Professor Dr. Emil Brunner and the Reply "No!" by Dr. Karl Barth*, Intro. by John Baillie, trans. Peter Fraenkel (London: Geoffrey Bles: The Centenary Press, 1946). On Kraemer's reflections on his exchange with Hocking, see *Religion and the Christian Faith* (London: Lutterworth Press, 1956), 222–24. In what follows, this work will be referred to as *RCF*. Further on the Hocking–Kraemer debate, see J. Wesley Robb, "Hendrik Kraemer Versus William Ernest Hocking," *Journal of Bible and Religion* 29/2 (Apr. 1961), 93–101.

18. See Hallencreutz, *Kraemer Towards Tambaram*, 273–74.

19. Cited in Hallencreutz, *Kraemer Towards Tambaram*, 275, n. 3. Further on Kraemer's immediate pre-Tambaram thoughts and activities, see Hendrik Kraemer, *Van godsdiensten en menschen. Reisindrukken van een Tambaram-ganger* (Nijkerk Netherlands: G. F. Callenbach, 1940), 9–23.

20. See Kraemer, *Van godsdiensten en menschen*, 11–12, 34f.; Van Leeuwen, *Hendrik Kraemer*, 105, 108.

21. See Kraemer, *CMNCW*, 101–41; "Continuity or Discontinuity," *The Authority of the Faith*, Tambaram Madras Series 1, ed. William Paton (London: Humphrey Milford/Oxford University Press, 1939), 1–23. For a compact summary of *CMNCW*, see

J. H. Bavinck, *De boodschap van Christus en de niet-Christelijke religies* (Kampen, Netherlands: Uitgave J. H. Kok, 1940), 8–76.

22. Kraemer has been criticized for his two-world view, that is, for thinking in terms of the so-called First and Third Worlds in absence of reflection on the so-called second world. See Elisabeth Adler, "Dialogue in the Second World," *The Ecumenical Review* 41/1 (Jan. 1989), 30–35; Bert Hoedemaker, "Kraemer Reassessed," *The Ecumenical Review* 41/1 (Jan. 1989), 42f.

23. See Kraemer, *CMNCW*, 6–21.

24. Ibid., 36.

25. Ibid., 41.

26. Ibid., 61–65.

27. Ibid., *CMNCW*, 65. Further on this pivotal concept in *The Christian Message*, see Bavinck, *De boodschap*, 94–101; Jathanna, *Decisiveness*, 512–20; Perry, "The Significance of Hendrik Kraemer," 39–43.

28. Kraemer, *CMNCW*, 65.

29. Ibid., *CMNCW*, 66. The position expressed in this quotation sounds remarkably similar to Karl Barth's methodological argument in *Church Dogmatics*. See *Church Dogmatics: The Doctrine of the Word of God*, I/2, trans. G. T. Thomson and H. Knight (Edinburgh: T. & T. Clark, 1956), 280–97.

30. Kraemer, *CMNCW*, 69.

31. Ibid., 70.

32. Ibid., 71. In "Continuity or Discontinuity," Kraemer sets down his fundamental presuppositions, which he believed it was his duty to do. To this end, he announces: "I take my standpoint *within* the realm of the Christian revelation. From it I take my standards of judgment and evaluation. The Christian revelation is my authoritative guide and no other principle or standpoint" ("Continuity," 7).

33. See Kraemer, *CMNCW*, 101–2, 112.

34. See Kraemer, "Continuity," 12, 14–23. See also Kraemer, *CMNCW*, 102–3. In terms of the options available in modern Protestant theology, the first option is represented by Schleiermacher and liberal Protestantism, and the second is represented by Barth and "neo-orthodoxy." It should be noted at this point that Christocentrism in the form of incarnational theology was part of Kraemer's theological makeup long before his encounter with Barth and Brunner. Kraemer's theological training in the Netherlands, both in the Netherlands Hervormde Kerk (Dutch Reformed Church) and at the University of Leiden, involved a sustained encounter with Dutch *ethische theologie* (ethical theology), a species of Schleiermacher-inspired German *Vermittlungstheologie* (mediating theology), which dominated Dutch Protestantism until the rise of dialectical theology in the 1920s. Although very much trained as an ethical theologian, Kraemer also distanced himself from ethical theology in important ways. On *Vermittlungstheologie*, see Felix Flückiger, *Die protestantische Theologie des 19. Jahrhunderts* (Göttingen, Germany, Vandenhoeck & Ruprecht, 1975), 44–61; Gottfried Hornig, "Die Vermittlungstheologie," *Handbuch der Dogmen- und Theologiegeschichte*, vol. 3, ed. Carl Andresen (Göttingen, Germany, Vandenhoeck & Ruprecht, 1988), 164–73; E. Schott, "Vermittlungstheologie," *Die Religion in Geschichte und Gegenwart*, 3rd ed., vol. 6, ed. Kurt Galling (Tübingen, Germany: J. C. B. Mohr [Paul Siebeck], 1962), 1362–64. On *ethische theologie*, see R. H. Bremmer, *Her-*

man *Bavinck als dogmaticus* (Kampen, Netherlands J. H. Kok, 1961), 65–114; T. L. Ha-itjema, *De richtingen in de Nederlandse Hervormde Kerk*, 2nd ed. (Wageningen, Neth-erlands: H. Veenman & Zonen, 1953), 46–101, 224–40; O. Noordmans, "Ontwikkeling en toekomst van de ethische theologie," *Geestelijke perspectieven* (Am-sterdam: H. J. Paris, [1930]), 125–77. On Kraemer and ethical theology, see Hallen-creutz, *Kraemer Towards Tambaram*, 86–99.

35. See Kraemer, *CMNCW*, 104.

36. Ibid., 102–3.

37. Ibid., 107.

38. Ibid., 110. It should be observed that Kraemer uses the term *Christianity* in two distinct senses. In the first sense, Christianity is equated with Christian revela-tion. In the second sense, Christianity is equated with the empirical, historical reli-gion. Christianity is discontinuous with the religions of the world in the first sense of the term but not in the second. Recognition of Christianity's continuity with the relig-ions of the world in the second sense, along with the reception of revelation as a di-vine gift, should summon forth, Kraemer stresses, an attitude of gratitude and humil-ity in the Christian believer.

39. Kraemer, *CMNCW*, 111. This question, unfortunately, never receives a com-pletely clear answer in Kraemer's corpus. He always seems to qualify any yes with a no and vice versa.

40. Ibid., 121.

41. Ibid., 119.

42. Ibid., 119.

43. Ibid., 118–21, 133. Kraemer points out that Barth did not deny *that* God works outside the sphere of Christian revelation but he did not say *how*—a criticism, ironi-cally, that could as well be applied to Kraemer. Barth, Kraemer argues, seems unwill-ing to address the question of Christianity's relationship to the world. In other words—bearing in mind Kraemer's dialecticism—Barth is too one-sided: "Even in this fallen world God shines through in a broken, troubled way: in reason, in nature and in his-tory" (*CMNCW*, 120). On the Barth-Brunner debate, see Brunner and Barth, *Natural Theology*. On Kraemer's view of the debate, see *RCF*, 178–79, 182–99, 356–58. Further on Kraemer's relation to Barth, see Jathanna, *Decisiveness*, 484–92. Jathanna, a more accurate analyst than most, correctly indicates Kraemer's independent position in re-lation to Barth and his consequent "dialectical relationship with Barth" (489). See also Johannes Aagaard, "Revelation and Religion: The Influence of Dialectical Theol-ogy on the Understanding of the Relationship between Christianity and Other Relig-ions," *Studia Theologica* 14 (1960), 148–85.

44. Kraemer, *CMNCW*, 121.

45. Ibid., 122.

46. Kraemer, "Continuity," 3. For Kraemer, the reality of Christic revelation does not entail the belief that general revelation does not exist. But the beliefs that general revelation manifests itself independently of Christic revelation and that the former naturally leads to the latter are mistaken.

47. Kraemer, *CMNCW*, 122.

48. Ibid., 123. In "Continuity or Discontinuity" (4), Kraemer proposes the phrase "contradictive or subversive fulfillment."

49. Kraemer, *CMNCW*, 128. Kraemer goes on to discuss the related matter of "points of contact," a key discussion point in the Barth-Brunner debate and in missiology. Kraemer concludes, emphasizing his posture of humility and his own missionary experience, that the only point of contact that exists between Christianity and non-Christian religions "is the disposition and the attitude of the missionary" (*CMNCW*, 140). See also *CMNCW*, 130–41.

50. Kraemer, *CMNCW*, 292.

51. Ibid., 295–99.

52. Ibid., 301–2.

53. See Lamin Sanneh, *Translating the Message: The Missionary Impact on Culture* (Maryknoll, N.Y.: Orbis Books, 1989), *passim* (see, however, especially 1–8); Andrew Walls, *The Missionary Movement in Christian History* (Maryknoll, N.Y.: Orbis Books, 1996), xvii, 22–23, 26–42, 28, 47, 51–54. Further on Kraemer's view of "adaptation," see Perry, "The Significance of Hendrik Kraemer," 49–53; M. M. Thomas, "An Assessment of Tambaram's Contribution to the Search of the Asian Churches for an Authentic Selfhood," *International Review of Mission* 78 (July 1988), 390–97. Thomas argues that Kraemer did well to argue that the revelation in Christ must be incarnated and adapted in non-Western cultures but that he did not win the day at Tambaram, with the consequence that the "antiadaptionists" won out. This lost battle marginalized Asian Christians and hindered their progress toward the articulation of an "authentic selfhood."

54. See Kraemer, *CMNCW*, 308–23.

55. Ibid., 318. Kraemer worries, however, about the limits of "translation." The use of improper terms and concepts can distort and confuse. Remembering that the "Christian truth as embodied in the revelation in Christ is incommensurable" (*CMNCW*, 326) with other religions, the missionary must use great care in translation and adaptation. In any event, the "real programme is not to *relate* the thought of Christianity to the thought of India or China or another civilization, but to *express* it through these different heritages" (*CMNCW*, 328).

Although Thomas claims that the "antiadaptionists" won the day at Tambaram ("An Assessment," 390–97), it seems as though Kraemer's position on adaptation found general acceptance at Tambaram, for in the Findings of Section I, the view is expressed that "witnesses for Christ must have a deep and sincere interest in the religious life of those among whom they are sent." Non-Western churches must, accordingly, draw sustenance from both the Christian tradition and indigenous traditions: "the Gospel should be expressed and interpreted in indigenous forms." See "The Faith by Which the Church Lives," in Paton, *Authority of the Faith*, 185–86.

56. Kraemer, *CMNCW*, 433. Given Kraemer's sense that *The Christian Message* was but an incomplete sketch, one contributor to the post-Tambaram discussions sought to supplement Kraemer's position in his tome, which he generally endorsed, by providing biblical warrant for his position. See Karl Hartenstein, "The Biblical View of Religion," in Paton, *Authority of the Faith*, 117–36. Relatedly, see Karl Ludvig Reichelt, "The Johannine Approach," in Paton, *Authority of the Faith*, 83–93. Kraemer, however, did not regard Reichelt as a theological ally. See Kraemer, *RCF*, 225.

57. See Kraemer, *RCF*, 231–33. See also Kraemer, *Van godsdiensten en menschen*, 28–9, 38f; Hallencreutz, *New Approaches to Men of Other Faiths*, 30–39.

58. See Paton, *Authority of the Faith*. Tambaram Madras Series I, ed. Wm. Paton (London: Humphrey Milford/Oxford University Press, 1939). As noted in the foregoing, this volume also contains Kraemer's essay "Continuity or Discontinuity." For accounts of the reactions at and after Tambaram, see Bavinck, *De boodschap*, 6, 77–78; Kraemer, *Van godsdiensten en menschen*, 23, 28–29, 38f.

59. See Kraemer, "Continuity or Discontinuity," 7.

60. T. C. Chao, "Revelation," in Paton, *Authority of the Faith*, Tambaram Madras Series I, ed. Wm. Paton (London: Humphrey Milford/Oxford University Press, 1939), 28f.

61. Chao, "Revelation," 37.

62. See A. G. Hogg, "The Christian Attitude to Non-Christian Faith," in Paton, *Authority of the Faith*, Tambaram Madras Series I, ed. Wm. Paton (London: Humphrey Milford/Oxford University Press, 1939), 94–116. On Kraemer's view of Hogg as his most perceptive critic, see Kraemer, *RCF*, 226; Lesslie Newbigin, "A Sermon Preached at the Thanksgiving Service for the Fiftieth Anniversary of the Tambaram Conference of the International Missionary Conference," *International Review of Mission* 78 (July 1988), 328. Hogg apparently changed his mind about his criticisms of Kraemer in later years. See Stanley Samartha, "Mission in a Religiously Plural World: Looking beyond Tambaram 1938," *International Review of Mission* 78 (July 1988), 314 n. 12. Further on the Kraemer-Hogg debate, see Jathanna, *Decisiveness*, 275–79; Lesslie Newbigin, "Christ and the World of Religions," *Churchman* 97/1 (1983), 16–30.

63. Hogg, "Christian Attitude to Non-Christian Faith," 96.

64. Ibid., 99.

65. Ibid., 115–16. On Kraemer's response to Hogg, see *RCF*, 225–28. The Findings of Section V indicate the disagreement at Tambaram on the question of the presence of revelation in non-Christian religions. See "The Witness of the Church in Relation to Non-Christian Religions, the New Paganisms, and the Cultural Heritage of the Nations," in Paton, *Authority of the Faith*, 193–94.

66. See Walter Marshall Horton, "Between Hocking and Kraemer," in Paton, *Authority of the Faith*, 144–45.

67. Horton, "Between Hocking and Kraemer," 147.

68. Ibid.

69. H. H. Farmer, "The Authority of the Faith," in Paton, *Authority of the Faith*, 150–56. Farmer also discusses a third sense of the term that is uniquely Christian in application, namely, fulfillment of divine promises and preparatory activity. See "Authority of the Faith," 155–56. On Kraemer's view that Christ negates and cancels human religious striving, it is tempting to conclude that, like Barth, he has in mind a kind of Hegelian *Aufhebung*, which involves both cancellation *and* elevation. See Barth, "The Revelation of God as the Abolition [*Aufhebung*] of Religion," *Church Dogmatics*, I/2, 280–361. Further on this matter, see Aagaard, "Revelation and Religion," 148–85.

70. Farmer, "Authority of the Faith," 157–62.

71. For Kraemer's retrospective analysis of the reactions to *CMNCW* at Tambaram, see *RCF*, 221–33. Kraemer admits that "I certainly owed my readers a more elaborate exposition and account of the reasons for my point of view than I gave in the [Tambaram] book" (*RCF*, 232). He also contends that his objectivist critics at Tam-

baram held positions that were "philosophically naive and theologically inadmissible" (*RCF*, 145).

72. Kraemer, *RCF*, 8. For sample, relatively immediate, postpublication reactions to *Religion and the Christian Faith*, see Wilhelm Andersen, "Dr [*sic*] Kraemer's Contribution to the Understanding of the Nature of Revelation," *The International Review of Missions* 46 (Oct. 1957), 361–71; Kenneth Cragg, "Hearing by the Word of God," *The International Review of Missions* 46 (July 1957), 241–51. While Andersen is generally appreciative of *Religion and the Christian Faith*, Cragg calls it "a book of . . . erudition and . . . exasperation" (241), "magisterial and disconcerting" (242). It should be noted that some authors see a change of stance on Kraemer's part from *The Christian Message* to *Religion and the Christian Faith* (a view not endorsed by Kraemer or by the present author). See Anderson, "Religion as a Problem for the Christian Mission," 104–5; Hallencreutz, *Kraemer Towards Tambaram*, 13; Walter Marshall Horton, "Tambaram Twenty-Five Years and After," *Philosophy, Religion, and the Coming World Civilization: Essays in Honor of William Ernest Hocking*, ed. Leroy S. Rouner (The Hague: Martinus Nijhoff, 1966), 231.

73. Kraemer, *RCF*, 6.

74. See Ibid., 18. Significant portions of *Religion and the Christian Faith* are dedicated to an assessment of the value and place of "the science of religion" and the philosophy of religion as well as a justification of a theological assessment of religion. See Kraemer, *RCF*, 35–95.

75. Ibid., 139.

76. See ibid., 139–99, 356–58. Kraemer's treatment of Barth, "this most pugnacious theological giant of modern times" (186), reveals great appreciation for the Swiss theologian's redirection of the course of modern Protestant theology. That said, however, Kraemer indicates a series of criticisms: Barth's emphasis on the sovereignty of God seems "artificial, somehow unreal, convulsive and overdone" (192); Barth's "repetitious pounding away . . . becomes oppressive" (192); and the religions of the world "fail to get a square deal" (193), owing to Barth's oversimplified verdict about something rather more complex: "One does not feel that this is dialectical theology!" (193).

77. Ibid., 237. As noted earlier, Kraemer does not centrally employ the much-maligned term *biblical realism* in his post-Tambaram writings.

78. Ibid., 251–52.

79. Ibid., 253.

80. Ibid., 293–308.

81. Ibid., 309.

82. Ibid., 310.

83. Ibid., 311.

84. Ibid., 313.

85. Ibid., 338.

86. Ibid., 338. See Kraemer, *CMNCW*, 128.

87. Kraemer, *RCF*, 341.

88. Ibid., 345. Kraemer pleads for the abandonment—or at least the severe qualification—of several other problematic terms used to think about Christianity's relationship to other religions, including *continuity*, *fulfillment*, and *preparation*. See Krae-

mer, *RCF*, 342–52. On the one case in which these terms could properly be used, that is, in the case of Israel, see Kraemer, *RCF*, 381–83.

89. Ibid., 353.

90. Ibid.

91. Ibid.

92. Ibid., 354.

93. Ibid., 373.

94. Ibid.

95. See Hendrik Kraemer, *Why Christianity of All Religions?* trans. Hubert Hoskins (Philadelphia: Westminster Press, 1962). In what follows, this work is referred to as *WCAR*. The original Dutch edition (*Waarom nu juist het Christendom?*) was published in 1960 and began life as a series of radio broadcasts in The Netherlands.

96. See Kraemer, *WCAR*, 15–17, 72–85.

97. Ibid., 89, 90.

98. Ibid., 93. Kraemer continues: In the light of Christ, other religions are seen to be "religions of self-redemption, self-justification and self-sanctification" (*WCAR*, 94). Revelation shows religions to be a *"fleeing* from God" (*WCAR*, 95 n. 1).

99. Ibid., 99–103.

100. Ibid., 104.

101. Ibid., 114.

102. Ibid., 116–17.

103. See *International Review of Mission* 78 (July 1988). For the account of the discussion, see Jean Stromberg, "Christian Witness in a Pluralistic World: Report on a Mission/Dialogue Consultation," *International Review of Mission* 78 (July 1988), 412–36, 449. Stromberg notes that there were sometimes tensions in the discussions (434), a point also made by Lamin Sanneh, who attended the 1988 conference (comment made by Professor Sanneh on June 30, 2000 in a summer seminar in Christian scholarship, "Christianity as a World Religion," held at Calvin College in Grand Rapids, Mich.).

104. Carl Hallencreutz, "Tambaram Revisited," 347. It bears pointing out once again that unlike both Edinburgh 1910 and Jerusalem 1928, which were dominated by Western Christians, half of Tambaram 1938's participants were Eastern Christians. See Van Leeuwen, *Hendrik Kraemer*, 105.

105. See note 5.

106. Samartha, "Mission in a Religiously Plural World," 311. Jathanna warns against two oversimplified historical assessments of Tambaram 1938. In the first case, Tambaram is wrongly interpreted as having presented simply a negative view of religions, in contrast with Jerusalem 1928's simply positive view (Jathanna sees both Jerusalem and Tambaram as correctives). In the second case, Tambaram is incorrectly depicted as the antithesis of interreligious dialogue. See Jathanna, *Decisiveness*, 493–511 and especially 509–11.

107. See Samartha, "Mission in a Religiously Plural World," 311–24. Further on Kraemer and Samartha, see J. A. B. Jongeneel, "Hendrik Kraemer and Stanley J. Samartha, Two Adverse Brothers," *Bangalore Theological Forum* (Jan.–June 1988), 3–15.

108. See Wilfred Cantwell Smith, "Mission, Dialogue, and God's Will for Us," *International Review of Mission* 78 (July 1988), 360–74 (the quotation is found on 372).

Smith's view that there is a divide between Kraemer's theology and his practice—that is, the view that deep down he knew better than he argued theologically—has also been expressed by Gualtieri, who indicates that late in his life Kraemer had doubts about his exclusivistic view of non-Christian religions. See Gualtieri, "Failure of Dialectic," 286 n. 25. Hoedemaker, however, disputes the view that there was a fundamental divide in Kraemer regarding his beliefs and his practice. See Hoedemaker, "Kraemer Reassessed," 48–49.

109. See Diana Eck, "The Religions and Tambaram: 1938 and 1988," *International Review of Mission* 78 (July 1988), 375–89 (the quotation is on 384).

110. Lesslie, Newbigin, "A Sermon Preached at the Thanksgiving Service," 327. This essay was reprinted in *Missionalia* 16/2 (Aug. 1988), 79–85, as "The Significance of Tambaram—Fifty Years Later." Newbigin's assessment of Kraemer, however, is not without reservation and criticism. Elsewhere, he cross-examines Kraemer on a number of critical issues raised by Jathanna and faults Kraemer for inadequately dealing with the Bible's teaching concerning election. See Newbigin, "Christ and the World of Religions," 20–29.

111. Newbigin, "A Sermon Preached at the Thanksgiving Service," 328.

112. See: Philip A. Potter, "WCC and the World of Religions and Cultures," *Ecumenical Review* 41/1 (Jan. 1989), 4–12; D. C. Mulder, "The Dialogue between Cultures and Religions: Kraemer's Contribution in the Light of Later Developments," *Ecumenical Review* 41/1 (Jan. 1989), 13–19.

113. See S. Wesley Ariarajah, "Christian Minorities amidst Other Faith Traditions: A Third-World Contribution," *Ecumenical Review* 41 (Jan. 1989), 20–29. For assessments from the other two "worlds," see: C. A. van Peursen, "Towards a Post-Secular Era: A First-World Contribution," *Ecumenical Review* 41 (Jan. 1989), 36–40; Adler, "Dialogue in the Second World," 30–35.

114. Hoedemaker, "Kraemer Reassessed," 41.

115. Ibid., 42. Potter makes a similar case in noting that "the content of Biblical realism ought to take into account the deep intent and scope of God's purpose for human beings in creation." See: Potter, "WCC and the World of Religions and Cultures," 10. In the concluding section of this chapter, I argue that Hoedemaker and Potter are essentially right in this claim.

116. See Ariarajah, "Christian Minorities amidst Other Faith Traditions," 27; Gualtieri, "Failure of Dialectic," 274, 279–81; Hoedemaker, "Kraemer Reassessed," 42; J. A. B. Jongeneel, "Christianity and the -Isms: A Description, Analysis, and Rethinking of Hendrik Kraemer's Theology of Missions," *Bangalore Theological Forum* (Jan.–June 1988), 39–41; Mulder, "Dialogue between Cultures and Religions," 17.

117. See Kraemer, *RCF*, 358–59. Jathanna enumerates several criticisms of Kraemer's Christocentric position, including Kraemer's neglect of a discussion regarding the historical character and importance of the Christ event and his failure to pay sufficient attention to the content of the revelation in Christ. See Jathanna, *Decisiveness*, 248–52. See also Newbigin, "Christ and the World of Religions," 20–29.

118. Jathanna makes the point that Kraemer's Christology remains insufficiently articulated. See Jathanna, *Decisiveness*, 70. Accordingly, he attempts to formulate Kraemer's doctrines of God and Christ. See Jathanna, *Decisiveness*, 70–86.

119. Some of Kraemer's interpreters have divined an Islamic—that is to say, a

rigorously monotheistic and undifferentiated—view of God in his thought. See Jathanna, *Decisiveness*, 79 n. 6. Instructively, Farmer points out Kraemer's tendency to
view God as demanding and sovereign, rather than as loving and fatherly. See Farmer, "Authority of the Faith," 159–61. Relatedly, Bavinck takes issue with Kraemer's
voluntaristic doctrine of God: what is revealed for Kraemer is not the being of God
but the will of God. Bavinck finds fault with such an ontological-voluntarist distinction (although he does not argue, as I would, that what is revealed first and foremost
is neither the divine being nor the divine will but divine life and personhood). See
Bavinck, *De boodschap*, 101–7.

120. As Masatoshi Doi has pointed out, if something of the divine "shines
through" in the religions of the world, there must be revelation in them. See Masatoshi Doi, "From Tambaram to Kandy," *Japan Christian Quarterly* (Summer 1969), 144.
See also Gualtieri, "Failure of Dialectic," 284.

121. See Karl Barth, *Church Dogmatics. The Doctrine of the Word of God*, I/1, trans.
and ed. G. W. Bromiley and T. F. Torrance (Edinburgh: T. & T. Clark, 1975), 47–347.

122. Gualtieri has carefully examined Kraemer's dialectical attitude to non-
Christian religions. He argues that Kraemer's evaluation of religions, because of his
view that they are rooted not in revelation but in the human quest for transcendence,
is finally not dialectical but repudiational. See Gualtieri, "Failure of Dialectic," 274–90.

123. This is an argument that cannot be systematically made here in plenary
fashion. See the following loci classici in Christian scripture: Genesis 1–2; Psalm 19;
Acts 14: 8–20; Acts 17: 16–34; Romans 1: 18–25. See also the following theological
positions articulated throughout the Christian tradition: Justin Martyr, "The First
Apology," *Early Christian Apologists*, Library of Christian Classics 1, trans. and ed.
C. C. Richardson (Philadelphia: Westminster Press, 1943), 242–89; Thomas Aquinas,
Summa Theologica, trans. Fathers of the English Dominican Province, vol. 1 (West-
minster, Md.: Christian Classics, 1981), Part 1, Question 2 (see especially 1a.2.3); John
Calvin, *Institutes of the Christian Religion*, trans. F. L. Battles, ed. J. T. McNeill, Library
of Christian Classics, 20 (Philadelphia: Westminster Press, 1960), 35–69; Brunner,
"Nature and Grace" in Brunner and Barth, *Natural Theology*, 16–60; John Paul II,
Crossing the Threshold of Hope, ed. V. Messori (New York: Alfred A. Knopf, 1997),
77–83.

124. For a brief discussion of these terms, see Plantinga, *Christianity and Plurality*, 5–6.

125. Lesslie Newbigin argues in a general way along these lines. For representatives of the three positions, he chooses Kraemer, Rahner, and Hick. See Lesslie Newbigin, *The Gospel in a Pluralist Society* (Grand Rapids, Mich.: Wm. B. Eerdmans,
1989), 171–83.

126. Kraemer's theocentrism, it should be noted, is rather different than the
theocentrism espoused by John Hick. For Kraemer, theocentrism is the inverse of an-
thropocentrism and is defined by Christocentrism; for Hick, theocentrism is the inverse of Christocentrism and is therefore defined by non-Christocentrism. Hick, in
fact, argues that Christocentric approaches to the non-Christian religions do not allow
for other manifestations of the divine in the religions. See John Hick, *God Has Many
Names: Britain's New Religious Pluralism* (London: Macmillan, 1980), 5–6, 51–52. See
also Jongeneel, "Christianity and the -Isms," 36–39.

127. A phenomenological-theological approach would seem to be hospitable to "adaptation" and "translation" in the work of missions—another check in the plus column for Kraemer. However, Kraemer's general emphasis on discontinuity, hesitation about general revelation, and insistence on Christic revelation—which opens him to possible accusations of "positivism of revelation" (*Offenbarungspositivismus*), to employ a designation that Bonhoeffer coined in his critique of Barth (see Dietrich Bonhoeffer, *Letters and Papers from Prison*, enlarged ed., ed. Eberhard Bethge (New York: Macmillan, 1972), 280, 286, 328)—would seem to militate against adaptation or translation, which surely must presuppose some continuity as well as the existence of general revelation. Kraemer's commitment to missions, it should be added, did not prevent him from seeing or stating the importance of interreligious dialogue, which he took to be pressing in the increasingly religiously pluralistic world of the twentieth century. See Kraemer, *World Cultures and World Religions*.

128. See Jathanna, *Decisiveness*, 253–54, 257–58; Newbigin, "Christ and the World of Religions," 20; Plantinga, *Christianity and Plurality*, 13–24; Potter, "WCC and the World of Religions and Cultures," 10.

129. Perry, "Significance of Hendrik Kraemer," 39.

9

Contextual Theology:
The Last Frontier

Wilbert R. Shenk

Unlike many fields of Christian theological thinking, the theology of mission has not had a sustained and unbroken chain of development. Neither the British, the dominant mission-sending country until 1900, nor the Americans, the largest sending country in the twentieth century, saw the need for an explicit mission theology until after 1945. Even the concept of mission theology had not yet been developed. Missions were the premier channel for Christian activism, and from the time of William Carey they had captured support by staying focused on carrying out the Great Commission. They concentrated on the continuous mobilization of ever more missionaries to evangelize and found churches throughout the world. The call to missionary service was made in terms of "motives" that would inspire men and women to offer to go and stimulate others to provide financial and moral support.[1]

The great changes in world affairs following World War II decisively reshaped the outlook for missions. The European colonial empires were about to be dismantled. Western and Soviet blocs arose and were soon locked into the Cold War. A bombshell struck the missionary enterprise in 1949 when the Communists came to power in China and began expelling all missionaries and other foreigners. Many people said that the "closing of China" signaled that Christian missions to China had failed.[2] Elsewhere, as national movements pushed for independence, the role of Western missions came under question as well. Mission-founded churches wanted their independence, but they also asked to be regarded as full partners in future missionary witness. This new climate and the new questions it prompted called for soul searching, self-criticism, and theological reflection. More than ever, it seemed, the Christian mission had to have an adequate theological foundation.

The International Missionary Council (IMC) took the lead in developing mission theology after 1945. This work was carried out in two ways. First, IMC assemblies in 1947, 1952, and 1958 featured substantive addresses on theological themes.[3] Second, the IMC initiated several research projects that contributed to mission theology. In 1954 the IMC introduced a Research Pamphlet series for the purpose of stimulating theological and missiological exploration. Wilhelm Andersen's essay in this series, *Towards a Theology of Mission,* summarized the key insights from the 1952 Willingen (Netherlands) Assembly that demonstrated the need for an explicit and articulated theology of mission. In 1962 a new series, "Foundations of the Christian Mission: Studies in the Gospel and the World," was launched with publication of two important books: Johannes Blauw's *The Missionary Nature of the Church* (1962), a biblical survey, and D. T. Niles's, *Upon the Earth* (1962), a theology of mission.[4] At this time, Gerald H. Anderson also edited a volume, *The Theology of the Christian Mission* (1961),[5] consisting of essays by eminent scholars on a range of biblical and theological topics relating to mission. Important as these initiatives were, the focus remained on the *Western* mission sending, what D. T. Niles aptly called the overshadowing "Westernity of the base."[6]

The second stage of this rethinking overlapped with the first. By the 1950s, various mission-founded churches in Asia, Africa, and Latin America were beginning to wrestle with the future of theological education in societies undergoing rapid transition. India, Pakistan, and Indonesia had each gained their independence from European colonial powers in the late 1940s, and many more nations would soon follow suit. Countries moving from being colonies to independent nations now faced the immense task of nation building.[7]

The churches in these new nations confronted two challenges: (1) to define their responsibility as formers of citizens ready to contribute to national construction and (2) to develop a theology rooted in their own context that could guide them in their lives and witness. The only theology available had been forged in the West and bequeathed to them by missionaries. It is no surprise that nineteenth-century Western theologians had not anticipated the urgent issues these churches now faced. Questions of identity and witness were uppermost in the minds of perceptive church leaders. Furthermore, the theological training in all these countries was thoroughly Western. What was needed, however, was an appropriate theology combined with new approaches to theological education. Both theology and theological training had to be attuned to the historical and cultural context of the church.

A key figure in this effort to reconceptualize the task of theology and adapt theological training to this new reality was Shoki Coe (who was known as C. H. Hwang until 1966), a leader of the Taiwanese Presbyterian Church and principal of Tainan Theological College since 1948. Over the course of a decade, Coe wrestled with these problems. Finally, he came to the insight that only a theology that emerged out of the life context of a particular church could be life giving and support that church in its witness to the world. This conceptual shift effectively repudiated the *modern* notion that Western knowledge, including theology, was universally valid. In 1966 Coe became director of the Theological Education Fund, an ecumenical agency for the development of theological schools and programs of study in the non-Western world, with major funding from the Rockefeller philanthropies.[8] In his new role, Coe now had to grapple with these issues on a global scale.

In 1972 Coe introduced the terms *contextuality* and *contextualization* to describe this way of doing theology.[9] This new conceptualization and terminology triggered a massive reorientation of Christian thought, both East and West, North and South, truly a paradigm shift. In the following years, all the major Christian traditions have grappled with the implications of *contextualization*, the term used by Protestants, and *inculturation*, the term preferred by Roman Catholics.[10] The concept has proved to be as relevant to the church and theology in the West as anywhere else.[11] As modern culture is evolving toward a new stage—usually called postmodernity—increasingly it is recognized that Western theology, developed in response to the realities of a Christendom that no longer exists, must adapt to this changing culture if it is to serve the church.

My argument is that the movement to develop contextual theology could emerge only outside the historic Christian "heartland" under non-Western leadership. Theology in the West had long ago lost its missionary dimension; it was oblivious to how fully embedded in Western culture it was. Although missionaries were well aware of the gathering forces of nationalism in the early twentieth century, they seemed to be paralyzed by conflicting loyalties—to the West and to the emerging churches they served. Some saw the need to prepare for the inevitable ending of Western colonialism by handing over leadership to indigenous people. Rarer were those missionaries who understood that for these churches to thrive they needed to develop a theology that responded to their particular historical, political, and cultural contexts. In effect, Western missions had reserved the most critical issue for the final phase of the modern missions movement.

The "indigenous church" ideal, introduced in the mid-nineteenth century by Henry Venn and Rufus Anderson, was exhausted. Proponents of contextual theology recognized that a fresh start had to be made if the churches in Asia, Africa, Latin America, and the South Pacific were to get fresh purchase on their reality. They urgently needed to establish their authenticity as Christians and as members of their culture. To do this, they had begun developing a missionary theology that would support them in their continuing witness in their societies.[12]

This quest for authenticity in Latin America, Africa, Asia, and the Pacific has been taking place at the same time that Western Christendom has been disintegrating. The steady decline in the number of Christian adherents in Europe and the marginalization of religion from public life throughout the West over the past generation has left no doubt as to the drastic changes that have taken place in the historical heartland of Christianity. The Western church has lost its authenticity for the opposite reason of the non-Western church. It has been suggested that the Western church is suffering from an advanced case of syncretism. The most promising remedy seems to be the church re-newed as a *missional* church whose identity is formed by a missionary theology. The rise of contextual theology out of the global East and South offers pow-erfully suggestive examples of an approach to theology that might better equip Western churches for mission in a post-Christendom era.

Twentieth-Century China: A Case Study

Shoki Coe's path-breaking teaching about the need for new Christian theolo-gies to arise out of the encounters of the gospel and non-Western cultures comes, of course, from a uniquely Chinese context. The story of Chinese Chris-tian leaders' engagement with these questions is the focus of this chapter (figure 9.1). It is set primarily in twentieth-century China with sideways glances at developments in other countries. By 1920 China had the largest number of foreign missionaries of any country, and China, the world's most populous nation, was in constant turmoil. It lurched from one political crisis to another until it reached a watershed with the Communist assumption of power in 1949. Inevitably, these political tensions spilled over into the churches and their related foreign missions.

Pre-Twentieth Century Background

Protestant missions emerged in the seventeenth century as modernity was dawning. The Enlightenment and the quickening development of scientific knowledge and technology had not yet added to the sense that Europeans could boast of a superior culture to that of Asia's ancient civilizations, but Europeans in the seventeenth and eighteenth centuries were busily engaged in geograph-ical exploration and in extending their trading operations into other parts of the world. From the seventeenth to the twentieth century, the assumption grew that Western culture was superior to others. By the mid-nineteenth century, if not before, growing Western economic, scientific, technological, and military power reinforced this presumed cultural superiority of the "Christian" West.

    Western people were insensitive to the deep resentment their attitude of superiority ignited in other peoples. A condescending and patronizing attitude is unfailingly corrosive, robbing those on whom it is bestowed of their dignity

FIGURE 9.1. China

and pride, and diminishing rather than enhancing their self-worth. Even when forward-looking mission theorists in the nineteenth century shifted from the *replication* model of mission, introduced in the seventeenth century to transplant Western Christendom in new lands, to the *indigenization* model, which called for the development of native Christianity, they failed to solve this problem. The new model still left the missionary—the foreign agent—in control.[13] Notwithstanding eloquent pronouncements about the importance of the "indigenous church," the model provided no real guidance in turning theory into practice, *for it never addressed the underlying issue of power*. Thus, when the communists defeated the Kuomintang and assumed control of the government of China in 1949, the main weapon they deployed against the Christian church was the charge that the Christian religion was merely a tool of foreign powers, and Christians were "lackeys" and "the running dogs" of capitalist interests. In the new China, it was asserted, one could not be both a loyal citizen and a Christian.

The Ambiguous Role of the Missionary in China

The Communists did not have to invent this idea, however. Resentment against foreign powers and suspicions that missionaries served as their cultural agents had a long history. It is difficult today to understand the extent to which in Chinese eyes the missionary had become a powerful symbol of foreign meddling in China's domestic affairs. After all, in the contemporary Western imagination, Christian missions were an enterprise of a fringe group of overly zealous and rather eccentric individuals. But from the Chinese viewpoint, the missionary put a face on the detested Western incursion into the Middle Kingdom. The basis for this image was established early in the nineteenth century.

Already at the time when Robert Morrison, the first Protestant missionary to China, arrived in Macau in 1807, the country was gripped by widespread instability and insecurity. The missionaries soon came to rely on the protection and intervention of their home governments to continue working in China. In 1868 Hudson Taylor, whose fledgling China Inland Mission had entered the country in 1865, established a station at Yangzhou. When the mission building was attacked by a mob, at Taylor's request the British government sent four gunboats to force the Chinese governor-general to take action against the local officials for failing to control the mob. Two years later, 19 foreigners were killed in an incident involving French Catholic missionaries at an orphanage at Tientsin. This outrage nearly triggered a war between France and China. In the aftermath, the French government imposed a settlement that included the execution of 18 Chinese.[14] Clearly, missions could command political and military resources when it served their interests.

The fact that Christian missions resorted to these tactics to protect their work in China put them under permanent suspicion. The failure of Western missions to recognize the nature and depth of the problem is reflected in the choice of banner under which missions to China operated through the late nineteenth and early twentieth centuries: "the Christian occupation of China." The unself-conscious use of a military metaphor to describe missionary activity suggested that Western missions operated according to the same calculus as Western governments and military. "To most Chinese," argues John King Fairbank, "Christian missionaries seemed to be the ideological arm of foreign aggression."[15]

Once established in China, Protestant missionaries soon involved themselves in the country's social, cultural, and political problems by advocating various reforms and developing an ever-expanding institutional infrastructure of schools, clinics, and hospitals according to Western ideals. This put them at odds with the traditional Confucian leadership. "To the scholar-gentry," historian Fairbank observes, "missionaries were foreign subversives, whose immoral conduct and teachings were backed by gunboats."[16] Measured by the number of converts gained—about 100,000 by 1900—the missionaries appeared to have made little impact on China's population of more than 400 million, but in cultural terms their influence was out of all proportion to their numbers.[17]

The Boxers

The Boxer Rising that ran from mid-June to August 14, 1900, brought the nineteenth century to a horrible end. The Boxer affair was fueled by deep antiforeign, antimissionary, and anti-Christian sentiment that had been seething for years. When the Boxers were finally routed, 250 foreigners, many of them missionaries, and thousands of Chinese Christians had been murdered across northern China.[18] The Boxer episode made it unmistakably clear that *missionary* Christianity had forged a contradictory identity in China.

One missionary eyewitness to the Boxers' action in Beijing, a young Anglican priest named Roland Allen, wrote an account titled *The Siege of the Peking Legations*.[19] He had observed at close range the hostility of the Boxers toward the Christian community and helped to care for victims of the violence. Allen was especially disturbed at the taunts thrown at Chinese Christians. He felt something was profoundly wrong that these believers would be called "foreigners" because of their faith in Jesus Christ. He became convinced that the "mission system" had created an unwarranted burden for Chinese Christians. In effect, Western missions had required Chinese converts to submit to cultural circumcision that, in turn, created a high barrier between them and their fellow Chinese.

A decade later in his seminal book, *Missionary Methods: St. Paul's or Ours?* Allen rendered a searching critique of modern missions. He noted that "three very disquieting symptoms" characterized the mission system: (1) mission Christianity remains "exotic," (2) these missions are dependent on foreign resources, and (3) "mission" Christianity looks the same the world over.[20] For Allen, the telling clue was that mission-sponsored churches everywhere exhibited dependency on the foreign missions. This relationship was shaped by the model and assumptions of the missions rather than by the cultures of the peoples among whom missionaries worked. And it created dependency on the mission rather than indigenous resources. He contrasted the modern missions system and its fruit with what he called the New Testament model, which treated each local church as a responsible faith community fully capable, under the Holy Spirit, of functioning as the Body of Christ in that place. Notwithstanding his penetrating analysis, Allen's contemporaries resisted his critique throughout his lifetime.

Rising Nationalism

Wherever Western powers had established colonies in Asia and Africa, nationalist movements such as the Indian Congress Party were springing up.[21] In

West Africa, Edward Wilmot Blyden promoted African nationalism and Pan-Africanism as a way of freeing Africa from Western domination.[22] William Wadé Harris, a Liberian prophet, preached his way across Côte d'Ivoire from 1913 to 1915. His message to the coastal peoples was to turn to the true and living God. He attracted such a following that the French colonial officials feared the political potential of such a grassroots movement and banned him permanently from the country.[23] Nationalist sentiment was on the rise in the Dutch East Indies and Sri Lanka as well.[24]

Although China was not colonized by any Western power per se, six nations—Russia, Japan, Great Britain, Germany, France, and Italy—had forced China to grant them "spheres of influence," a euphemism for trading enclaves over which they exercised control. In addition, American power was on the rise in East Asia. By 1900, the Manchu or Qing dynasty was crumbling, and revolutionary elements, inspired by political ideas from the West, were calling for a new kind of government based on democratic ideals, a modern constitution and self-government. Although some in the Qing regime recognized that reorganization of the system of governance was needed all the way from the local level to the top, this was countered by a strong conservative impulse to centralize power at the top. Even so, the increasingly enfeebled regime was unable to muster the resources needed to carry through any real reform.

The decade 1901–10 was a period of political confusion as the Qing Dynasty foundered. On 10 October 1911, a group of army officers revolted. In December, a republic was declared, and by February 1912 the Qing emperor had abdicated, making way for a new government to be established. But the situation remained unsettled with continuing power struggles between the president, Yuan Shikai, and the parliament. In 1913, the president dissolved parliament and assumed dictatorial powers. Upon Yuan's death in 1916, the country was plunged into another period of political chaos and insecurity. In the absence of a strong central government, warlords controlled much of China until 1923, when Sun Yat-sen set about organizing a new national government. Unfortunately, Sun died in 1925 before he could implement his reforms.

The next two years were a period of intense nationalism directed against Great Britain as the most visible imperial power. Fearing a new wave of anti-foreignism, several thousand missionaries deployed throughout China moved from the interior to Shanghai and other coastal cities.[25] In 1927, Chiang Kaishek finally emerged as nationalist leader.

Racism

With uncommon prescience, in 1868 Henry Venn, secretary of the Anglican Church Missionary Society, had warned that the specter of racism would rise to haunt missionaries in the future. Indeed, it would be a driving force in the nascent nationalist movements. Venn's concern was soon eclipsed by the growing enthusiasm for "scientific" ideas of race sponsored by proponents of evolution.[26]

More than 40 years later, addressing the World Missionary Conference at Edinburgh in 1910, V. S. Azariah, soon to be the first Indian bishop in the Anglican Church, said: "The problem of race relationships is one of the most serious problems confronting the Church today."[27] He asserted that the power and integrity of the gospel were being put at risk by behavior on the part of both Westerners and others that betrayed gospel ideals. "The burden of my message is that . . . the relationship too often is not what it ought to be, and things must change, and change speedily, if there is to be a large measure of hearty co-operation between the foreign missionary and the Indian worker."[28] In this constructive but forceful speech, Azariah pleaded that the issue be taken seriously by all concerned.

In the event, the momentum generated at Edinburgh 1910 was largely stalled by the outbreak of war in Europe. Only after the end of World War I did missionary leaders regroup and follow through on important initiatives proposed at Edinburgh.

At its founding meeting in 1921, the International Missionary Council instructed J. H. Oldham, as a part of his duties as secretary, to devote time to the study of race relations. Oldham's book, *Christianity and Race Relations* was published in 1924.[29] He observed that the present situation stemmed from the fact that since 1492 European peoples had been extending themselves and their interests into other parts of the world on a growing scale. But by the turn of the twentieth century, Oldham noted, a tide could be observed flowing in the opposite direction, and Western hegemony was being relativized. The Japanese had defeated Russia and the Ethiopians had routed the Italians. "No longer was the European to be regarded as invincible. . . . The day of his unquestioned supremacy was over."[30] Oldham believed that the key question was how the various races of the world could live together harmoniously. The old power imbalance had to be redressed.

Well aware that he was not writing in a historical vacuum, Oldham warned, "Doctrines of racial domination are being sedulously preached by writers whose books have an extensive circulation."[31] Theories of race that would be foundational to the National Socialism propounded by Adolf Hitler and to the policy of apartheid in South Africa were being vigorously promoted. Over and against such ideas Oldham proposed a Christian view that accepted the primacy of the kingdom of God, God's love for every person, and the calling of the Christian to follow God in loving and serving all.[32]

The *International Review of Missions*, of which J. H. Oldham was editor, regularly featured articles and reviews that dealt with race, imperialism, and nationalism. D. D. T. Jabavu, from South Africa, observed, "The aboriginal black people of South Africa have not remained unaffected by the general world movement of awakening race-consciousness that is stirring all colored peoples in Japan, China, Egypt, the United States and the British West Indies."[33] Jabavu reported a disturbing trend on both sides of the color line: "White men both locally and in Britain have become hardened, while on the other hand the black man himself, under the guidance of an ambitious younger generation, has developed intelligence and some feeling of independence that has made him less easy of management." He forecast that "some ugly collision between white and black" would occur unless a change of attitudes was introduced.[34] Here the question of race could not be separated from social justice, politics, and the rights of self-determination. Jabavu credited World War I with awakening race consciousness in Africans, for they now saw how fallible the nations of Europe were. One evidence of this freedom to pursue an independent line was "the spread of religious separatist movements."[35] He reported a total of 106 African-initiated churches that had been registered with the government with names such as Bethesda Zion Apostolic, African United Gaza, Natural Church of Ethiopia, Pentecostal Holiness, and Christian Catholic Church in Zion. Jabavu concluded: "The European races of South Africa will solve their Native Question when, and probably only when, they as a whole make a serious endeavor to deal with the Bantu people in a sympathetic spirit, which in the last analysis is founded on our Lord's gospel dictum 'Love thy neighbor as thyself.'"[36]

Shortly thereafter, reports began to come from the Congo of a new "prophet movement" that started in May 1921 and was affecting Roman Catholic and Protestant missions. A secretary of the British Baptist Missionary Society wrote a report on the movement that he believed demonstrated "a new and growing sense of solidarity and African race consciousness which must be reckoned with . . . [and] because of the indication found in it of a desire for leadership."[37] This was an account of the initial ministry of Simon Kimbangu, a movement that quickly became a threat both to colonial and ecclesiastical authorities. This "indigenous" Christian movement revealed how wide was the gap between missionary Christianity and indigenous religiosity. But as the report makes clear, it also had to do with the desire of the Congolese to free themselves from European control and leadership. "It was suspected that a connexion existed between this uprising and the general world-wide pan-African agitation."[38] The charismatic Kimbangu, who was attracting throngs of people, stirred anxiety on the part of the public officials, who feared this movement might turn into political revolt. But the report recognized the "evident revival of real religion throughout the whole of the Lower Congo region."[39]

The Turbulent Twenties

The 1920s were a critical decade for the churches in China. It was a period of ferment and rising expectations. With the Meiji restoration in 1868, Japan had made a fundamental decision to modernize by overhauling its government, economy, and educational systems based on Western science and technology while retaining its traditional cultural values. Many Chinese intellectuals hoped that China might pursue a similar course. In 1919 the American philosopher John Dewey visited China. A student of Dewey's at Columbia University, Hu Shi, was active in advocating the modernization of China. In 1921 British Fabian Socialist Bertrand Russell spent several months in China. "Both made a considerable impression on one wing of intellectuals, the middle-of-the-road liberals. . . . Chinese intellectuals to their left, however, were coming under a rival Western influence."[40] This competing influence was, of course, Marxism. It appeared that China was on the verge of moving in a new direction. But the political situation was volatile and the country on the brink of chaos.

National Christian Conference of 1922

In the aftermath of the Boxer affair in 1900, Chinese Christians had gone through deep soul searching. Fusan Zhao summed up the situation: "To Chinese Christians, the hundred years of western missions was a sufficient lesson for them to realize that the Church in China, if it was to survive, should sever herself from foreign missions backed up by unequal treaties and gunboats. As early as 1906, the Rev. Yu Kuo-chen of Shanghai started an independent Chinese church though it was only a tiny beginning."[41] This stream of independent churches would grow, especially after 1920, and influence the future shape of the church in China. At the same time, the majority of Chinese Christians continued their membership in the churches related to foreign missions.

In May 1922, the National Christian Conference convened a meeting of mission and church leaders from all over China in Shanghai.[42] Churches, missions, Christian universities and colleges, and the Young Men's and Young Women's Christian Associations all sent delegates. This was not a meeting of Chinese churches or of missions, like earlier conferences, but something far more representative. China was in a new situation, the participants recognized. "The past five or six years had brought world-wide and powerful influences making for the augmenting and intensifying of the spirit of nationalism in the Chinese Church."[43] This meeting was called out of a sense of urgency. "We do not want to build a Church that is foreign," said Dr. Chen Ching Yi in his keynote address, "but we must admit that there is still little or no sign that the Christian Church in China is becoming Chinese. The most serious aspect of this problem is not the dependence of the Chinese Church upon the liberality of Christians in other lands. *Its dependence upon the thoughts, ideas, institutions and methods of work of others is an even more difficult problem*" [emphasis added].[44] China could now boast of outstanding Christian scholars, medical doctors, and intellectuals, and they were embarrassed that the church continued to be regarded as foreign. In his opening address to the conference, Chen said, "Christianity in China is seriously handicapped at the present time by being regarded as a foreign religion."[45] This had become the burning concern.

Other Chinese church leaders as well as missionaries delivered plenary addresses. While all agreed that the "indigenous church" was the most important issue, the Chinese and missionary views did not coincide. Missionaries continued to express the hope that the Chinese would assume greater responsibility for making Christian institutions and churches self-supporting. Formally, the Chinese expressed their strong dissatisfaction with the denominationalism the missionaries had brought, and they voiced a desire to have a united church, but this scarcely concealed their impatience with continued missionary control of institutions and churches. In a forceful and eloquent concluding statement, the Chinese leaders said:

> We wish to voice the sentiment of our people that the wholesale, un-
> critical acceptance of the traditions, forms and organizations of the
> West and the slavish imitation of these are not conducive to the
> building of a permanent genuine Christian Church in China . . . the
> rapidly changing conditions of the country all demand an indige-
> nous Church which will present an indigenous Christianity, a Chris-
> tianity which does not sever its continuity with the historical
> churches but at the same time takes cognizance of the spiritual in-
> heritance of the Chinese races.[46]

This conference did advance the discussion but fell short when it came to proposing concrete actions. The conference unanimously elected Chinese officers to preside, and the issues of highest priority to Chinese Christians were the ones addressed. But one cannot escape the impression that the Chinese church leaders were too constrained by their polite manners to break new ground.

"Indigenous Church" Revisited

During the 1920s, one issue dominated the Christian conversation in China: the *indigenous church*. Magazines, journals, and books from this period are filled with discussions of how to make the church in China indigenous.[47] C. Y. Cheng spoke for many of his compatriots when he said: "Eventually there will be no foreign missions in China except those of the Chinese Church. . . . The sending and supporting of missionaries from the West can hardly be expected to continue as a permanent method." And yet the present arrangement was at odds with this vision of the future. Cheng said forthrightly, "The mission is still overshadowing the Church, but by rights it is the Church, and not the mission, that is the more permanent organization. *Today the mission holds the reins of the work and controls the policy*" [emphasis added].[48] The challenge was to find a way to break the old patterns in order to trigger the transformation that was patently required to move toward the ideal of a church in China no longer labeled "foreign."

As a secretary of the National Christian Council, C. Y. Cheng continued to wrestle with this question in an essay, "Some Thoughts regarding the Indigenous Church."[49] He suggested that over the past century, under missionary guidance, the church in China had moved through four stages: (1) cultivation of personal religion, (2) discovering and applying the social aspects of Christianity, (3) an emphasis on the church becoming self-reliant, and (4) the essential unity of all Christians in China and the need to discard Western denominationalism. The church in China had now reached the fifth stage: the quest to become "indigenous." Cheng observed that although Buddhism and Islam "are foreign in their origin, they are not generally regarded as foreign religions."[50] By contrast, Christianity alone continues to be regarded as foreign to China. For Christianity to get rid of this stigma, a new understanding had to be developed. In this regard, Christian history provided an important clue. The Christian faith had repeatedly moved and made its home in new cultural contexts without losing "its vital principles."[51] Rather than being fearful of such adaptation, the Chinese church should undertake this step courageously.

What have been the constraints on such a development in the modern period? Cheng never answers this question that is implied in all that he said. He is too restrained and courteous to offer specific recommendations. Instead, he proposed two leading questions: (1) "How can Christ be so presented as to ensure meeting the real needs of the East?" and (2) "How can the Church be so developed in China as to place direct responsibility for its development on the Chinese themselves?"[52] There is no evidence that any group undertook to address the challenge Cheng had laid down.

Perhaps the most useful contribution to this discussion was a brief article by Roland Allen, "The Essentials of an Indigenous Church."[53] Allen asks two fundamental questions: (1) What constitutes the church? and (2) What makes something indigenous? Based on the example of the apostolic church, Allen argues that the only kind of church planted by the apostles was "native Churches." Of course, a nonnative person was instrumental in planting the church, but from the outset the local group was answerable to no other authority than the Holy Spirit. In contrast to missionary practice today, in which baptizing new believers and administration of the sacraments had been reserved to the missionary, the apostle Paul was careful to avoid baptizing people lest they claim his authority over them. Thus, Allen answers his first question saying that as soon as a viable nucleus of believers is formed, a church is constituted. This body has the power of "recognizing its own members, admitting and excluding."[54] They are not answerable to any other authority.[55] With regard to the second question, Allen argued that "native" or indigenous means that the church is composed of and belongs to the people indigenous to a particular place. They are not under the administration or control of nonnatives.

The thrust of Allen's argument is that the modern missions system violated both of these principles. The missions system reserved to itself authority over the church—that is, setting the rules for who can be baptized, who can commune, and who is to be excommunicated. And missionaries, themselves nonnative, typically kept leadership in their own hands. The system maintained control over the church, a system that by the 1920s had been in place for a century.

Allen did not address the question that was most urgent: How does one transform a complex system of local churches, schools, universities, clinics, hospitals, and other programs from one controlled by nonnatives into an indigenous enterprise?[56] As is well known, he was rather dismissive of institutionalized programs. Nonetheless, these were an important and visible part of "the church in China" as it had developed and could not be ignored. Allen's diagnosis was perceptive, but he had no constructive suggestions for those who had to make the difficult decisions about the future of existing institutions and programs.

On balance, this outpouring of concern about the indigenous church did little to solve the perplexing problems facing both missions and churches. Nonetheless, an important alternative was developing.

The Indigenous Church Movement

As noted before, in 1906 Yu Kuo-chen founded an independent church, but this hardly constituted a movement. A new stage for indigenous Christian movements in China started around 1920. Almost immediately, these new groups were stigmatized by the established churches as schismatic and sectarian. The best known of these is the Little Flock—or Local Church movement—associated with Nee Tuo-sheng (Watchman Nee). Whatever their defects, these movements represent attempts to develop a fully indigenous Christian church with an appropriately contextualized theology. They understood themselves as overcoming the liabilities associated with the mission-founded churches.

Nee credited missionaries with nurturing him in the Christian faith in his youth, but he had grown disillusioned with the Methodist Church to which his family belonged because he perceived a lack of genuine spirituality. Nee became increasingly critical of the foreign missions and their related Chinese churches. Like many other Chinese Christians, he was troubled by Western denominationalism and the charge that the Christian faith was a foreign religion. Nee's relations with missionaries were marked by ambivalence. Clearly, he wanted to avoid falling into the same trap as the mission-related churches by coming under the sway of foreigners.

Nee was convinced that the mission-founded churches were compromised by their "foreignness" and lukewarm spirit. In other words, he saw the problem to be profoundly theological. Consequently, these churches could not respond to the spiritual needs of the Chinese people. For him the only answer was to establish a "wholly independent Chinese Christian movement by returning to a more simple New Testament form of Christianity."[57] Accordingly, Nee developed an ecclesiology that was nonhierarchical and local in organization. He wanted no name for his movement other than Christian Assembly in such-and-such a place. Each assembly practiced believers' baptism and observed the Lord's Supper weekly. Local assemblies had their own elders and were self-governing, self-supporting, and self-propagating. Nee taught that "the church has only one power, one authority, and one life, which is the Holy Spirit. . . . Where there is not the Holy Spirit, there is not the church."[58]

Watchman Nee was a powerful preacher and leader but is probably best known for his prolific theological writings, most of which were produced for the use of leaders and members in local assemblies. Although Nee had an idiosyncratic style, he saw his kind of biblical theology as attuned to the Chinese cultural context, on the one hand, and offering to the members of the assemblies resources for developing and sustaining a practical discipleship, on the other.

The long-term influence of these indigenous movements from the 1920s is reflected in the House Church Movement of post-1949 China. These churches had been taught to be self-reliant—not to depend on either organizational or physical structures—and to emphasize the inner life of faith of the believer.[59] Their continued existence despite intense persecution gives the lie to the charge that the Christian faith could not become indigenous in China.

Post-1949 China and Contextualization

The communist takeover in China in 1949 plunged Christian missions into a decade-long crisis. The maelstrom in which all foreigners, including several thousand missionaries, were arrested, interrogated, jailed, and expelled formed a major scene in the drama of the Cold War between the Communist bloc and the West. Equally devastating was the knowledge that thousands of Chinese Christians were being persecuted because of their friendships with Westerners and loyalty to Christ. Many predicted that this spelled the end of the church in China. At every opportunity, the Communists reminded Chinese Christians that they were disloyal to the motherland, and their ilk a disgrace. It was generally concluded that missions had failed in China. The China "debacle" could be attributed, a number of observers reflected, to the failure to develop an authentically indigenous church.[60]

Contextualization

There is a certain poetic justice, therefore, in the fact that the lead in developing a new theory for understanding the relationship between "gospel and culture" should come from Taiwan, where President Chiang Kai-shek had fled when the Chinese Communists wrested control from the Kuomintang in 1949. Here he set up the Republic of China (ROC).

Shoki Coe [C. H. Hwang], a Presbyterian Church leader in Taiwan, had been principal of Tainan Theological College since 1948.[61] He received his theological education in Great Britain, and his wife was British. The Taiwan Presbyterian Church early took positions critical of the ROC's policies with respect to its treatment of indigenous Taiwanese and found itself under government surveillance. Coe thus was acutely aware of the complexities of intercultural relations. For him, it was an existential reality.

Coe was active in international discussions of theological education that eventuated in the establishment of the Theological Education Fund under the International Missionary Council in 1957. Initially, this movement was preoccupied with the goal of raising the standards of theological education. But it soon became apparent that the nature of theological training had to be rethought in the light of the rapidly changing sociopolitical situation. In a major statement, "A Rethinking of Theological Training for the Ministry in the Younger Churches Today," Coe observed that theological educators were trying to serve "churches in lands undergoing revolutionary developments in almost every sphere of their existence." [62] Juxtaposed with this observation was the comment by Dean Liston Pope of Yale Divinity School, who on a visit to Asia praised the Asians for the good quality of their training programs but said that they were simply imitating the Western pattern. Coe acknowledged that this comment had provoked deep reflection. He feared that in their enthusiasm to improve programs, theological educators were unaware that "we are in fact *uncritically repeating* and *imitating* the particular pattern we happened to inherit" [emphasis in original].[63] Excellence in theological education is a laudable goal, provided that education is focused on the correct object. Coe was convinced that the so-called younger churches were facing a *new missionary situation* that the old curriculum could not address. He urged that what was needed was a leadership prepared to guide the churches' participation in the *missio Dei* in complex and revolutionary situations. Coe insisted that effective theological education should lead to "a deeper understanding of the Gospel in the context of the particular cultural and religious setting of the Church." Such an education, he believed, would lead the church to "a deeper understanding of itself as a missionary community sent into the world and to a more effectual encounter within the life of the society."[64]

Another senior Asian Christian leader, D. T. Niles, insisted that no one "should be invited to accept Jesus Christ without, at the same time and in the same act, accepting the world for which Jesus died and to which Jesus belongs as its Lord and Saviour."[65] A new angle of vision was emerging. The long-running struggle to become indigenous and throw off the yoke of colonialism was ending. It was time the churches shifted their efforts to the task of discovering their mission in this changed historical context.

In 1966 Shoki Coe moved to Great Britain, and that year he was appointed director of the Theological Education Fund. He now devoted his full attention to the reform of theological education. The life and ministry of the church must always be indigenous. What was needed, however, was a new way of thinking that shifted attention away from the institutional dimensions—finance, leadership, and outreach that the traditional "three-selfs" had emphasized—to relationships and processes.

Thinking and theorizing about the "indigenous church" had taken place during the colonial era. By definition, the West represented power and control. This power and control were expressed in multiple ways: political, military, economic, cultural, religious, and psychological. To become indigenous meant breaking free of Western control. By 1960, the decolonization process had been under way for more than a decade, and the remaining colonies were scheduled to receive their independence from the Western colonial powers, a transition largely completed by 1970. A parallel transfer was under way between Western missions and the churches of Asia, Africa, and the Pacific. The changed geopolitical and ecclesiastical situation had many implications for the churches, including the character of theological education. Now the focus of thought needed to shift from churches' independence from Western control to their ability to bring their message to bear on the culture in which they resided.

In 1972, Coe unveiled his new conceptualization of this way of thinking. He proposed that the key terms were *contextuality* and *contextualization*. To prepare the church to fully enter into the *missio Dei*, it must learn to carry out "that critical assessment of what makes the context really significant in the light of the *Missio Dei*." To think in context was to engage in "missiological discernment of the signs of the times." The locus of discernment and action was now lodged with the local church.[66]

The move Coe proposed would bring to a conclusion the process envisaged by Rufus Anderson and Henry Venn in the nineteenth century of developing fully indigenous churches. In this postcolonial time, churches urgently needed to be set free of the burdensome cultural baggage that had been imported and that proved to be a barrier to effective witness. This entailed a radical rethinking of the nature and purpose of the local church in its particular context. The theological precedent for contextualization is the Incarnation—God in Christ entering history and culture. The existential imperative is the *missio Dei*, in which the church is called to follow Jesus Christ in redemptive engagement with the world. Coe and his colleagues played an indispensable role in clearing the ground for the new stage. The important work of actually developing *contextual* theologies could now begin.

The Promise of Contextual Theology

The quest for authentic expressions of the Christian faith in Asia, Africa, Latin America, and the Pacific Islands on the part of the so-called younger churches is having a "reflexive" impact on the West as well. The *modern* concept of theology as universal theological knowledge independent of ecclesial context has been weighed in the balance and found wanting. The Western church has been floundering, insecure in its identity, timid and unsure of its witness. The Christian movement in other parts of the world is characterized by growth and vitality. Notwithstanding the fact that the church remains a distinct minority in most of these societies, it shows its greatest strength and vitality wherever it has achieved an identity that combines cultural authenticity and theological integrity. From this, there emerges dynamic missionary engagement and witness.

This clue is of singular importance for the future of the church in the West. A century ago, the German theologian Martin Kähler criticized Western theology for its lack of vitality. He pointed out that originally theology was simply—and profoundly—reflection on missionary action. Consequently, "mission is the mother of theology."[67] Two thousand years of Christian experience bears witness that only engaged theology empowers the church. The contextual theology movement is giving needed impetus for recovery of such a theology today.

NOTES

1. This can be documented by examining mission studies bibliographies for the twentieth century. Some Europeans were engaged in studies of mission theology by the 1920s, but these studies remained largely unknown in the English-speaking world. The fine book by Godfrey E. Phillips, *The Gospel in the World: A Re-Statement of Missionary Principles* (London: Duckworth, 1939) is representative of the Anglo-American approach up to 1945. The book contains a 10-page bibliography of "Suggestions for Further Reading" that covers the field of mission studies quite adequately.

2. A widely read postmortem was David Paton, *Christian Missions and the Judgement of God* (London: SCM Press, 1953).

3. See these conference-derived symposia: C. W. Ranson, ed., *Renewal and Advance: Christian Witness in a Revolutionary World* (London: Edinburgh House Press, 1948); Norman Goodall, ed., *Missions under the Cross* (London: Edinburgh House

Press and International Missionary Council, 1953); and Ronald K. Orchard, ed., *The Ghana Assembly of the International Missionary Council* (London: Edinburgh House Press and International Missionary Council, 1958).

4. Johannes Blauw, *The Missionary Nature of the Church: A Survey of the Biblical Theology of Mission* (New York: McGraw-Hill, 1962); Daniel Thambyrajah Niles, *Upon the Earth: The Mission of God and the Missionary Enterprise of the Churches* (New York: McGraw-Hill, 1962).

5. Gerald H. Anderson, ed., *The Theology of the Christian Mission* (New York: McGraw-Hill, 1961).

6. Niles, *Upon the Earth*, part 2, chap. 3.

7. Rajah B. Manikam, ed., *Christianity and the Asian Revolution* (Madras: Joint East Asia Secretariat of the International Missionary Council and the World Council of Churches, 1954), is one example of the kind of reflection that was being conducted at this time.

8. Christine Linemann-Perrin, *Training for Relevant Ministry: A Study of the Contribution of the Theological Education Fund* (Madras: Christian Literature Society, 1981).

9. Shoki Coe, "In Search of Renewal in Theological Education," *Theological Education* 9 (Summer 1973): 233–43, gives a concise presentation of the developing theory of contextualization.

10. John R. W. Stott and Robert T. Coote, eds., *Down to Earth: Studies in Christianity in Culture* (Grand Rapids, Mich.: Wm. B. Eerdmans Co., 1980), papers from the 1978 Willowbank consultation convened by the Lausanne movement, shows that evangelicals had embraced the key ideas of contextualization by this time. Indeed, Charles H. Kraft's *Christianity in Culture* (Maryknoll, N.Y.: Orbis Books, 1979) worked out a comprehensive theory of contextualization based on the concept of dynamic equivalence from the field of linguistics. Louis Luzbetak, SVD, *The Church and Cultures* (Maryknoll, N.Y.: Orbis Books, 1988), Aylward Shorter, WF, *Toward a Theology of Inculturation* (Maryknoll, N.Y.: Orbis Books, 1988); and Robert J. Schreiter, *Constructing Local Theologies* (Maryknoll, N.Y.: Orbis Books, 1984), represent major work by Catholic scholars on this theme.

11. Max L. Stackhouse, *Apologia: Contextualization, Globalization, and Mission in Theological Education* (Grand Rapids, Mich.: Wm. B. Eerdmans Co., 1988), reflects the ferment and discussion that took place among American theological schools in the 1980s in response to the challenge of contextualization and globalization to theological education.

12. Wilbert R. Shenk, "Recasting Theology of Mission: Impulses from the Non-Western World," *International Bulletin of Missionary Research* 25:3 (July 2001): 98–107, identifies four defining themes in the emerging missionary theology in Asia, Africa, and Latin America: Christological openness to culture, pneumatological drive, missional Christology, and missional ecclesiology.

13. Wilbert R. Shenk, *Changing Frontiers of Mission* (Maryknoll, N.Y.: Orbis Books, 1999), chap. 4, discusses these models in greater detail.

14. J. A. G. Roberts, *A Concise History of China* (Cambridge, Mass.: Harvard University Press, 1999), 196.

15. John King Fairbank, *China: A New History* (Cambridge, Mass.: Belknap Press, 1992), 221.

16. Ibid., 222.

17. Estimates of the number of Christians in China in 1900 range from 100,000 to more than 700,000. The larger figure usually is based on the total Christian community, whereas the lower figure is based on baptized membership. Even so, the way membership is counted varies from one tradition to another. Concerning the source of antimissionary sentiment, see Paul A. Cohen, *China and Christianity: The Missionary Movement and the Growth of Chinese Anti-Foreignism, 1860–1870* (Cambridge, Mass.: Harvard University Press, 1963), examines the roots of Chinese antipathy toward Christian missions.

18. Fairbank, *China*, 230–32; Diana Preston, *The Boxer Rebellion* (New York: Walker, 2000), Prologue, describes effectively the background of this episode.

19. Roland Allen, *The Siege of the Peking Legations, Being the Diary of the Rev. Roland Allen, with Maps and Plans* (London: Smith, Elder, 1901).

20. Roland Allen, *Missionary Methods: St. Paul's or Ours?* (Grand Rapids, Mich.: Wm. B. Eerdmans Co., 1962; orig. 1912), 141–42.

21. For a reflection on the Indian situation in the 1920s, see A. C. Cumaraswamy, "The Indian Christian Church and the Spirit of Nationality," *International Review of Missions* (hereafter *IRM*) 13:1 (Jan. 1924): 60–66.

22. Edward Wilmot Blyden (1832–1912), born at St. Thomas, Virgin Islands, migrated to Liberia in 1850; there he was ordained to the Presbyterian ministry. By 1886, frustrated by the arrogance of Christian missionaries, Blyden withdrew from the Presbyterian Church. He served the governments of Liberia and Sierra Leone as ambassador to the United Kingdom, published several books, and promoted the idea of "African personality" as the basis for developing African society. Blyden's legacy is competently summarized by Jehu Hanciles, *Euthanasia of a Mission: African Church Autonomy in a Colonial Context* (Westport, Conn.: Praeger, 2002), 164–70.

23. Gordon M. Haliburton, *The Prophet Harris* (London: Longmans, 1971), chap. 10; Sheila S. Walker, *The Religious Revolution in the Ivory Coast* (Chapel Hill: University of North Carolina Press, 1983), chap. 3; and David A. Shank, *Prophet Harris, The "Black Elijah" of West Africa*, abridged by Jocelyn Murray (Leiden: E. J. Brill, 1994), especially chap. 12.

24. N. Adriani, "Spiritual Currents among the Javanese," *IRM* 6:1 (Jan. 1917): 113–25; H. Kraemer, "Spiritual Currents in Java," *IRM* 13:1 (Jan. 1924): 101–8. The "currents" discussed combine religious, social, and political elements. For Sri Lanka (Ceylon), see H. W. Mediwaka, "Christianity and Nationalism," *IRM* 13:1 (Jan. 1924): 52–59.

25. Fairbank, *China*, 283.

26. Henry Venn, "Instructions to Missionaries, *Church Missionary Intelligencer* NS 4:10 (Oct. 1868), 316; Philip D. Curtin, "'Scientific' Racism and the British Theory of Empire," *Journal of the Historical Society of Nigeria* 2 (1960): 40–51.

27. V. S. Azariah, "The Problem of Co-Operation between Foreign and Native Workers," *World Missionary Conference: The History and Records of the Conference*, Vol. 9 (Edinburgh and London: Oliphant, Anderson and Ferrier, 1910), 306. For historical context, see Susan Billington Harper, *In the Shadow of the Mahatma* (Grand Rapids, Mich.: Wm. B. Eerdmans/London: Curzon Press, 2000), 147–49.

28. Azariah, "Problem of Co-Operation," 306.

29. J. H. Oldham, *Christianity and the Race Problem* (New York: George H. Doran Co., 1924). Cf. Robert E. Speer, *The Gospel and the World* (New York: Fleming H. Revell Co., 1919), chap. 3, "Christianity and the Race Problem"; Speer, *Of One Blood* (New York: Missionary Education Movement, 1924); Speer, *Race and Race Relations* (New York: Revell, 1924); Basil Mathews, *The Clash of Colour: A Study of the Problem of Race* (London: UCME, 1924).

30. Oldham, *Christianity and the Race Problem*, 3.

31. Ibid., 9.

32. Ibid., 18–20.

33. D. D. T. Jabavu, "Native Unrest in South Africa," *IRM* 11:2 (Apr. 1922): 249.

34. Ibid.

35. Ibid., 254. In fact, these movements were emerging in other parts of Africa. As noted previously, the Prophet Harris of Liberia had won a major following during his itinerant ministry from Liberia to Western Ghana, 1913–15, leading to his expulsion by the French colonial authorities. These movements consistently produced great anxiety on the part of governments.

36. Ibid., 259.

37. P. H. J. Lerrigo, M.D., "The 'Prophet Movement' in Congo," *IRM* 11:2 (Apr. 1922): 270. Cf. Marie-Louise Martin, *Kimbangu: An African Prophet and His Church* (Grand Rapids, Mich.: Wm. B. Eerdmans Co., 1975), chaps. 4–7.

38. Lerrigo, "'Prophet Movement,'" 275.

39. Ibid., 277.

40. O. Edmund Clubb, *Twentieth Century China* (New York: Columbia University Press, 1964), 110–11.

41. Fusan Zhao [Fu-San Chao], "The Penitence and Renewal of the Church in China," in David M. Paton, ed., *Essays in Anglican Self-Criticism* (London: SCM, 1958), 87.

42. Fletcher Brockman, "The National Christian Conference in China," *IRM* 11:4 (Oct. 1922): 502–14.

43. Ibid., 505.

44. Ibid., 506.

45. Ibid.

46. F. Rawlinson, Helen Thoburn, and D. MacGillivray, eds., *The Chinese Church as Revealed in the National Christian Conference* (Shanghai: Oriental Press, 1922), 502. Cf. The Secretaries, "The National Christian Council of China," *IRM* 13:1 (Jan. 1924): 90–100, a programmatic statement of the purpose and program of the council, in light of the National Christian Conference, on behalf of the Christian community.

47. I have made no systematic attempt to document this observation. It is based on a cursory survey of books and journals published during this period. Especially important sources are *The Chinese Recorder* and *International Review of Missions*. The 1922 conference proceedings is a special resource.

48. C. Y. Cheng, "The Development of an Indigenous Church in China," *IRM* 12:3 (July 1923): 384.

49. Cf. English summary by D. Willard Lyon, "Dr. C.Y. Cheng's Thoughts on the Indigenization of the Chinese Church," *The Chinese Recorder* 61:12 (Dec. 1925): 814–20.

50. Ibid., 816.

51. Ibid., 817.

52. Ibid., 818.

53. *The Chinese Recorder* 61:8 (Aug. 1925): 491–96. Reprinted from *World Dominion*.

54. Ibid., 493.

55. Allen lists five apostolic principles that ought to guide missionary practice in cultivating a truly indigenous church: (a) teach converts so they can readily apply in practice what they have been taught; (b) church organization must be culturally appropriate and supportable within the local economy; (c) the economic basis of the church must be attuned to the culture and economy of the people; (d) believers must be taught mutual responsibility and church discipline; and (e) the church should immediately begin exercising spiritual gifts in the service of Christ and the church. *Missionary Methods: St. Paul's or Ours?* (Grand Rapids, Mich.: Wm. B. Eerdmans Co., 1962), 196.

56. It is known that Roland Allen stirred deep anxiety and resentment among his contemporaries. The only written critique I have discovered is Kenneth Scott Latourette, "The Light of History on Current Missionary Methods," *IRM* 42:2 (Apr. 1953): 135–43. The normally irenic Latourette does not conceal his irritation with Allen.

57. Ya Ding Li, "The Distinctive Characteristics of the Little Flock Church," unpublished Ph.D. tutorial, Fuller Theological Seminary, 2002, 1, 3. I am indebted to Mr. Li for the use of his material in this section.

58. Ibid., 3.

59. Cf. Daniel H. Bays, "The Growth of Independent Christianity, 1900–1937," in Daniel H. Bays, ed., *Christianity in China: From the Eighteenth Century to the Present* (Stanford, Calif.: Stanford University Press, 1996), 307–16.

60. Paton, *Christian Missions and the Judgement of God*. When Deng Xiaoping opened the bamboo curtain in 1979, many were surprised to learn that a growing and vigorous Christian movement had survived 30 years of intense persecution in China.

61. Ray Wheeler, "The Legacy of Shoki Coe," *International Bulletin of Missionary Research* 26:2 (Apr. 2002): 77–80.

62. Shoki Coe, "A Rethinking of Theological Training for Ministry in the Younger Churches Today," *South East Asia Journal of Theology* 4:2 (Oct. 1962): 7–34.

63. Ibid.

64. Shoki Coe [C. H. Hwang], "In Search of Renewal in Theological Education," *Theological Education* 9 (Summer, 1973): 236.

65. Niles, *Upon the Earth*, 107.

66. Coe, "In Search of Renewal," 241.

67. Cited by David J. Bosch, *Transforming Mission* (Maryknoll, N.Y.: Orbis Books, 1992), 16.

Conclusion

The Current Transformation
of Christianity

Lamin Sanneh

The diverse, complex reality of the world Christian resurgence defies
any simple explanation or, indeed, any single cultural formulation,
as this book demonstrates. Yet at the time when the editors were
putting the final touches on this project, the cultural clash they predicted arose in sharp detail in the continuing controversy over homosexuality in the church in the West. Third World churches are being judged in the light of that issue. At its general convention in
Minneapolis in August 2003, the liberal leaders of the American
Episcopal Church, reacting to the conflict over its confirmation of an
Episcopal gay bishop, dismissed the dissenting Third World bishops
as backward, misguided, and ill informed.

That judgment, based on a single-issue view of religious teachings, tends, nevertheless, to carry over into a judgment about the
objectionable character of Christian expansion in its Third World
phase and suggests that collective cultural convictions carry the
weight and authority that doctrines once did. A logjam has been
broken, as one official at the Minneapolis meeting put it, and now
the church is freed to pursue unencumbered its mission of enlightened cultural assimilation. In the eyes of Third World critics, such a
position is, in effect, the virtual reinstatement of Western enlightened cultural finality for the universal theological finality of Jesus. In
this contest, the variety and scope of a resurgent Christianity have
become instances of cultural schism. Nonconforming churches in
the global South and East are deemed to have seceded from the
West's ascendant cultural mandate. Still, given the scale of the opposition, it is not clear whether cultural victory in line with prevailing

liberal sentiment, declared as God's answer to prayer, represents an advance for tolerance and unity in the church. Instead, it makes for a fault line on a global scale, a fact to which a new Western skepticism seems to point, as I shall describe below here.

At any rate, because a single-issue view of Christianity and a do-as-you-please religion is the way in which a post-Christian West prefers to characterize itself, we may take note of the variety of other cultural factors accompanying contemporary religious developments. To begin with, the revolution of information technology, including the Internet and satellite TV, has had a direct impact on the transmission of ideas and values, and world Christianity stands in the front line of this impact. The missionary impulse and religious itinerancy of an earlier age have coalesced with indigenous reception and adaptation to field Christianity in new cultural contexts and idioms. Christianity has become *ambicultural* as the faith of multiple language users straddling national and social boundaries.

Translation, Transmission, and the Variety of Culture

Cultural variety and plurality of idioms were inscribed into the original character of Christianity. The religion was a translated faith right from the start: the Gospels are not a verbatim transcript of the preaching and acts of Jesus. The Bible of Christianity is not the Qur'an, the untranslatable scripture of Islam. Through the Western missionary movement, this linguistic fact about Christianity turned it into an active translation force, resulting in the production of grammars, dictionaries, and primers of local languages for the purposes of Bible translation and religious instruction. Where it was undertaken, Bible translation became the vehicle of indigenous cultural development and the basis of establishing churches. Whatever the cosmopolitan predilection of new urban Christian groups in Africa, Asia, Latin America, and the Pacific, we should not overlook the hinterland and vernacular background of by far the largest proportion of the world's 2 billion Christians. Grammars and dictionaries existed at all for the great majority of the languages of the world, we should recall, by virtue of the missionary movement, and the effect of those linguistic resources on internal developments and options in the affected cultures cannot be emphasized enough.[1]

For coastal peoples, reports of the first encounters are similar in pattern to those of subsequent encounters with hinterland groups. The story is told about the New England missionary to Hawaii, Hiram Bingham (1789–1869), who, in 1822, barely two years after arriving on the islands, opposed the teaching of English to young people in spite of the great demand for it. His reason was that English was "a language unintelligible to their parents and [to] the mass of the community around them . . . and a perseverance in such an attempt would have given over the adult and aged population to incurable ignorance and degradation." Bingham had sounded the note of Hawaiian cultural authenticity.[2] In Hawaii, too, the changing face of Christianity assumed Hawaiian features.

Richard H. Dana Jr. noted in a report in the *New York Tribune* in June 1860 that the missionaries of the American Board of Commissioners for Foreign Missions had in 40 years taught the people of Hawaii "to read and write, to cipher and to sew. They have given them an alphabet, grammar, and dictionary; preserved their language from extinction; given it a literature, and translated into it the Bible and works of devotion, science and entertainment."[3]

The issue of reviving the Hawaiian language has been recently rejoined, with the churches at the forefront of the drive. Frank Kaulanaula Pestana, a senior pastor at a Hawaiian church that has roots in the New England missionary tradition, declared, "Hawaiian has been part of who we are from the beginning. The fact that we speak it and we sing it and we read it, that's our role. We keep it alive by doing all these things."[4] A *New York Times* reporter investigating the question concludes that Hawaiian churches can claim credit for keeping the language alive in periods of the most serious threat.

> The missionaries learned it so that they could convert the islanders, but they also preached in it and became the first to transcribe it into a written language, translating the Bible and documenting centuries of Hawaiian culture and history. And although many of the missionary churches supported the 1893 overthrow of the Hawaiian monarchy, a role for which they apologized 100 years later, they nonetheless provided one of the few places where the language was promoted after it was largely banned in schools, in favor of English, near the turn of the last century.[5]

Pila Wilson, a scholar of Hawaiian studies at the College of Hawaiian Language, said the Sunday schools "were the primary formal institution [whose work was] conducted in the Hawaiian language. They are the reason the Hawaiian language made it into the time we are."[6]

The documenting of centuries of Hawaiian culture and history as a corollary of Bible translation invested Christianity with the rules of Hawaiian self-understanding. You could be Hawaiian and Christian, or be Christian and Hawaiian, it amounted to the same thing as far as Christianity was concerned, for parallel conjunctions occurred at the religion's source and almost everywhere else since: Jewish and Christian or Christian and Jewish, Gentile and Christian or Christian and Gentile, and so on. Expanded over time and across space, we hear repeated echoes of this theme of one God active in the midst of many cultures, and of many cultures renewed from a common faith in one

God. As Irenaeus in the second century observed, the church is distinguished by the diversity of cultures that have embraced the gospel, sometimes "without ink or paper."

The Sanctions of Power and the Bounds of Endurance

It is tempting to see in the scope, momentum, and magnitude of the worldwide Christian resurgence a ringing endorsement of religious triumphalism, but that temptation must be resisted because the reality is a great deal more complex than that. The face of world Christianity bears the pockmarks of adverse circumstances. Global forces have been at work within and beyond the new religious resurgence. The AIDS pandemic in that regard, with its epicenter in Africa, has spread through patterns of urban and labor migration, rural dislocation, casual and seasonal labor, the drug traffic, travel and mobility, and fertility rates. The pressures of economic and political forces have sparked an urgent, desperate, and wide-ranging ferment in traditional societies vis-à-vis national and global issues, and that has made the religion especially appealing to migrant and transient populations. The social agency role of religious organizations has grown in the midst of political upheaval and economic challenge, with Christianity offering, or perceived as offering, hope and assurance against mass disenchantment.

The rolling machinery of messianic political tyranny has not spared Third World churches, whose leaders have suffered horrendous persecution at the hands of the redeemer state. The story of what happened in Ethiopia may stand as an object lesson for all concerned. Shortly after he came to power in 1974, Mengistu Haile Mariam, styling himself after Lenin, unleashed what has come to be called the reign of Red Terror that engulfed the monarchy and the church. In 1977 and 1978 alone, the regime killed half a million people, according to reports by Amnesty International.

Mengistu created in Ethiopia a Soviet satellite with close ties to the Kremlin and instituted scientific socialism as exclusive state dogma. "The USSR helped us materially, not only with words. And from that moment on, [Leonid] Brezhnev was like a father to me," Mengistu acknowledges proudly. "We met thirteen times in all, always in the Soviet Union. Each time, before I told him anything else, I would say, 'Comrade Leonid, I am your son. I owe you everything.' And I truly felt that Brezhnev was like a father," Mengistu affirmed, heady still from the thrill of filial righteousness. Working from the authoritative dogma he learned at Brezhnev's knee, Mengistu was disappointed with Mikhail Gorbachev for having abandoned the Communist ideology with his glasnost and perestroika reforms. Living in exile in Zimbabwe since his overthrow in 1991, Mengistu denounced Gorbachev and his alleged partner in crime, Ronald Reagan, for their rearguard conspiracy against progress. He continued to sing the praises of two former allies, North Korea's Kim Il Sung and Cuba's Fidel Castro. "Fidel is deeply patriotic, a true revolutionary. . . . Fidel is very human." As for Kim Il Sung, he "drank, smoked, and told jokes. He gave me power stations, shipyards, and military advisors, asking nothing in return."[7]

Unrattled in his gilded cage, Mengistu still reveled in the killings, mutilations, terror, and brutal repression by his regime, including the summary execution of counterrevolutionaries, reactionaries, and the purge of undigested elements. He showed deadly contempt for the church and spared no one connected with it. His reign of terror in Ethiopia evoked a nightmare without parallel even in the dark catalogues of religious intolerance. Mengistu lived the truth of the dictum that Communism does not cry over spilled blood. It has scapegoats enough for that. Mengistu's lethal brand of secular fundamentalism, complete with apostolic protocols from the Kremlin, amplifies the strains of extremist intolerance on the left that we all too readily associate with the flaming fatwas of religious fundamentalists on the right.

To this toll must be added a similar one exacted of the church in Angola, giving us the picture of Christianity under fire in much of Africa. In November 1975, Angola declared its independence from Portugal amid an intractable and fractured armed liberation movement, and amid the shreds of a deeply conflicted society. The new MPLA (Popular Movement for the Liberation of Angola) government adopted Marxist-Leninism under a centralized party machinery as the vanguard of the revolution. Political militancy was at once declared the official antidote to religion, and the party adopted a warpath toward the churches. In December 1977, the official organs of the state announced that Catholics and Protestants did not qualify as members of the party or of the government.

A widespread harassment of religion ensued, including the confiscation of property and the forcible removal of children from their parents for reeducation in indoctrination camps. When the Catholic Church responded in January 1978 to the escalating situation, with Vatican Radio denouncing the arbitrary measures against the church, the party answered back with menacing anticlerical threats. Lucio Lara, the secretary of the party central committee, threatened reprisals for dissent, announcing that the government had provided itself with the legal instruments to consider "as illegal and therefore punishable any activity which places faith or religious belief in opposition to the revolutionary transformation of society."[8]

Attacks on the church proceeded unabated, with the torture and deaths of priests, nuns, pastors, and others, as the grim logic of a political vendetta took its toll. The government invoked scriptural warrant by producing what it called Ten Principles of Pioneers, modeled on the Ten Commandments, and followed that by promulgating another parallel document called Ten Commandments for Christian Youth. Church leaders protested that what the government required of religion was that religion should remain a target for repression.[9] What the leaders did not say but could also have said was that a negation of God was being remorselessly erected into a system of government. On those grounds, compromise or conciliation was inconceivable, as was stability.

Ethiopia and Angola at different ends of the continent offer examples of state capture of religion in order to bolster claims of omnipotence and domination, with organs of power sequestered as tools of party dogma. The irony of Africa's reputation as a religious continent was sharpened into the command dogma of comprehensive state power, and religion's moral capital was made to yield the premium of state salvation. A comparable development in Europe had produced in reaction the phenomenon of the confessional Christian and other variations on the theme. In Africa, it inspired an urgent, demonstrative piety that grasped the eternal promises of religion as a shield against the fickle promises of institutional power. In conditions of law and order and political stability, such a maneuver, perhaps, might be deemed evasive or escapist, but in the provocative context of state repression and incompetence, the maneuver represented enlargement of the bounds of endurance. The pathos of repression and anarchy did not enfeeble the moral will necessarily, and so the will to believe found a moral outlet.

The disasters of the day have not slowed the pace of expansion; sometimes, as in Sudan or Nigeria, they have strengthened or precipitated the resurgence. We get a sense of what is afoot in the charismatic fervor of Pentecostalism as it sweeps through the ranks of restive youth and migrant groups. In its popular practices, charismatic faith has hints enough of surviving memories of spirit power and possession in the local culture to be able to transmit ideas of global reach and personal fulfillment. The Pentecostal message of material prosperity as proof of divine approval gives location a global Good Housekeeping Seal of Approval. Neighborhood arenas and megachurches resound with testimonies of newfound health, wealth, and success, with promises of more to come. The religious network and the enterprise culture have converged with the movement of globalization to transform indigenous religious expectation and expression and to foster a new idiom fused of the global and the local. As a consequence, people's thoughts, feelings, and anxieties have been concentrated on the present moment and its possibilities. The new expectations, and the accompanying perplexities, of world deliverance are not just a wish to restore old customs but to repossess them at the level of personal liberation with a global resonance, often in situations of gross economic deprivation and human rights violation.[10]

Blossoms in the Dust

The role of women across the domains of public and private has similarly grown, reflective of a world undergoing rapid social change. The economic basis of traditional role exclusion between men and women has been eroded by buoyant new ideas. Furthermore, the vastly increased consumer options of a global economy have fed appetites and raised expectations that go above and beyond what domestic capacity can satisfy or tribal sanctions constrain. The mass-market brand of evangelical and Pentecostal mobilization, for example, fits into this youth culture of buoyant expectations and an awakened appetite for personal possibility.

These are the forces that have pushed world Christianity forward and shaped its reigning convictions of promise and destiny. As the *World Christian Encyclopedia*[11] put it, in spite of the vogue enjoyed by the phenomenon of the prosperity gospel, a good proportion of the world's Christians are poor, young, and uneducated. According to statistics of membership, the new converts are characterized by extraordinary persecution and suffering. In spite of that, the rate of conversion to Christianity is greatest among these populations, and for good reason.

The missionary momentum of the religion, similarly, has been at its most vigorous among the recently evangelized peoples of the world. Only a small proportion of Christian and church leaders have had any theological education, and people of necessity have turned to open-air meetings, along with compound and house fellowship gatherings, for prayer, teaching, and nurture. Religious observance for the new believers has been a spirited performative blend of song, dance, and music, enlivened with active personal supplication, mediation, and encounter.

The institutional structures that have maintained Christianity in the West are largely missing in post-Western Christianity or, where they exist, are demonstrably weak. The impetus behind Christian growth seems surprisingly unrelated to structural strength or to Western aid, though Pentecostalism in Africa and Latin America, for example, has fostered an American-style organizational structure, with coliseumlike mass auditoriums flanked by parking lots, schools, and banks. In the absence of central planning and the requisite material provision, and outside any satisfactory theories to account for the phenomenon, Christianity has continued to grow and expand in previously non-Christian societies.

Western Skepticism

The West is confronted with a striking fact of our times in the rapid change overtaking Christianity in terms of its current distinct non-Western cultural and anticultural forms. A strictly political and chronological view of the expansion of Christianity would probably stress the originating Euro-American cultural mode of the religion, especially at the point of missionary conception and transmission, and nowhere is this chronological view more pronounced than in the colonial empires that sheltered Christian missions. On the basis of the West's religious chronology, observers have spoken of a global menace threatened with the worldwide Christian resurgence. They forecast an age of new political instability and interreligious conflict fomented by the resurgence.

That uncompromising attitude of contending with Third World religious orthodoxy dominated discussions at the 1998 Lambeth Conference in England. Some senior churchpeople there accused Third World Christianity of being bankrolled by conservative groups in the United States. Third World Christianity was set up to promote a reactionary cultural agenda, they charged. Implicated in the uncontrolled fallout of national political breakdown, this new Christianity, critics claimed, would hatch witch hunts of enemies and opponents as happened in the pre-Enlightenment West. World Christianity, accordingly, they believe, constitutes a threat to the West's hard-earned liberal achievements. All of that seems like a prescription for a major cultural schism.

Taking offense at the Third World bishops for their antigay stance at this meeting, Bishop John Shelby Spong of Newark, for example, declared, in a remark for which he issued a halfhearted apology afterward, that the witch-hunting and superstitious societies from which these bishops came represented a threat to the Anglican church as a force in Western civilization. What he saw and heard at Lambeth, he reaffirmed, "was the sunset of the Anglican communion."[12] This was not only an instance of the West defining itself against Christianity but also, more tellingly, of a post-Christian West, still recovering from religion as contagion, mobilizing behind a domesticated highbrow view of culture as a new manifest mandate. The attitude survives from previous generations, as when a nineteenth century American critic said that religion "degenerates among [American] blacks into mere wild-fire, with as little tendency to transform the character as the heathen rites of their ancestors in their native jungles."[13] Spong and his backers defied the new face of Third World Christianity for lacking the refinement of culture and suppleness of character that would make it acceptable to the West. Still, Spong's attack begs the question: What motives have defied the law of self-preservation to make Africans and others convert to Christianity in circumstances of acute travail at home and persistent abuse abroad? Perhaps these converts really are genuine when they say they believe in God, hard as that may be for us to accept. Their defiance under attack does not bode well for encounter with the coming new Christianity.

At Lambeth itself and subsequently, there was widespread consternation among Western bishops that the Third World bishops seemed misguided enough to think that the Bible could replace enlightened reasonableness as a standard of guidance for faith and conduct. The unprecedented large conversions taking place in Africa and elsewhere were viewed as an instance of simplistic Third World literalism that must give way to the West's subtle style. Yet, instead of wilting, Christianity has continued to blossom against nationalist intolerance at home and Western objections abroad, provoking a skeptical West to add the culture gap to the poverty gap to distance itself from the new Christianity. The West limits its role in the new Christianity to taking precautions against too close an encounter with it, except where the West can tame it. Secular constitutions in the new nations that give marriage and family life, for example, no higher merit than other lifestyle choices, are more acceptable to Western Christians than any appeal to scripture and church teaching on such issues. Many of the Western strategies of promoting global pluralism, accordingly, are directed at such attempts at co-optation. It is the White man's burden by another name,[14] and it portends a future culture clash perhaps as profound as the Reformation.

We sense the magnitude of that clash from the fact that World Christianity remains striking for its antistructural popular roots that show up in charismatic revival and spiritual formation in the midst of widespread state collapse and social disenchantment. The scruples of the West against reverting to the orthodox convictions of classical Christianity have not constrained the global Christian resurgence. A collision seems all but inevitable.

Alternative Christianities

The inexorable transcultural expansion of Christianity suggests something about the obdurate character of religious loyalty against the political pressure to conform and contrasts strikingly with the modern West, where political commitment defines our fundamental priorities, including the distinction between public and private. It is not difficult, however, to discern in the antistructural, popular roots of world Christianity the rough outlines of the coming global political realignment and its accompanying cultural retrenchment, involving as it does the emergence of new forms of civil society outside the sphere of state power and without the dogma of a strident individualism.

A new international order in which the principal players will be members of civil society united by allegiance grounded in spiritual claims will look very different from one in which, as at present, national states are the exclusive and final international actors. It might mean, for example, that nongovernmental organizations (NGOs), assuming more and more a religious character, will accede to a more important role as arbiters of international affairs.[15] It behooves us to prepare ourselves for that possibility and with it the need to modify, or even abandon, national state jurisdiction as the prerequisite of the international order. Nation-states have been more often the problem than the solution. It is certainly the case now that the global religious resurgence has undermined confidence in the standard cultural consensus on the relations among church, state, and society that has defined the modern world.

The current transformation of Christianity in a postcolonial world should allow us to track on a global scale the coming structural changes of faith and the public order. In this highly unstable milieu, the real challenge for the churches is no longer what it once so clearly was—namely, the largely conceded case for the populist overthrow of colonial hegemony in favor of uncontested national state power—but rather the still underdeveloped case for a moral bill of rights that would serve as a foundation for new forms of society. Hatred of the foreigner, decisive in the fervor of the nationalist struggle, is a false alibi in conditions now of grave national failure, and in any case the realities today of globalization smudge the line between friend and foe without advantage necessarily to local needs or to spiritual values—yet another sign of the approaching debacle. The alternative ways of being Christian today mean that cultural compromise and political moderation are unlikely to be a restraining or a galvanizing standard anymore, and so a radical choice implicating church, state, and society seems unavoidable.

Conclusion

There are worse ways to try to account for the current global Christian resurgence than to echo the sentiments of Will Durant in his massive, 11-volume, panoramic, unifocused study, *The Story of Civilization*. He showed how Christianity's new cultural idiom of creative synthesis was the key to the civilizational shift involved in eventually superseding pagan Europe. Durant's penetrating verdict is pertinent to an understanding of the contemporary phase of Christianity, in which issues of cross-cultural origin have reasserted themselves under the pressures of cross-cultural expansion and adaptation. In the medieval West, Christian and pre-Christian ideas and values were intermixed in a process of mutual transformation, Durant argued. He would thus resonate with the notion that to understand the changing face of Christianity today, we must forget our modern rationalism, our proud confidence in reason and science, our restless search after wealth and power and after an earthly kingdom. We must enter sympathetically into the mood of populations disillusioned with old assurances, as well as with the new call of the pursuits of secular preeminence. The new Christians are standing, as it were, between the shipwreck of the old order and the tarnished fruits of self-rule of the new, finding all the dreams of a worldly utopia shattered by betrayal, war, vanity, anarchy, poverty, epidemics, and endemic hostility. They are seeking refuge in the justification of the righteous kingdom, flocking to the churches because the old fences of what used to be home have crumbled. They are inspired and comforted by the narratives of ancient scripture, throwing themselves upon the mercy and goodness of God and upon one another's charity. They are living in the reality of a fellowship established, a cause vindicated, a judgment fulfilled, and a hope rekindled. The dramatic response of compressed, preindustrial societies of the non-Western world to Christianity has opened a new chapter in the annals of religion.

NOTES

1. See L. Sanneh, *Translating the Message: The Missionary Impact on Culture* (Maryknoll, N.Y.: Orbis Books, 1989).

2. G. S. Parsonson, "The Literate Revolution in Polynesia," *Journal of Pacific History* (1967), 39–57, 52.

3. *The New York Tribune*, 5 June 1860, cited in *Missionary Album: Portraits and Biographical Sketches of the American Protestant Missionaries to the Hawaiian Islands* (Honolulu: Hawaiian Mission Children's Society, Sesquicentennial Edition, 1969), 17. Such language work has been essential to the development of the science of anthropology, as the Oxford anthropologist Godfrey Lienhardt testifies in his book *Divinity and Experience: The Religion of the Dinka* (Oxford: Clarendon Press, 1961). He writes: "Without Fr. Nebel's work on Dinka language and thought, my own would have been made immensely more difficult" (p. vii).

4. Quoted in Michelle Kayal, "Churches Try to Protect Hawaii's Native Tongue," *New York Times*, February 22, 2003, B4.

5. Ibid.

6. Ibid.

7. Ricardo Orizio, "The Lion Sleeps Tonight," an interview with Megistu Haile Mariam, translated from the Italian by Avril Bardoni, *Transition*, Issue 89, vol. 11, no. 1.

8. *Jornal de Angola*, 5 Feb. 1978, cited in Lawrence W. Henderson, *The Church in Angola: A River of Many Currents* (Cleveland: Pilgrim Press, 1992), 357.

9. In Liberia, similar protest was made by Archbishop Michael Kpakala Francis in a long-running confrontation with the country's rulers, whom he accused of using death and violence as tools of oppression. He spoke of the evil done by the country's rulers who took Liberia through dark periods of unspeakable suffering and thereby destroyed a generation. They made a mockery of the Ten Commandments, which they read as "Thou shalt steal," "Thou shalt rape," "Thou shalt lie," and "Thou shalt kill." These men have to answer to God and to man for their conduct, the archbishop challenged. Tim Weiner, "Peace and Reason Amid Chaos, a Balm for Pain," *New York Times*, 13 September 2003, A4.

10. For some poignant personal stories see R. Werner, W. Anderson, and Andrew Wheeler, *Day of Devastation, Day of Contentment: The History of the Sudanese Church Across 2000 Years* (Nairobi: Paulines Publications Africa, 2000).

11. David Barrett et al., *The World Christian Encyclopedia* (New York: Oxford University Press, 2 vols., 2001).

12. John Shelby Spong, "Anglicans Get Literal," *New York Times* Op-Ed essay, 13 Aug. 1998.

13. Cited in James McPherson, *The Abolitionist Legacy* (Princeton, N.J.: Princeton University Press, 1975), 189.

14. For an examination of the theme in Rudyard Kipling, see Andrew F. Walls, *The Cross-Cultural Process in Christian History*, chap. 10, "Carrying the White Man's Burden: Some British Views of National Vocation in the Imperial Era" (Maryknoll, N.Y.: Orbis Books, 2002).

15. See, e.g., Douglas Johnston, ed., *Faith-Based Diplomacy, Trumping Realpolitik* (New York: Oxford University Press, 2003).

Index

Abban, Isaac 118
Abbot, Elisha 139, 142–145, 148
Abogaye-Mensah, Robert 125
abolitionists 141
Accra 81, 84
acculturation 47
Action Chapel International (ACI) 84
Adamawa State 50, 54
Africa 192, 193, 197, 198, 207, 208, 214, 216–220
African Christianity: Its Public Role 118
African Baptist Seminary 68
African diaspora 120
African Independent Churches 29, 48, 87
African nationalism 198
African religions 152
Africanization 45, 47, 59
Afro-Caribbean 35
afterlife 10
AIDS 92, 216
Akanda 24
Ako-Adjei 126
Akrofi-Christaller Memorial Center 10
Akufo-Addo 126
Akyem-Abuakwa Kingdom 127
Aladura 48
Alive Chapel International 85

All Africa Conference of Churches (AACC) 9, 97, 105, 107
Allen, Roland 16, 197, 203–04
Alliance of Baptists 75, 76
American Baptists 8, 12, 137, 142, 144–150
  Home Missionary Society (ABHMS) 150, 151
  Missionary Union (ABMU) 144, 145, 148, 150
American Board of Commissioners for Foreign Missions 101
American Colonization Society 140
American Episcopal Church 213
Amerindian slaves 24
Amnesty International 216
Andersen, Wilhelm 192
Anderson, Gerald H. 192
Anderson, Rufus 193, 207
Anglican Church 220
  Missionary Society 198
Anglo-Saxons 150, 163
Angola 217, 218
Annan, Kofi 118
Annie Armstrong Easter Offering 73
Anthropology and missions 48, 49
Antigua 36
apartheid 108, 199
Arawaks 24
Ariarajah, S. Wesley 176
Arracan 142

Asare, Bishop Charles Agyin 83
Ashimolowo, Matthew 93, 94
Ashmore, William 151
Asia 192–194, 197, 198, 206–208, 214
Asian culture 146
Asian missions 176
Authority of the Faith, The 168, 170
Azariah, V.S. 199

Baeta, C.G. 45
Bahamas 36
Bamba, Amadou 11
Bambara 24
Banaras 167
Bantu people 200
Baptist
    Convention in Zimbabwe (BCZ) 67,
        71, 72
    Convention of Angola 76
    English 141
    Missionary Magazine 151
    missionary spokespeople 137, 146
    Mission of Central Africa 69
    in Zimbabwe 8, 64, 66
    Theological Seminary of Zimbabwe
        (BTSZ) 66, 70, 71, 73, 74, 76
Barbados 36
Barth, Karl 165, 170, 176, 177
    Barthians 162
    Barth-Brunner debate 166, 171
Baschulte, Lawrence 30
Bassein region 139
Bediako, Kwame viii, 10
Beijing 167, 197
Belloc, Hilaire 5
Benjamin, Leayle M. 30
Bethesda Zion Apostolic United Gaza
    200
Bhagavat-Geeta 159
Bible Society of Angola 76
Bible Victory Church 85
Biblical realism 165, 167
Bingham, Hiram 214–215
Blauw, Johannes 192
Blue Water Bible College 29
Blyden, Edward Willmot 198
Boahen, Albert Adu 117
Boardman, George 135–137, 139, 141, 142
Boardman, Sarah 135, 136
Boasian anthropology 140

Boer government 108
Book of Common Prayer 135
Bowlin, Betty and Ralph 68
Boxer Rising 197, 201
brain drain 30
Brazil 151
breakthrough 86, 90
Brezhnev, Leonid 216
Brockett, L.P. 149
Bronnum, Dr. Neils 51
Brown University 145
British Baptist Missionary Society 200
British West Indies 200
Brunner, Emil 167, 171, 177
Bryan, Adelbert 29
Buddhism 159, 203
Bulawayo 67
Burma 135, 139, 141, 146–148, 151
Burmese
    Buddhists 139
    culture 141
    government 141
    Karen tribe 12
    people 141, 142
    society 138
Busia, K.A. 129
Byu, Ko Tha 136, 139, 143, 151

Calvin, John 33, 166, 171, 177
calypso 36, 38
Carey, William 141, 191
Caribbean
    culture 5
    music 32–34, 38
Carobs 24
Carpenter, C.H. 149
Carstens, Mrs. 25, 26
Castro, Fidel 217
Catholic Church 104, 217
Catholic Parish of Christ the King 84
Chao, T.C. 168, 169
charismatic missionaries 6
Charlemagne 122
Cheng, C.Y. 202, 203
Cherokee 141
China 15, 151, 191, 193, 195, 196, 197,
    198, 200–05
    Inland Mission 196
Chiusaru, David 76
Christianborg 25

Christian Catholic Church in Zion 200
Christian Council of Ghana 124–25
Christian Message in a Non-Christian World, The 14, 161, 163–5, 167–68, 171–173, 175
Christian-Muslim tensions 55
Christian Recorder 152
Christianity
    African 75, 81, 120–123, 128
    Asian 137, 146, 148, 150
    Burmese 139
    "charismatic" 84
    Chinese 193, 201, 202
    European 58
    expansion and acculturation of 5
    Ghanaian 83, 88, 91, 92
    Hawaiian 215
    Karen 136, 137, 138–40, 142, 143, 144–50
    Longuda 140
    missionary 197
    post-Enlightenment 7
    post-Western 10
    Third World 10, 15, 220
    variety of 5
    Zimbabwean 148
Christianity and Race Relations 199
Christianity Today 27
Christ paradigm 124
Church of the Brethren 26, 27
"church planting movements" (CPMs) 73, 74
Civil War 150
Clarke, Viola 35
Clement of Alexandria 165, 170
Coe, Shoki 192, 194, 206–208
Cold War 191
College of Hawaiian Language 215
colonialism 64
Columbia University 201
Columbian Exposition (1849) 150
Columbus, Christopher 22–24
Communism 217
    as ideology 216
    in China 15, 191, 194, 196, 205, 206
    in Ethiopia and Angola 216–218
    in Mozambique 103–105
Concord 159
Confucian leadership 196
Congo 200

Connecticut 145
Connoly, Ron 39, 66
contextual theology 15, 16, 193, 208
    contextuality 193, 207
    contextualization 193, 206–08
    top-down approach 6, 16, 46
Continental missionary 162, 163
"Continuity or Discontinuity" 164
corpus christianum 98, 99
Côte d'Ivoire 198
Covenant Christian Center 30, 34
Creole 6, 27, 30, 31, 36, 38
creolization 36
Crosby, Fanny 34
Cuba 217
cultural appropriation 13
cultural imperialism 29
cultural originality 46

Dana, Richard H. Jr. 215
Danish branch of the Sudan United Mission (DSUM) 51
Danish Creole 25
Danish government 24
Danquah, J.B. 126
Darwinism 13
democratization 98
Dewey, John 201
diakonia 105
diaspora community 6
disenfranchisement 28
disestablishmentarianism 144, 145, 148
diversity 15
Domestic Mission Board (DMB) 72
Dominica 31, 36
Donoghue, Eddie 22, 24, 26, 27
Donovan, Violeta 33
Dotson, Clyde T. 66, 68, 69
DuBois, W.E.B. 151
Duncan-Williams, Bishop Nicolas 83
Durant, Will 222

East Indies 198
Eck, Diana 175
eclecticism 6
Ecuador 67
Ecumenical Institute 170, 171
Ecumenical Review 175
Edinburgh (1910) 161, 162, 199
Edwards, Jonathan 141

Egypt 200
Emerson, Ralph Waldo 159
Englishmen 163
Enlightenment, The 194
"Essentials of an Indigenous Church,
    The" 203
Ethiopia 123, 216–218
ethnocentrism 140
Eurocentric 46
Europe 140, 170, 218
Evangelical theology 141
extraversion 9, 66, 67, 70

Fairbank, John King 196
faith gospel 88, 91, 92, 94
Faith Tabernacle 11
Farmer, H.H. 169, 170
FM radio 91
Foreign Mission Board (FMB) of the
    Southern Baptists 66, 68, 70–72, 74
Fort, Giles and Wanna Anna 68
France 196, 198
Fraser, Sir James 8
Frelimo government 9, 103–105
Freud, Sigmund 177
Fulani 54
fundamentalism viii, 122
Funzamo, Isaias 104

gangster rap 29
Gates, Bill 87
General Assembly 9
General Secretary of the United Nations
    118, 125
Germany 198
Ghana 10, 81–84, 87, 125, 127, 128
Ghana Academy of Arts and Sciences
    127
Gifford, Paul 118–121, 124
global Christian resurgence 16
global pluralism 221
globalization 39, 118
Goatley, Dr. David 75
Goerner, Cornell 69
Gold Coast 66
Goodwin, Harella 36
Gorbachev, Mikhail 216
Grace Thrillers 36
grassroots 6, 13, 29, 45, 49
Great Britain 198, 200, 206, 207

Great Commission 191
Grenada 36
Groupes Bibliques Universitaire 112
Guyuk 55
Gwelo/Gweru 68, 71, 75

Habyarimana, President 110
Haiti 30
Hallencreutz, Carl 174
Harare 64, 67
Hausa 54
Hawaiian churches 215
Heward-Mills, Bishop Dag 83
Hick 177
Highfield, Arnold R. 36
Hinduism 29
Hitler, Adolf 199
Hocking, W.E. 163, 170, 176
Hoedemaker, Bert 176
Hogg, A.G. 169, 170, 175
Holiness and Pentecostal movements
    140
Holy Family Parish on St. Thomas 30
homosexuality 213
Horton, Walter Marshall 169, 170
House Church Movement 205
Hu Shi 201
Hwang, C.H. 192–93, 206

Ibo 24, 27
Idahosa, Benson 84
inculturation 193
India 30, 141, 160, 164, 192
Indian Congress Party 197
indigenous
    culture 214
    religious expectation 218
indigenous church 193, 195,
    in China 202–207
indigenization 6, 7, 16, 59, 195
Indonesia 14, 163, 164, 192
International Central Gospel Church 84
International Missionary
    Conference 160, 161, 164
    Council (IMC) 160, 162, 163, 192, 199,
        206
    Research Pamphlet 192
International Missions Board (IMB) 72–
    74, 83

International Review of Mission 174, 175, 199
interreligious encounter 14
Inyati 64
Irenaeus 216
Isert, Paul Erdman 25, 26
Islam 14, 29, 123, 163, 203, 214
Italy 198

Jabavu, D.D.T. 199, 200
Jamaica 36
Jankombum 22, 24–29
Japan 198, 200–01
jazz 35
J.B. Danquah Memorial Lectures 127
Jerusalem 161, 162, 169
Jim Crow legislation 13, 150
John-Lewis, Monseigneur William 30
Journey of the Soul, The 32

Kähler, Martin 208
Kaishek, Chiang 198, 206
Kanea, Okyeman 127
Kano 55
Kaplin, Steven 46
Karen New Testament 139
Karen people 12, 13, 135, 137, 139, 141–149
Kayibanda, President 110
Kenya 48, 98
Kimbanguism 48
Kimbangu, Simon 200
Kingdom Crew 36
Kingdom Life Christian Center 34
King Obstinate 36
King Short Shirt 36
Kingsway International Christian Center 93
Kraemer, Hendrik 14, 15, 160, 163–179
Kremlin 216, 217
Kuffour, John Agyekum 83, 91, 117
Kumebe (healers) 56
Kuomintang 206
Kwandalha (spirits) 56
Kyaw, Matt 143

Lagos 10, 11
Lambeth Conference in England 220
Lamptey, Obetsebi 126
Lara, Lucio 217

Latin America 192, 193, 208, 214, 219
Laundry, Piper 39
Laymen's Inquiry 163, 169, 175
Legio Maria 48
Lenin 216
Lewis, Lester 36, 38
Liberia 66
Life of David Brainerd, The 141
Lifeline International Music Ministry 38
Lighthouse Chapel International (LCI) 84, 85, 93
Little Flock (Local Church Movement) 204
Lloyd, Jerry 39
London Missionary Society 64
Longuda 50, 58
  beliefs 38, 49, 51
  cosmology of evil and original sin 56
  externalization of evil 57
  personal sin 57
Lord's Supper 205
Lott Carey Baptist Mission Convention 75
Lottie Moon Christmas Offering 73
Lutheran Church of Christ in Nigeria (LCCN) 45, 49–51, 53, 56, 58, 59

Macau 196
Machel, President Samora 9, 105
Madras Christian College 160
Mahama, Alhaji Aliu 118
Malaya 67
Manchu (Qing dynasty) 198
Manganhela, Zedequias 103
Manifest Destiny 140
Mariam, Mengistu Haile 216, 217
Martyr, Justin 170
Marx, Karl 177
Marxist-Leninism 217
Marxist philosophy 103, 104
Mason, Francis 139, 143, 144, 148
Mason, Harriett 35, 36
Mason, Stan 35
Mbaké, Shaykh Mourtada 11
Mbefo, Luke 46
Mbiti, John 46
McKinley, Dr. Hugh and Rebecca 71, 74
Meiji 200

Methodists 147, 151
  Africa University in Mutare 76
  Black 152
  church 151, 152, 204
Mhalamhala, Yosépha 101
Middle East 30
millennialism 87
Mills, John Atta 117
Minneapolis 213
miracles 10
missionaries
  Anglican 29, 64, 83
  Baptist 8, 12, 13, 29, 64, 66, 69, 139,
    140, 150
  Catholic 24, 64, 83, 100
  charismatic African 30
  Dutch Reformed 29
  Lutheran 26
  Methodist 29, 64, 83
  Morovian 25, 26, 29, 30
  Pentecostal 29, 83
  Protestant 29, 83, 101
  Roman Catholic 29, 64
  Seventh Day Adventist 64
Missionary Methods: St. Paul's or Ours?
  197
Missionary Nature of the Church, The 192
misso Dei 206, 207, 208
Moffat, Robert 64
Mokko 24, 27
Moorehead, Mario 29
Morehouse, Henry 151
Morning Star 139
Morrison, Robert 196
Mount of Olives 162
Mouride Brotherhood 11
Mozambican Christian Council (CCM)
  105–107
Mozambique 9, 99–101, 107, 112
Mugabe, Henry 8, 74
Mulder, D.C. 176
multiculturalism 15
Murray, Gilbert 123
Mwase, Isaac M. T. 148

"name it and claim it" gospel 88
National Association of Evangelicals of
    Ghana (NAEG) 125–26
National Christian
  Conference 201

  Council 203
National Democratic Congress (NDC)
  117, 125
"Nationalization Plan" 76, 77
National Socialism 199
Native Americans 140, 142
Natural Church of Ethiopia 200
Ndhlovu, Aaron 69
Neely, Alan 72, 73
Nee Tuo-Sheng (Watchman Nee) 204–05
Newbigin, Lesslie 14, 175
New Patriotic Party (NPP) 117, 125
Newsweek 118
New Testament 147, 168, 171, 205
  church model 197
New Touba 12
New Vision Ministries 34
New York 11, 12, 147
New York Tribune 215
Nigeria 8, 10, 11, 26, 46, 48, 50, 66, 140,
  218
Niles, D.T. 192, 207
Niles, Joseph 36
Nkrumah, Kwame 81, 82, 126–128
Nobel Peace Laureate 118
Nogomo, King Mutapa 100
nongovernmental organizations (NGOs)
  221
North America Mission Board 72
North Korea 217
Nyati, Joseph 69
Nziramasanga, Abel 69, 70

Ofori-Atta, William (Paa Willie) 125–127,
  128, 129
Okyeman Council 128
Ogun 29
Oldham, J.H. 199
Old Testament 152, 171
organic unity 48
Otabil, Mensa 11, 83–85, 91, 93
Other-wordly 58

Pacific 193, 207, 208, 214
Pakistan 192
Palestine 164
Pan Africanism 198
Panama Canal 24
Paton, Wiliam 163, 168
PCG (Presbyterian Church of Ghana) 127

Peacock, James 49
Peale, Norman Vincent 87
Peel, John 58
Pentecostal Holiness Church 200
Pentecostalism 218, 219
Peru 67
Pestana, Frank Kaulanaula 215
Phillips, Pastor George E. 32
Pierre, Glenworth 34, 36, 38, 39
Pilate, Pontius 124
Pinkerton, E.H. 101
Plumbtree 70
political pluralism 128
Pope, Dean Liston 206
Portugal 102, 217
    colonialism 102, 103
post-Christian West 10, 16
post-colonialism 27, 28, 63
post-missionary era 63
Potter, Philip A. 175
Po, Tway 143
Powell, Mary 39
praeparatio evangelica 167
pre-Christian religion 88, 91, 92
Prince Henry the Navigator 99
Programme to Combat Racism (PCR)
    103, 104
prophet 83, 90
Protestant liberalism 170
Protestant missions 101, 160, 161, 194
Provisional National Defense Council
    (PNDC) 126
psalmist 38
Puerto Rico 30

Qur'an 11, 214

Rahner, Karl 121
Rangoon Baptist College 148
Rastafarianism 29
Rawlings, Jerry John 82, 83, 91, 117
Reagan, Ronald 216
Reconstruction 151
Red Terror 216
Reformation 221
reggae 35, 38
Religion and the Christian Faith 171–173
"Religion Bridge" 39
Renamo government 9, 105
replication model 195

Republic of China (ROC) 206
*Rethinking Missions: A Laymen's Inquiry
    after One Hundred Years* 163
Richards, E.H. 101
Rhodes, Cecil John 64
Rhodesia 64, 65, 70
Rhodesia Front 65
Rhodesian Baptist Mission 68
Rhodes Pioneer Column 64, 65
Roberts, Oral 88
Rochester, New York 147
Rockefeller philanthropies 193
Roman Catholics 193, 200
Roman Empire 124
Rushdie, Salman 21
Russell, Bertrand 201
Russia 198, 199
Rwanda 98, 109, 112
Rwanda Patriotic Front (RPF) 110, 111

Sadler, Dr. George 67
Salamone, Frank 48
Salisbury 64, 67
Samartha, Stanley 174
Sanneh, Lamin 22, 26, 27, 39, 46, 122,
    137
Santeria 29
Santo Domingo 30
Sanyati 64, 68
    Baptist Hospital 67, 70
    Primary School and Secondary
        Schools 67
    Reserve 67
Schoffeleers, Matthew 48
Schreiter, Robert 47
Scotland 164
Sears, Barnas 147, 148
Second Anglo-Burmese War 139
Second Republic (Ghana) 82, 126, 129
secularization 21
Senegal 11
sensus divinitatis 166, 171, 177
Seventh Day Adventist Philadelphia
    Church 33
Shanghai 198, 201
Shango 30
Shikai, Yuan 198
Siege of the Peking Legations, The 197
Singing Rose 36
Smith, Bernard 34, 36, 38

Smith, Ian 8, 65
Smith, Wilfred Cantwell 175
social Darwinism 150
South Africa 48, 100, 101, 103, 108, 109,
    111, 112, 199, 200
Southern Baptist Convention 64, 66, 68,
    72, 73, 74
Southern Rhodesia 8, 67, 68
Spong, John Shelby 220
Sri Lanka 198
St. Croix 23–26, 31, 34, 36
St. John 168
St. Paul 168, 177, 203
St. Thomas Assembly of God 32
Stevens, Phillips 58
Stipe, Claude 48
Story of Civilization 222
Story of the Karen Mission in Bassein, The
    149
Student Volunteer Movement 161
success 87, 90
Sudan 218
Sufi 11
Sundkler, Bengt 87
Sung, Kim 217
Swanba (witches) 53–56
Swanmbraha (evil spirits) 56
Swanya (witch) 53, 54
Switzerland 171
Synagogue Church of All Nations 83
syncretism 48, 49, 58

Tainan Theological College 193, 206
Tainos 24
Taiwan 206
Taiwanese Presbyterian Church 192, 206
Talented Tenth 151
Tambaram 160, 161, 163, 164, 168, 169,
    170, 174, 175, 176, 179
Tavoy 135, 137, 139
Taylor, Hudson 196
Temple, William 4
Ten Commandments 217
ter, Harr, Gerrie 120
Thee, A-Pyah 135, 139, 141
Theological Education Fund 193, 206,
    207
Theology of the Christian Mission, The 192
theory of mission 14
Third Republic 83

Third World
  bishops 213
  Christianity 220
  churches 213
  literalism 220
Tientsin 196
tolerance 15
Toussant, Naomi 36
Towards a Theology of Mission 192
Tranformaçâo de Armas em Enxadas 107
Travellers Rest Farm 68
Trinidad 30
Troeltsch, Ernst 176
Turnbull, Judy 36
Turnbull sisters 36
Tutsi refugees 110
Tutu, Desmond 109
Twi language 125
Tyson, George F. 36

UNICEF 107
Unilateral Declaration of Independence
    (UDI) 65
United States 140, 200, 220
universal truth claims 14
University of Geneva 171
University of Leiden 163, 170
University of Zimbabwe 76
Upon the Earth 192
U.S. Virgin Islands 21, 22, 27–30, 32
  colonial era 27

Vanden Berg, Todd M. 140
Vatican Radio 217
Venn, Henry 193, 198, 207
vernacularization of the Gospel 39
V.I. Christian Ministries 34
Vodun 30
Voice Print: An Anthology of Oral and
    Related Poetry from the Caribbean 35

Walls, Andrew 137, 146
Ward, Kevin 122
Wayland, Francis 13, 14, 145–148
West Indies 23
  Danish 26, 28
white Baptists 64
White-dominated media 29
white supremacy 13
Williams, Pastor Amaran 33

Willingen (Netherlands) Assembly 192
Wilson, Pila 215
Winners' Chapel 10, 11, 83, 85, 88
witches 51, 52, 57
witchcraft 6, 45, 58, 59
    accusation 54
    acquisition 53
    and the devil 54–56
    protection 57
    victims of 55
Wolterstorff, Nicolas 34
Woodward, Kenneth 119, 120
Word Miracle Church International
    (WMCI) 84
World Bank 83, 87
World Christian Encyclopedia 219
World Council of Churches (WCC) 104–
    106, 162, 170
World History of Christianity, A 122
World Missionary Conference 199

World War I 162, 200
World War II 191

Xintomane, Lois 101

Yale Divinity School 206
Yangzhou 196
Yat-sen, Sun 198
Yi, Dr. Chen Ching 201
Young Men's Christian Association 201
Young Women's Christian Association
    201
Yu Kuo-chen 201, 204

Zaire 48, 98
Zambia 69, 98
Zhao, Fusan 201
Zimbabwe 8, 63–66, 71, 75, 76, 216
Zion Church 48
Zuppi, Don Matteo 106, 107